Handbook of Food Preparation

Food and Nutrition Section
American Home Economics Association

Ninth Edition

KENDALL/HUNT PUBLISHING COMPANY
4050 Westmark Drive   Dubuque, Iowa 52002

ACKNOWLEDGEMENTS

The American Home Economics Association is indebted to many persons and organizations who over the years have assisted in the tremendous task of collecting the information contained in this Handbook. Among the organizations are the American Egg Board, the Agricultural Marketing Service and the Agricultural Research Service of the United States Department of Agriculture, American Amaranth Inc., Arrowhead Mills, California Bean Commission, Fleischmann's Yeast Inc., Florida Department of Natural Resources, Frito Lay, Inc., High Altitude Services, Idaho Bean Commission, Jenn-Air Company, Malt-O-Meal Company, National Barley Foods Council, National Dairy Council, National Live Stock and Meat Board, National Marine Fisheries Service of the National Oceanic and Atmospheric Administration, United States Department of Commerce, National Pasta Association, Prism Associates, Quaker Oats, Rival Manufacturing Company, Sandoz Nutrition, The Sugar Association, Inc., the United States Rice Council, the Food and Drug Administration of the United States Department of Health and Human Services, and the Wheat Foods Council.

Contributions and helpful criticisms have come from many Association members. Among those in particular are:
Judi Adams
LaVerne Anderson
Joan Gehle
Larry Hendershot
Klaus Lorenz
Richard Myron
Kristen O'Brien
Ruth Pearce
Nancy Rodie
Carol Walton

1992
COMMITTEE MEMBERS
Joyce Ostrander, Chairman
Gertrude Armbruster
Patricia E. Aune
Karen Basinger
Marlys Bielunski
Jeannette Bohnenkamp
Helen C. Brittin
Teresa Broadbent
Caroline H. Cannon
Anne S. Cooper
Phyllis M. Denee
Terry Egan
Kay Engelhardt
Karen Fabian
Patricia Godfrey
Rowena L. Hardinger
Barbara Harvey
Rosemary Hedlund
Rita Held
Ruth Holecek
Zoe Ann Holmes
Libby Hoyle
Janet M. Johnson
Nancy Johnson
Julie M. Jones
Noelle L. Kehrberg
Pat Kendall
Melissa Larsen
Nan Lenhart
Janice R. Leno
Joanne Z. Lytton
Linnet McGoodwin
Sandra J. Mitchell
Julia A. Mode
Kathryn Moore
Linda Nierman
Susam Lamb Parenti
Carolyn Raab
Susan Reynolds
Marilyn Rose
Alice Jo Shannon
Camilla Shilling
Janet Sim
Marguerite Stetson
Nancy C. Stutzman
Janelle Walter
Myrna M. Wesley
Cynthia Wilks
Margy Woodburn

PREFACE TO 1993 REVISED EDITION

It has been more than a decade since the eighth edition of the *Handbook of Food Preparation* was first available. In fact, it has been nearly fifty years since the first edition of the *Handbook* was published. During those intervening years, several generations of home economists and other food and nutrition specialists have been educated in the area of foods using this resource. Professionals have used it as a reference in various employment settings, as have homemakers, who have used it to answer a broad spectrum of food-related questions.

Two years ago, when the publication temporarily was out of print, the urgency of revising the handbook became obvious. A survey was sent to all members of the Food and Nutrition Section of AHEA asking them what portions of the book they most frequently used and what sections they wished to see revised or what new sections they would like to have included in a new edition. Respondents to the questionnaire were very helpful in providing suggestions for new and revised material, as well as generous in volunteering to work on the revision project.

In the last two years, long overdue major Federal legislation dealing with nutrition labeling has been enacted, and with it, a mandate for education related to the topic. It is hoped that this newest edition of the *Handbook of Food Preparation* incorporates the many suggestions from members regarding needed revisions and additional material, as well as provides up-to-date information on food product labeling regulations, which then can be used in nutrition education programming.

Execution and completion of this project would not have been possible without the organizational and editorial skills of Joyce Ostrander, Seattle Pacific University, coordinator and editor for this ninth edition, and the many people who served as writers and reviewers of various sections of the manuscript. The final editing of the publication was very ably handled by Margaret McWilliams, California State University — Los Angeles, retired, who also served as editor of the eighth edition.

Joanne M. Pearson, Chairperson
Food and Nutrition Section, 1991-1993

TABLE OF CONTENTS

General Food Information

CONSTRUCTION OF RECIPES

The writing of recipes carries with it a double responsibility. First, each recipe must be accurate and complete in essentials and written so simply and clearly that it cannot be misunderstood. At the same time it is important to present the recipe in a way that appeals to users while keeping within space limits.

A recipe is made up of two major parts — the list of ingredients and the method of preparing the product. These should be as practical as possible. Readily available ingredients, level measurements, and a simple procedure are ideal components of a recipe and should be used whenever possible. However, when the quality of a dish depends upon special ingredients or an unusual procedure, the recipe should include this information also.

Following are some well-tried rules for editing and setting up recipes. These should be a useful guide in the writing of new recipes or in the editing of recipe material for publication. Guidelines for metric usage also are presented.

INGREDIENTS

1. List all ingredients with measurements in the order used.

2. Do not abbreviate unless space is a problem.

3. Give ingredients in the easiest units of measure, as 1/4 cup instead of 4 tablespoons. Use standard measurements.

4. Use weights instead of measures when it is helpful, as for uncooked meat, poultry, fish, cheese and similar foods. Include weight or fluid measure for canned products.

5. Specify types of products needed, as *cake flour, all-purpose flour, dark corn syrup.*

6. For eggs, list *egg yolks* or *egg whites* or *eggs,* and include simple preparation, as *eggs, slightly beaten.* If special preparation is needed, as for meringue, explain in the method, detailing all necessary steps.

7. Safeguard a recipe by giving the exact names of products used. Or use descriptive names. *(Many commercial firms will supply generic names for products upon request.)*

METHOD

1. Use short sentences and clear, simple directions that anyone can follow easily.

2. Give word pictures, like *chill until syrupy*, or *beat until foamy throughout*, or *mixture thickens as it cools*. These are always helpful, especially with unfamiliar mixtures.

3. Without being wordy, use methods for combining or cooking ingredients that represent best accepted procedures. For example, specify the best way to sift dry ingredients together, or to thicken a sauce, or to fold in beaten egg white — these can be expressed in the same terms whenever they occur in recipes. This practice results in a standardized consistency of phrasing, from recipe to recipe.

4. Give thought to the most efficient order of work to avoid using extra bowls, cups, measuring tools, extra beating, and so forth.

5. Specify sizes of baking pans or casseroles, as: *9-inch round layer pans, 1 1/2 inches deep* or *shallow 1-quart casserole*.

6. Try to give both general and specific tests or temperatures. Then the recipe provides a double check on important stages. For example: *Cook to 238°F or until a small amount of syrup forms a soft ball in cold water*.

7. For the yield, give the number and size of servings to expect or the total measure, as: *Makes 4 1-cup servings*, or *makes 1 quart*.

ACCURACY

1. Read over the edited recipe. Does it say exactly what is meant? Is it simple, clear, and complete, yet as brief as it can be?

2. Recheck the ingredients, amounts, and method against the original recipe data. Recheck the order of ingredients as listed against the order used. Check for any omissions in temperatures, times, yields, and so forth.

3. With every typing of the recipe, read the new copy carefully against former copy.

4. With every printing of the recipe, check first proofs against original correct copy then proofread at each succeeding stage. And read proofs just for sense at least once.

RECIPE FORMS

The most-used forms for presenting recipes are given here. Each has advantages.

Standard form. This familiar form gives all ingredients first, then the method. The listed ingredients show just what is needed to make the recipe.

In this form, when an ingredient is modified the exact measurement should be given. For example: *2 cups sifted flour*, not 2 cups flour, sifted; *2 cups diced cooked carrots*, not

2 cups carrots, diced and cooked; *2 cups packed brown sugar*, not 2 cups brown sugar, packed. But *1 cup heavy cream, whipped*, not 1 cup whipped cream.

The method follows in paragraphs or steps. This form is especially good for recipes using many ingredients. Following is an example of the *standard form*:

Soft Gingerbread

1 2/3 cups sifted cake flour
  1/4 cup sugar
    1 teaspoon double-acting baking powder
  3/4 teaspoon soda
  1/2 teaspoon salt
  1/2 teaspoon cinnamon
  1/2 teaspoon ginger
  1/4 teaspoon cloves
  1/4 cup shortening (at room temperature)
  1/2 cup molasses
  1/2 cup water
    1 egg, unbeaten

1. Preheat oven to 350°F (moderate).

2. Sift dry ingredients together into mixing bowl. Add shortening. Combine molasses and water and pour three-fourths of this mixture into mixing bowl.

3. Beat 2 minutes at a low speed of electric mixer or 300 vigorous strokes by hand.

4. Add egg and remaining liquid, then beat 1 minute longer in mixer or 150 strokes by hand.

5. Pour batter into greased and lightly floured 9 x 9 x 2-inch pan.

6. Bake at 350°F 30 minutes, or until toothpick inserted in center comes out clean.

7. Serve hot with butter or lemon sauce.

Standard form in metric units. The following recipe is a rather literal conversion, using acceptable replacement units with minimal rounding of measures to provide the metric measurements. The 250 milliliter (ml) measurer with 25 ml graduations is a standard and "measuring spoons" are available to measure 1, 2, 5, 15 and 25 milliliters. Dry measurers are 250, 125 and 50 ml. All recipes converted to metric units must be tested and adjustments made to provide the best product.

Soft Gingerbread

375 milliliters sifted cake flour
 50 milliliters sugar
   5 milliliters double-acting baking powder
   4 milliliters soda
   2 milliliters salt
   2 milliliters cinnamon
   2 milliliters ginger
   1 milliliters cloves
 50 milliliters shortening
    (at room temperature)
125 milliliters molasses
125 milliliters water
   1 egg, unbeaten

1. Preheat oven to 180°C (moderate).

2. Sift dry ingredients together into mixing bowl. Add shortening. Combine molasses and water and pour three-fourths of this mixture into a mixing bowl.

3. Beat 2 minutes at a low speed of electric mixer or 300 vigorous strokes by hand.

4. Add egg and remaining liquid, then beat 1 minute longer in mixer or 150 strokes by hand.

5. Pour batter into greased and lightly floured 23 x 23 x 5 centimeter pan.

6. Bake at 180°C 30 minutes, or until toothpick inserted in center comes out clean.

7. Serve hot with butter or lemon sauce.

Action form. This recipe style combines narrative action with listed ingredients. Although this style is easy to follow, it takes more space and is difficult to arrange economically or attractively on paper. The ingredients are described in the same way as in the standard form. Following is an example of the *action form.*

Soft Gingerbread
Preheat oven to 350°F (moderate).
Measure and sift together into mixing bowl:
1 2/3 cups sifted cake flour
  1/4 cup sugar
   1 teaspoon double-acting baking powder
  3/4 teaspoon soda
  1/2 teaspoon salt
  1/2 teaspoon cinnamon
  1/2 teaspoon ginger
  1/4 teaspoon cloves

Add 1/4 cup shortening (at room temperature)

Mix together:
  1/2 cup molasses
  1/2 cup water

Pour three-fourths of this molasses-water mixture into dry ingredients.

Beat 2 minutes at a low speed of electric mixer or 300 vigorous strokes by hand.

Add remainder of liquid and 1 unbeaten egg.

Beat 1 minute longer in mixer or 150 strokes by hand.

Pour batter into greased and lightly floured 9 x 9 x 2-inch pan.

Bake at 350°F 30 minutes, or until toothpick inserted in center comes out clean. Serve hot.

Descriptive form. In this recipe form, each ingredient is followed by the necessary modification. For example: *carrots, diced, cooked*; *cake flour, sifted*; *evaporated milk, whole or skim*; *brown sugar, packed*; *eggs, slightly beaten*; *process Cheddar cheese, if desired*. This enables the cook to see readily what ingredients are needed.

The amounts of the ingredients are given in a separate column. Each step in the procedure is a separate paragraph, which appears parallel to the ingredients involved. To save space, the procedure may be placed below the ingredients. This is the newest recipe form and is easy to follow. An example of the *descriptive form* (Hot Chicken Sandwich) illustrates this construction.

Hot Chicken Sandwich
6 servings

Toast, whole-wheat, dry	6 slices	Preheat broiler.
Chicken,	1/3 to 1/2	Place toast slices

cooked, sliced	pound, as desired	in a shallow baking pan Cover with slices of chicken.
Cream of chicken soup, condensed, canned	10 1/2-oz. can	Combine soup and milk in saucepan. Heat to simmering.
Evaporated milk	1/3 cup	Pour hot soup over sandwiches.
Tomato slices	6 large or 12 small	Arrange tomato slices on top of sandwiches.
Bacon slices, cut in thirds, partly cooked	4	Top with bacon slices and olives.
Olives, stuffed, sliced	6	Broil until sandwiches are hot and bacon is crisp.

Narrative form. This form includes the amounts of ingredients with the method. It is especially suited to the short recipe, the spoken recipe, or the recipe of few ingredients where the method is more complex. It can be expanded for detail or condensed for offhand recipe ideas. Unless the recipe is short, this is the hardest form to follow, but it uses very little space. An example of the *narrative form* follows:

Baked Cod Fillets

Thaw one pound (500 g) frozen cod fillets. Cut into serving portions. Arrange fillets in a well-greased baking dish. Brush with melted butter or margarine and sprinkle with salt and pepper. Pour 3/4 cup (175 ml) milk over fish. Combine 2 tablespoons (30 ml) melted butter or margarine with one cup (250 ml) soft bread crumbs and sprinkle over fish. Bake at 400°F (200°C) about 40-45 minutes or until fish flakes easily when tested with a fork. Makes 3-4 servings.

OVEN TEMPERATURE TERMINOLOGY

Most recipe writers in giving oven temperatures state the degrees first and follow with the descriptive term, thus, 400°F or 200°C (hot) oven. The following listing shows the commonly accepted descriptive terms for each temperature range in degrees Fahrenheit and Celsius:

250°F to 275°F
    Very slow oven   (120°C to 140°C)
300°F to 325°F
    Slow oven   (150°C to 160°C)
350°F to 375°F
    Moderate oven   (180°C to 190°C)
400°F to 425°F
    Hot oven   (200°C to 220°C)
450°F to 475°F
    Very hot oven   (230°C to 240°C)
500°F to 525°F
    Extremely hot oven   (260°C to 270°C)

MODIFICATION OF RECIPES TO MEET DIETARY GUIDELINES

The link between diet and health is so important that the U.S. Departments of Agriculture and Health and Human Services have suggested the following **Dietary Guidelines for Americans**.

1. Eat a variety of foods.

2. Maintain healthy weight.

3. Choose a diet low in fat, saturated fat and cholesterol.

4. Choose a diet with plenty of vegetables, fruits and grain products.

5. Use sugars only in moderation.

6. Use salt and sodium only in moderation.

7. If you drink alcoholic beverages, do so in moderation and do not drive.

These guidelines do not apply to people who need special diets because of diseases or conditions that interfere with normal nutrition requirements. Such persons need special instructions from a registered dietitian or physician.

Most people, however, can benefit by modifying what they already eat. One way to modify the diet is to make adjustments in the types and amounts of ingredients in recipes so that the end result is just as satisfying, but fits better with the Dietary Guidelines.

When To Modify Recipes

Not all recipes need to be modified. Consider the following questions.

1. **Is the recipe already low in fat, cholesterol, sugar or salt?**
   If so, only minor or no changes may be needed. For example, if a recipe calls for an egg, and the dish serves eight people, the amount of cholesterol per serving already is low.

2. **How often is the food eaten?**
   It is not as important to modify a recipe for a dish eaten once or twice a year as it is for food eaten frequently. For example, it is more important to cut the fat in a weekly tuna fish salad sandwich than it is to cut the fat in a birthday cake.

3. **How much of the food is eaten?**
   Sometimes the best way to modify the intake of a certain food is to eat less of it. Decreasing the quantity eaten may be more satisfying than decreasing the quality.

How to Modify Recipes

1. **Identify the dietary goal and decide which nutrients to modify.** To cut calories (joules), identify what ingredients contribute the most calories (joules) and try to reduce the fat and/or sugar. To reduce sodium or to increase fiber, identify the ingredients that contain these components.

Calories: Fat is the most concentrated source of calories (joules). Each gram of fat supplies nine calories (38 kJ), compared to four calories (17 kJ) per gram of protein or carbohydrate and seven calories (29 kJ) per gram of alcohol. Reducing the amount of fat in a recipe is the most effective way to cut calories (Kj).

Fat: Fatty acids are basic components of fat. They are either saturated, monounsaturated or polyunsaturated. All fats in foods are mixtures of these fatty acids.

Saturated fats are found in the largest proportions in fats of animal origin such as whole milk, cream, cheese, butter, lard, meat and poultry. They also occur in large amounts in coconut oil and palm kernel oil.

Monounsaturated fats are found in large amounts in canola oil, olive oil and peanut oil, as well as in many margarines and semi-solid vegetable shortenings.

Polyunsaturated fats are found in the largest proportions in fats of plant origin such as liquid vegetable oils (safflower, sunflower, corn, cottonseed and soybean) and margarines and salad dressings made from them.

Cholesterol is a fat-like substance found only in food of animal origin. Significant sources include egg yolks, meats (particularly organ meats), butter, cream, and cheese.

Sugar comes in many forms, for example, white sugar, brown sugar, raw sugar, honey, corn syrup, molasses and maple syrup.

Sodium is found in salt (salt is 40 percent sodium), baking soda, baking powder, monosodium glutamate (MSG), soy sauce, bouillon, pickles, olives, cured meats, many canned vegetables and frozen dinners, most cheeses, sauces, and soups.

Fiber (important in a good diet) is found in whole grain breads and cereals; dry beans and peas; nuts and seeds; and fruits and vegetables, especially those with edible skins or seeds.

2. **Determine how to change the ingredient(s) to achieve the dietary goal.** Ingredient(s) can be:

a. eliminated completely,

b. reduced in amount, or

c. substituted with a more nutritionally acceptable ingredient.

To choose the best approach, it is helpful to have a general idea of the function of the ingredients, and what will happen if they are modified. Table 1.1 (page 10) lists the function and nutritional contribution of several ingredients.

TIPS FOR
HEALTHY MODIFICATIONS
Here are a few ways to modify recipes. These suggestions can be applied to most food; exceptions include those in which specific proportions of ingredients are essential to prevent spoilage or to create a certain product consistency (such as salt in cured meats or pickles, or sugar in jams and jellies).

1. **To Decrease Total Fat and Calories:**
■ Reduce fat by one-fourth to one-third in baked products. For example, if a recipe calls for 1 cup (250 ml) hydrogenated shortening, try 2/3 cup (150 ml). This works satisfactorily in many quick breads, muffins and cookies.

■ Cut back or even eliminate added fat in casseroles and main dishes. For example, browning meat in added fat is unnecessary, because some fat will drain from the meat as it cooks. Use a microwave oven, non-stick pan, or cooking spray.

- Saute or stir-fry vegetables with little fat or simmer in water, wine or broth.

- To thicken sauces and gravies without lumping, eliminate fat and instead mix cornstarch or flour with a small amount of cold liquid. Stir this mixture slowly into the hot liquid to be thickened and bring it back to a boil, stirring constantly. Add herbs, spices, or flavorings.

- Chill soups, gravies, and stews and skim off hardened fat before reheating to serve.

- Select lean cuts of meat and trim off visible fat. Remove skin from poultry before cooking.

- Bake, broil, grill, poach, or microwave meat, poultry or fish instead of frying in fat.

- Decrease the proportion of oil in home-made salad dressings. Try one-third oil to two-thirds vinegar. Low-fat cottage cheese, yogurt and buttermilk seasoned with herbs and spices also make low-fat dressings.

- Use reduced-calorie sour cream or may-onnaise. To reduce fat further, use plain low-fat or non-fat yogurt, buttermilk or blended cottage cheese instead of regular sour cream or mayonnaise for sauces, dips and salad dressings. If a sauce made with yogurt is to be heated, add one table-spoon of cornstarch to one cup of yogurt to prevent separation.

- Use nonfat or low-fat milk instead of whole milk. For extra richness, try undi-luted evaporated skim milk.

- Choose low-fat cheeses such as feta, Neufchatel and mozzarella instead of high-fat ones such as Swiss or Cheddar. Also use less cheese.

2. **To Decrease Saturated Fat and Cholesterol**
- Use two egg whites or an egg substitute product instead of one whole egg. In some recipes, simply decrease the total number of eggs. This is especially true if the fat and sugar also are decreased in the recipe.

- Use margarine instead of butter. Look for margarines in which liquid vegetable oil is the first ingredient.

- Use vegetable oils instead of solid fats. To substitute liquid oil for solid fats, use about one-fourth less than the recipe calls for. For example, if a recipe calls for 1/4 cup or 4 tablespoons (60 ml) of solid fat, use 3 tablespoons (45 ml) of oil. For cakes or pie crusts use a recipe that specifically calls for oil, because liquid fats require special mixing procedures.

3. **To Decrease Sugar**
- Reduce sugar by one-quarter to one-third in some baked goods and desserts. Add extra spice or flavoring to enhance im-pression of sweetness. This works best with quick breads, cookies, pie fillings, custard, puddings and fruit crisps.

- Decrease or eliminate sugar when canning or freezing fruits. Buy unsweetened frozen fruit or fruit canned in its own juice or water.

- In cookies, bar and drop, replace one-quarter of sugar called for with an equal proportion of nonfat dry milk; this reduces calories and increases calcium, protein and riboflavin in recipe.

- Choose fruit juices, club soda or skim milk over soft drinks and punches. Make fruit juice coolers with equal parts fruit juice and club soda or seltzer.

- Non-sugar sweeteners are available and work well in some applications. Be aware, however, that aspartame (Equal®) will not work well in products that are heated. Saccharin can be used in hot and cold foods, but may leave a bitter aftertaste. Neither product can enhance the volume or tenderness of baked products the way sugar does. Therefore, rather than substitute non-sugar sweeteners for sugar in recipes, it is best to choose recipes especially tested for use with non-sugar sweeteners.

4. To Decrease Sodium
- Salt may be omitted or reduced in most recipes. Do not reduce the salt in cured meats or pickled or brined vegetables, because it acts as a preservative. A small amount also is useful in yeast breads to help control the rising action of the yeast.

- Start with a gradual reduction. For example, if a recipe calls for 1 teaspoon (5 ml) of salt, try 1/2 teaspoon (2 ml). If the amount of salt is reduced gradually, an individual soon adjusts to a less salty taste.

- Choose fresh or low-sodium versions of products. For example, choose low-sodium soups and broths, soy sauce, canned vegetables and tomato products.

- Rely on herbs and spices rather than salt for flavor.

- Use garlic or onion powder instead of garlic or onion salt.

- Reduce the salt used in cooking pasta, noodles, rice or hot cereals.

- Dilute broth or bouillon with water when using as the cooking liquid.

- Read labels. Any ingredient that includes "sodium" as part of its name contains sodium.

5. To Increase Fiber
- Choose whole grain instead of highly refined products (for example, whole-wheat flour and bread, bulgur, brown rice, oatmeal, whole-corn meal, and barley).

- Whole-wheat flour usually can be substituted for up to one-half of the all-purpose refined flour. For example, if a recipe calls for 2 cups (500 ml) of all-purpose flour, try 1 cup (250 ml) of all-purpose and 1 cup (250 ml) of whole-wheat flour.

- Add extra fruits and vegetables to recipes.

■ Add fruits to muffins, pancakes, salads, and desserts, and add vegetables to quiche fillings, casseroles, and salads.

PUTTING IT INTO PRACTICE

To begin, look at the ingredients in the recipe and review their functions (Table 1.1). Then look at the general guidelines for modifying ingredients. Use the following steps when modifying a baked product.

1. **Compare the recipe with the basic recipe proportions given in this book.** To do this, express ingredients in terms of 1 cup of flour (250 ml). For example, if the recipe calls for 2 cups of flour (500 ml) and 1/2 cup sugar (125 ml), it calls for 1/4 cup (60 ml) sugar for every 1 cup flour (250 ml).

2. **Decide what ingredients to reduce.** Compare the amounts of fat, eggs, sugar and salt per 1 cup (250 ml) flour with amounts given in a basic recipe proportion table. Those on the high end of the range are the ones to reduce. Reduce fat and/or sugar to at least the midpoint of the range. Reduce eggs, if needed, to within range. Reduce sodium if desired.

3. **Decide which ingredients to increase.** Fat and sugar provide moistness and richness to recipes. When they are reduced, liquid needs to be added back, usually in the form of water, milk, fruit juice, applesauce, or fruit or vegetable pulp. Fruit and vegetable pulp also add fiber; milk adds calcium. Add back at least half as much liquid as sugar and fat reduced.

Table 1.1
FUNCTION AND NUTRITIONAL CONTRIBUTION OF BAKING INGREDIENTS

Ingredient	Function	Kilocalories Kilojoules	Nutritional Value
Flour	Contributes structure and rigidity. Gives stretch or elasticity. Provides thickening.	460/cup (1925)	Provides complex carbohydrates some protein, source of B vitamins and iron if enriched or whole grain.
Liquid	Dissolves dry ingredients (flour, sugar, salt). Moistens flour to develop structure. Dissolves leavening agents, e.g. baking powder, baking soda	Water = 0/cup Milk = 80-160/cup (335-670)	Milk is a good source of calcium, riboflavin, protein; also provides some vitamin A thiamin. Whole milk contains some saturated fat.
Salt	Helps improve taste. Slows rising in yeast products.	0/tsp	Provides 2,000 mg. sodium/tsp (5 ml).

Ingredient	Function	Kilocalories Kilojoules	Nutritional Value
Leavening	Important for structure and lightness.	0/tsp	Baking powder and soda contain sodium; yeast does not.
Sugar	Adds sweetness. Increases volume. Helps tenderize product. Aids in browning. Rapid browning.	Sugar = 770/cup (3222) Honey = 1020/cup (4269) Molasses = 700-825/cup (2930-3453)	Provides energy. Molasses provides some calcium and iron.
Fat	Helps tenderize. Adds flavor to product.	Lard, shortening, oil = 120/Tbsp (502) 1920/cup (8032) Butter/ Margarine = 110/Tbsp 1760/cup (460-7366)	Provides only fat calories. Butter, lard, vegetable shortening and palm and coconut oil higher in saturated than polyunsaturated fat. Margarine and other oil higher in polyunsaturated fat. Butter, lard and other animal fats contain cholesterol. Butter and margarine provide some sodium and vitamin A.
Eggs	Contribute to elasticity and structure. Beaten whites incorporate air into batters. Yolks add color and emulsify fats.	80/egg (335)	Provide protein and small amounts of several nutrients. Egg yolk rich in fat, saturated fat and cholesterol.
Nuts	Flavor and variety.	750-850/cup (3139-3557)	Provide some protein, B-vitamins, iron and fiber. Generally rich in fat and polyunsaturated fat.
Fruits and Vegetables	Flavor and variety.	Fruits = 100-200/cup (418-837) Vegetables = 20-150/cup (84-628)	Generally good source of vitamins A and/or C. Good source of fiber, especially when skins and tiny seeds are consumed.

For example, if you reduce the sugar in a recipe by 2 tablespoons (30 ml) and fat by 4 tablespoons (60 ml), add 3 tablespoons (45 ml) milk or fruit juice. Because honey and molasses have greater moisture retaining properties than sugar, replacing a portion of the sugar that remains in the recipe with honey or molasses may improve softness and moistness in the resulting product.

4. **Consider adding nonfat dry milk to increase calcium content.** In many baked recipes nonfat dry milk can replace up to one-fourth of the sugar in the recipe with good results. Two to 4 tablespoons (30 to 60 ml) of nonfat dry milk powder per cup (250 ml) of flour also may be added to cookies and cakes as an additive. Look at the recipe and add nonfat dry milk powder equal to the reduction in sugar.

5. **Try recipe with modifications made.** Use the tooth pick or touch test, not visual appearance, to evaluate doneness. Because sugar slows protein coagulation and slows starch gelatinization, products made with reduced sugar will bake more quickly and be less brown when done.

6. **Evaluate the quality and taste of the product.** If the recipe still seems richer than desired, make further reductions in fat and sugar and increase liquid. If the product seems dry, be careful to not over bake. If still dry and not over baked, try adding more liquid (water, fruit juice, applesauce, fruit or vegetable pulp), or substitute a portion of the sugar in the recipe with honey or molasses.

7. **Try reformulated recipe and repeat steps 5 and 6 until pleased with the results.** Remember to record the modifications that work. Recipes that meet the Dietary Guidelines are worth repeating. The Carrot Bread (on the following page) is an example of an original recipe with modifications.

HIGH-ALTITUDE FOOD PREPARATION

At altitudes above 3000 feet (914 m) food preparation by traditional, microwave, or campfire methods may require changes in time, temperature, recipe proportions, microwave power levels and/or pan size. The reason is reduced atmospheric pressure at higher elevations; the pressure decreases about 1/2 pound per 1000 feet or 2.2 Newtons per 305 meters increase in elevation. Pressure per square inch (0.645 square meter) at sea level is 14.7 pounds (6.7 kg), at 5000 feet (1524 m) is 12.3 pounds (5.6 kg), and at 10,000 feet (3048 m) is 10.2 pounds (4.6 kg). This decreased pressure affects food preparation in several ways:

Water and liquids evaporate faster and boil at lower temperatures.

Leavening gases in breads and cakes expand more.

Liquids foam more quickly, and cakes and breads rise more during baking; liquid or cakes may flow over the sides of the pan.

Microwaved foods thaw and reheat at a slightly slower rate.

Carrot Bread

ORIGINAL RECIPE	kcal/(kJ)	MODIFIED RECIPE	kcal/(kJ)	Improvement(s) Made
Sugar, 3/4 cup (175 ml)	578 (2419)	1/4 cup sugar (60 ml)	192 (804)	Decreased sugar
		1/2 cup orange juice (125 ml)	60	Increased vitamin C and moisture
Soybean oil, 1 cup (250 ml)	1920 (8035)	1/3 cup corn oil (80 ml)	636 (2662)	Decreased fat
Eggs, 2	160 (670)	One egg	80 (335)	Decreased cholesterol
Vanilla, 1 1/2 tsp (7 ml)	0	Same	0	———
All-purpose flour, 2 cups (500 ml)	910 (3808)	1 cup all-purpose flour (250 ml)	862 (3607)	
		1 cup whole wheat flour (250 ml)		Increased fiber
Baking Powder, 1 tsp (5 ml)	0	Same	0	———
Baking Soda, 1/2 tsp (2 ml)	0	Same	0	———
Cinnamon, 1 Tbsp (15 ml)	0	Same	0	———
Salt, 1/2 tsp (2 ml)	0	Salt, 1/4 tsp (1 ml)	0	Decreased sodium
Carrots, grated 1 1/4 cups (300 ml)	50 (209)	Carrots, grated 1 1/2 cups (375 ml)	60 (251)	Increased vitamin A and fiber
TOTALS: Recipe	3618 (15141)		1890 (7910)	
1/2-inch slice (1.25 cm)	201 (841)		105 (439)	

Directions: Beat together sugar, oil, eggs, orange juice and vanilla. Stir dry ingredients together and add to sugar and oil mixture. Blend in grated carrots. Bake in oiled 9 x 5-inch (23 x 13 cm) loaf pan at 350° (180°C) for 40 to 50 minutes.

Foods microwaved at 5000 feet (1524 m) versus sea level are often more moist, but they cool and dry out rapidly. Store baked goods covered.

Foods cook more slowly in boiling water as altitude increases.

Approximate boiling temperatures of water at various elevations:

sea level	212.0°F/100.0°C
2000 feet/ 610 meters	208.2°F/ 97.8°C
5000 feet/1524 meters	202.5°F/ 94.5°C
7500 feet/2286 meters	197.8°F/ 91.8°C
10,000 feet/3048 meters	193.0°F/ 89.0°C

Each 1000 feet (304.8 m) elevation increase decreases the boiling point temperature 1.9°F (1.1°C). Determining microwave wattage with the boiling water test may not be accurate over 2500 feet (762 m).

BOILED, COOKED, AND FRIED FOODS GUIDELINES:

Since water boils at lower temperatures at higher altitudes, food products require a longer cooking time to reach the desired end point.

Beverages/soups: Increase the amount of coffee/tea and brew time for similar flavors. Brew pot versus cup to release flavors and maintain heat. Above 8000 feet (2438 m), brewed beverages are not very hot. Homemade soups need more time and water. Milk-based beverages boil over easily.

Vegetables: Increase boiling time 4-11 percent at 5000 feet (1524 m), 20-25 percent at 7200 feet (2194 m), and 55-66 percent at 10000 feet (3048 m) and add more water. Foil-wrapped potatoes with roast at 325°F (160°C) need 2-2 1/2 hours at 5000 (1524 m) and 7500 feet (2286 m), and 3 hours at 10000 feet (3048 m). Prick potatoes to prevent explosions during baking. A general rule for microwaving fresh whole vegetables is to heat on high for 7 minutes/pound (454 g) for cut vegetables, then add 1-2 tablespoons (15-30 ml) water and microwave 1/2-1 minute more. For frozen vegetables, add 2-4 tablespoon (30-60 ml) water and 1-3 minutes more time. To prepare dried beans, soak over-night, and then cook using 2-3 times more water and greatly increased time; a pressure saucepan is recommended for cooking soaked, dried beans at altitudes above 7500 feet (2286 m).

Meat/poultry: For moist heat cooking at 5000 feet (1524 m) 25-50 percent more time is needed for braising or simmering meat and 5 to 35 minutes more time for microwaving. Watch the liquid levels, and use tight fitting lids. Microwave for the first braising period on High for 8-10 minutes until boiling, then cook at lower power until fork tender. For dry heat roasting in a hot oven, use the same or slightly longer times; check for doneness with a thermometer. Large or dense pieces may need 10-25 percent more time. A three-pound (1.36 kg) chicken needs 10-15 minutes more roasting time or 3-5 minutes more when microwaving. Pan-fry at slightly higher settings; increase electric skillet/wok temperature by 25°F (14°C). For grilling, a partial precook and frequent basting are helpful to prevent drying of meat. Note: Charcoal briquets need 45 minutes to become 70 percent ashed-over at 5000 feet (1524 m) versus 20-25 minutes at sea level. In the microwave one pound (454 g) ground meat needs 1-3 minutes more time.

Fruits and steamed puddings: More time for all cooking methods may be needed. Above 7500 feet (2286 m), precooking pie fruit is desirable.

Egg cooking:

Soft cooked

5000 feet/1524 meters	5-6 minutes
7500 feet/2286 meters	7 minutes
10,000 feet/3048 meters	9 minutes

Hard cooked

5000 feet/1524 meters	20-25 minutes
7500 feet/2286 meters	23-27 minutes
10,000 feet/3048 meters	26 minutes

Slight time increases are needed for poached eggs.

Sugar cooking: Candies, syrups, frostings, and jellies need a decrease in the final cooked-stage temperature. The temperature should be decreased by the difference in the boiling water temperature at the preparation altitude and that of sea level. Example: A thermometer in boiling water reads 202°F (94.5°C) or ten degrees below 212°F (5.5 below 100°C). For soft ball candy, subtract 10 degrees from 238°F (114.5°C) and cook only to 228°F (5.5 from 114.5°C or 109°C). The cold water candy and jelly sheeting tests are the same as at sea level. Microwaved candies foam up more, so use a larger dish or make half of the recipe.

Starch Cooking: At altitudes of 5,000 feet (1524 m) or higher, problems may be encountered in the use of cornstarch for thickening. Direct heat, a heavy sauce pan (not a double boiler) and constant stirring to prevent scorching are needed for the starch to reach maximum gelatinization. Overcooked sauces may break down and become watery. Above 7500

feet (2286 m), replace 1 tablespoon (15 ml) of cornstarch with 2 tablespoons (30 ml) flour in pudding/filling. When microwaving, make sure the whole mixture is boiling and thickened; add time if necessary.

Rice/pasta: Add 1 teaspoon (5 ml) oil per cup of rice/pasta to prevent sticking and boiling over. For rice at 5000 feet (1524 m) add an additional 4-8 tablespoons (60-120 ml) water per 1 cup (236.6 ml) of water in the recipe and increase time by 25-30 percent. When microwaving, cook on high 5-8 minutes until boiling and continue at 50 percent power, increase time by 30-40 percent. For pasta, keep water at an adequate boil, taste test and generally add more time. When microwaving cereals, use a large bowl. In casseroles with rice, pasta, dried beans and firm vegetables, precook these items. For milk-based casseroles, use a larger dish to prevent boiling over.

Deep fat frying: The lower boiling point of water in foods requires lowering the temperature of the fat to prevent overbrowned but raw foods. A rough guide is to lower the frying temperature about 2-3° F for each 1000 feet (1 to 1.5°C per 304.8 m) increase in elevation. Example: At 8000 feet (2438 m), doughnuts need fat at 359°F to 351°F or 24 to 16°F(183 to 177°C or 13 to 7°C) lower. Cake-like doughnuts may need less baking powder, sugar and/or shortening.

Canning, pressure canning and freezing: See Section 13 Food Preservation. Pressure saucepans designed only for pressure cooking should not be used for canning.

Pressure saucepans: Pans which are designed

ONLY for pressure cooking and NOT canning require an increase in pressure to achieve the required processing temperature.

STEAM PRESSURES AT VARIOUS ALTITUDES

Altitude		Pressure Required for 240°F 116°C		Pressure Required for 250°F 121°C	
Feet	Meters	lb.	kPa	lb.	kPa
Sea Level	0	10	68.9	15	103.4
1000	305	10.5	72.4	15.5	106.8
2000	610	11	75.8	16	110.3
3000	914	11.5	79.3	16.5	113.8
4000	1219	12	82.7	17	117.2
5000	1524	12.5	86.2	17.5	120.7
7000	2134	13.5	93.1	18.5	127.6
10000	3048	15	103.4	20	137.9

LEAVENED AND BAKED FOODS GUIDELINES:

Since the atmospheric pressure is less at higher elevations, leavened baked products can rise excessively, stretching the cell structure, producing a coarse, irregular texture, overflowing the pan sides, and even falling in the center with a sway or depression and low volume. Quick breads, if low in sugar, are firm enough to withstand the excess rising and need only to have leavening reduced, liquid added and temperature and maybe pan size increased. For cookies, see "Hints" below. Generally microwaved cakes require fewer adjustments than do cakes baked in an oven. Accurate measurements are especially important at higher elevations. Most cakes, cake-like products and breads are affected slightly at 2000 feet (610 m) and significantly above

3500 feet (1067 m). Adjustments in the recipe are needed above 3500 feet (1067 m). There are no "formulas" for adjusting and only repeated tests can determine the most successful adjusted recipe.

Changes to improve baked products and adjust recipes: This includes cakes, quick breads, cookies, bar cookies, brownies, pancakes, and doughnuts. Try the smaller measurements first.

Oven temperature — Increase 15 to 25°F (8-14°C except for some chocolate or delicate cakes which might burn. High temperatures help to "set" the batter before the cells formed by leavening gases can expand too much. Cookies may or may not need a temperature increase.

Oven baking time — Decrease due to higher temperatures. For microwave baking, add 1-3 minutes if cake falls at end of the bake time when the door is opened.

Leavening — To prevent excess rising, reduce baking powder 1/8 teaspoon at 3000 feet (0.6 ml-914 m), 1/8-1/4 teaspoon at 5000 feet (0.6-1.25 ml-1524 m), 1/4 teaspoon at 7000 feet (1.25 ml-2134 m). Reduce soda in quick breads, muffins, pancakes/waffles by 1/4 of total amount. Use at least 1/2 teaspoon (2.5 ml) soda for each cup (236.6 ml) of acid liquids.

Sugar — For each one cup (236.6 ml), decrease 0-1 tablespoon at 3000 feet (0-15 ml at 914 m), 2-3 tablespoons at 5000 feet (30-45 ml at 1524 m), 4-5 tablespoons at 7000 feet (60-75 ml at 2134 m). Note: Fast evaporation of water leads to a higher concentration of sugar, which raises the temperature when the structure sets and may cause the cake to fall. Therefore, sugar is decreased and liquid increased. A sticky, overly browned crust and/or dip in center indicates excess sugar.

Liquid — To compensate for greater evaporation in cakes and quick breads, increase liquid. For each one cup (236.6 ml) add 1-2 tablespoons at 3000 feet (15-30 ml at 914 m), 2-4 tablespoons at 5000 feet (30-60 ml at l524 m), or 3-4 tablespoons at 7000 feet (45-60 ml at 2134 m). In cookies, add 1/2-2 teaspoons (2.5-10 ml) water per recipe with the flour addition. If biscuit dough seems dry, add 1 tablespoon per one cup (15 ml/236.6 ml) flour.

Flour — Since flour strengthens the structure, for each recipe, add 1-4 tablespoons at 5000 feet (15-60 ml at 1524 m) and 2-5 tablespoons at 7000 feet (30-75 ml at 2134 m). Cookies squeezed through a press may need less flour. For self-rising flour, use only high altitude-adjusted recipes.

Eggs — Since eggs strengthen the structure and add liquid, use large eggs, although some cooks prefer extra-large eggs. For angel food, sponge or foam type cakes or souffles, it is important not to beat too much air (leavening) into the eggs. Therefore, use cold eggs, beat whites to soft peaks that just fold over; do not beat until stiff and dry. With yolks or whole eggs, beat only until they are slightly thickened. For foam-leavened cakes, using less sugar, more flour and a higher baking temperature also helps. For a four-egg popover recipe, add 1 more egg and decrease shortening, if listed. Above 7500 feet (2286 m) an extra egg can help rich cakes.

Fats/oils — Excess fat weakens the cell structure. For high fat-high sugar quick breads, fat may need to be reduced 2-8 tablespoons (30-120 ml) per recipe. For waffles add 1 teaspoon (5 ml) extra oil to prevent sticking.

Pans — Use larger pan size or increase number of pans. Example: For two 8-inch rounds (20 cm), use three 8-inch (20 cm) or two 9-inch (23 cm) rounds. If a large hollow air hole develops in quick breads, increase pan size or number of muffins. Generous "greasing" (1-2 tablespoon per pan — 15-30 ml per pan) and flouring (if required) helps prevent sticking, an altitude problem.

Other hints: For microwaved cakes, begin with recipes developed for microwave use. Changes may not be needed, but if the cake does not rise as high, falls, has a wet center, or is too tender, then adjustments are recommended. If center bottom is underdone, bake on inverted plate.

Sea level recipes for cookies, bar cookies and brownies may give acceptable, but different results at high altitudes. It is best to bake a test cookie to determine if more flour, liquid, or temperature changes are needed. Note: Cookies continue to brown a little after removal from oven, so cookies should be baked to a lighter color than desired. Since high altitude cookies are more delicate, cool 1 minutes on baking sheet and carefully remove to rack. These changes may be needed for microwaved bar cookies or brownies, too.

For "mushroomed" muffins, adjust recipe for the altitude and increase number of muffins.

For pancakes, check that the insides are not doughy when the surfaces appear brown.

Commercial mixes — In cake, muffin, brownie, and other mixes, ingredients cannot be removed; therefore adjustments for conventional/microwave mixes are: adding flour, liquid, and/or an egg, plus increasing pan size or number of pans, or baking temperature/ time. Follow the high altitude directions printed on the mix boxes, or contact the food manufacturer for information on adjustments.

Yeast breads — Rising time can be from 15 to 30 minutes shorter; let dough rise just until doubled. Better flavor is developed by punching down the dough twice. During rising, loosely cover dough with foil to prevent a dry crust from forming. Automatic bread machine recipes may require experimentation to prevent too dry a dough, or overrising. Sometimes yeast is reduced and liquid added.

Pies, pastry, cheesecake and souffles — For slightly dry pastry dough, add water by teaspoon until the dough cleans the bowl. Thoroughly prick unfilled crusts to prevent bubbling. See: Boiled Foods: Fruits - pie fillings. Custard and pumpkin pies may need high-sided pie plates. Baked cheesecakes may have higher sides, and a center area which "settles back" during cooling. Cheesecakes require much experimentation to adjust. For souffles. See Leavened and Baked Foods: Eggs.

For questions about other commercial food products, contact the food manufacturer. It may have high altitude directions on file.

MICROWAVE COOKING BASICS

Most countertop microwave ovens have magnetron tubes that generate microwaves at a frequency of 2450 megahertz (MHz), while many combination (oven-microwave) units generate microwaves at 915 MHz. When microwaves are absorbed by food, the polar (charged) molecules such as water, fat and sugar attempt to align with the field, which changes 2450 million times (or 915) per second. Heat is evolved rapidly within the food, primarily due to this molecular friction. Heating also occurs by subsequent conduction of this heat. Microwaves are non-ionizing and do not cause chemical or molecular changes.

Cooking power for most consumer ovens is within a range of 400-720 watts; however, there are no standards. Ovens designed for both conventional and microwave cooking supply 300-400 watts cooking power. The higher the cooking power, the faster the cooking will be. The weight of food is the most accurate measure for cooking time.

Although some ovens are equipped with temperature sensing probes, most microwave heating is controlled by adjusting the time according to the cooking power, the mass and density of the food, and its starting temperature. Some ovens have variable speeds (power controls) which automatically cycle the magnetron tube off and on to vary the amount of energy used to cook foods during the specified period of time. Denser foods cook better with less energy. Size of the oven cavity, quantity of food and oven wattage determine cooking time. The glass tray on the bottom of the countertop oven elevates food to allow microwaves to reach the bottom of the food. The tray should not be removed during cooking. Do not operate oven without either food or liquid in it.

Cooking power may not be evenly distributed throughout the oven; however, new features are minimizing this problem. Microwave ovens designed for cooking more than one food at a time are constructed intentionally so that different amounts of energy are directed into different areas of the oven. Manufacturers are always updating their microwave ovens and products. Refer to the manufacturer's directions for use and care of the specified oven being used.

To Estimate Cooking Power (wattage)

In 4-cup (1 l) glass measuring cup, add 2 cups (500 ml) water. Record temperature of water. Microwave on high/full power for 1 minute. Record temperature. Subtract first temperature from second temperature and multiply this by 17.5 = actual wattage. Repeat this three times and figure the average of the three.

Testing Distribution of Cooking Power

Microwaves are directed by a stirrer fan, carousel tray, or baffle, but still they may not always be directed evenly; hence, food may cook unevenly. To avoid uneven cooking, rotate dish (1/4 turn) or stir food half way through cooking time.

To test distribution of power, select test material, such as cake batter. Place an **equal amount** of test material in nine to 12 **identical containers** such as custard cups. Space containers of test material evenly throughout the oven. Turn oven on full power for two minutes. Greater concentration of power will be indicated by visible signs of cooking in certain areas of the test product.

Water (equal amounts) may also be used for this test. The difference in water temperature from unit to unit may be determined after two minutes of heating. Higher water temperatures indicate a greater concentration of power in that area.

Mass and Shape of Food

As the mass of food increases, the length of time required to heat or cook increases. The relationship approaches linearity, but varies with each food. The major heating by microwaves penetrates only the outer 1 inch (2.5 cm) of the food. The center of large masses of food must be heated by conduction of heat from the hot portions during a "standing" period following heating. "Standing time" or "carryover cooking" allows the food to rest and continue cooking. The amount of time will vary depending on the size, volume, moisture and fat content, and density of the food. Standing time averages will usually be: 1-3 minutes for individual or small items; 5 minutes for vegetables, sauces and cakes; 10 minutes for dense main dishes; and 15 minutes for large items such as roasts and turkeys. Avoid additional cooking until standing time is completed. If necessary, add cooking time in increments of 1-2 minutes to avoid overcooking.

Techniques for Promoting Even Heating

Cooking may be assisted by subdividing food into uniform or smaller portions, rotating or stirring periodically, or periodically inverting large portions of food during cooking. Foods arranged in a circle cook more uniformly than they do in a rectangle. Avoid irregular shapes and square corners, or shield edges of foods that are thin, with a *small* piece of foil during cooking. Foil must not touch the side of the oven.

Place the thicker or more dense portions of food toward the outside of the container or arrange food in a doughnut shape. Do not overcook food. Allow for standing time after cooking. Do not remove cover during standing time.

For foods requiring long cooking times, use reduced power for part of the cooking, or manually cycle the energy on and off at intervals. The "off" interval allows time for the temperature to equalize in the food.

Initial Temperature of Food

The lower the initial temperature of the food, the longer the time required to achieve the desired end temperature by heating. Starting with frozen food increases the time even more, since additional energy is required to melt the ice (latent heat of fusion). Most foods except vegetables are thawed before cooking. (Thawing may be done in the microwave oven by using reduced power prior to the actual cooking period.)

Density of Food

The more dense the food, the greater the amount of microwave energy required for heating. When pieces of food differing in density or thickness are heated simultaneously, the less dense or thinner portions should be placed near the center of the container. For example, place peas in the center of a ring of mashed potatoes.

Water Content

Free water is the most polar food constituent and the most reactive to microwaves. The rapid conversion of water to steam, which occurs in microwave heating, necessitates the puncturing of food membranes or skins to prevent the food from exploding. Fats also heat very rapidly when subjected to microwaves.

When frozen foods are heated, pockets of free water can form and become superheated, resulting in an explosive release of steam. The defrost cycles on microwave ovens provide energy intermittently by pulsing on and off (cook-rest), allowing time during the off cycle for helping to equalize the temperature in the food and heating to the center of large pieces of food. Covering, during defrosting, helps to distribute the heat more evenly. Food will also need to be rotated.

Reheating Foods

Reheating foods is one of the microwave oven's greatest assets. Reheat refrigerated leftovers in serving containers, allowing 3-4 minutes/pound (0.5 kg). Frozen cooked foods will need a rest-cook cycle with rotation. To reheat foods on a dinner plate, loosely cover and allow 1-2 minutes on full power. Bread products are porous and will heat fast. A roll will heat in 10-15 seconds and may still feel cool to touch. Allow carry over time before heating again to avoid a tough, hard roll. Slotted roasting racks are helpful to reheat bread products wrapped in a paper towel or napkin. For each cup of pasta or rice, allow 1-2 minutes to reheat.

MICROWAVES AND FOOD SYSTEMS

Meat, Poultry, Fish

Tender, boneless cuts of meat are more suitable for microwave cooking than less tender cuts. Ground beef patties, steaks, or chops may be cooked with high power. For roasts, reduce cooking power, particularly after the meat is hot. Reduce power during the entire cooking period to slow the process for tenderization of pot roasts. Recommendations for promoting even heating are also applicable to cooking meats by microwaves.

Roasts may need 15-30 minutes of standing time for conduction of heat to the center of the roast after microwave cooking is stopped. From 5-15 minutes standing time is needed for fish or poultry, depending upon the size. The slower the cooking and the smaller the mass, the shorter the standing time required. Since the internal temperature of the meat will rise during standing, the following internal temperatures are suggested as a guide for terminating cooking:

Rare beef	125°F (52°C)
Medium beef	140°F (60°C)
Well done beef	158°F (70°C)
Lamb	158°F (70°C)
Pork	155°F (68°C)
Reheating fully cooked ham	131°F (55°C)
Poultry (>3.3 lb or 1.5 kg)	170°F (77°C)

Use only thermometers designed for microwave ovens, or use a conventional thermometer when the oven is turned off. If the meat does not achieve the desired internal temperature during the standing period, it can be sliced, covered and cooked a few minutes longer without detrimental effects on eating quality.

An even coating of fat (about 0.5 cm thick) provides a means of basting a roast during microwave cooking. Fat which collects in the bottom of the container during roasting should be removed midway during cooking so that it will not splatter or shield the underside of the meat from microwaves.

Since less evaporation occurs than with conventional heating, only about 1/4 cup (50 ml) liquid is required for moist heat cookery of less tender cuts of meat. Prepare meat for cooking by piercing with a long-tined fork. If a pot roast is large, cut it into chunks to lessen the time required to heat the interior to a temperature sufficient to start solubilization of collagen.

Small portions of meat, poultry or fish should be turned once during cooking. Place whole birds breast side down first and turn over midway in the cooking process. The larger the mass, the more often it should be turned. The skin of whole poultry or poultry pieces should be pierced in several places prior to cooking.

Browning aids, such as a browning utensil or coatings, may be preferred for meat patties, steaks, or chops. Coatings will be less crisp than with conventional cooking. Crisping can be achieved by placing the product under a conventional broiler after cooking. For products that tend to become dry, such as pork chops, cover with sauce.

Milk, Cheese, and Eggs

Milk tends to foam excessively when heated to the boiling point by microwaves. Therefore, a larger container is required for heating milk alone or for casseroles and other foods containing large amounts of milk. Products containing cheese should be cooked at reduced power or for a very short time to prevent a rubbery texture.

Since eggs or egg-milk combinations cook fast, the time span is reduced between optimum coagulation and over coagulation. Slow cooking and close attention are necessary. As a rule, egg foams and products composed largely of egg foam are less satisfactory when cooked by microwaves than when cooked conventionally.

Starch Pastes, Pasta, Rice

Since gelatinization of starch is enhanced by rapid heating, starch cookery is suited to microwave heating. Periodic stirring is necessary for lump-free starch-thickened sauces. The sauce should be brought to a boil to achieve maximum thickening, but boiling should not be continued because the swollen starch granules may rupture.

Rice and pasta require time to absorb moisture. They cook well by microwaves, but little time is saved by this method of cookery. Additional time, at reduced power, will be necessary after the water has been brought to a boil. Adding a small amount of oil reduces the tendency to boil over. Pasta, rice or cereal may be cooked for individual servings or in quantity. Cook in a dish large enough to boil water without boiling over.

Sugar Solutions

Microwave cooking of sugar solutions minimizes the problems of scorching and of crystal build-up on the sides of the cooking container. With candy, the solution can be brought to a rapid boil, and boiling can be continued at a reduced level of microwave power. A large container is essential to prevent boiling over.

Jams or preserves can be made in small batches by microwave heating. The power should be reduced after the mixture has reached the boiling point to minimize the possibility of overcooking.

Vegetables and Fruits

Vegetables and fruits are easily cooked by microwaves. The speed of cooking favors the retention of color and pleasing flavor. Overcooking may result in a rubbery texture. For vegetables which require short cooking by conventional methods, little time is saved by microwave heating. However, for long-cooking vegetables, such as whole potatoes, time may be reduced as much as 85 or 90 percent. Many vegetables can be cooked without added water, but for those with a high cellulose content, texture is improved by cooking with a small amount of water. Most vegetables and fruits should be covered. Skins on whole vegetables serve as a cover and should be pierced to permit steam to escape and to minimize the possibility of explosions.

Baked Products

Cakes, muffins and other quick breads cook well by microwaves, but do not form brown crusts. Leavening should be reduced by one-third for microwave cooking. For products prepared from mixes, the texture may be improved by allowing the batter to stand for 15-20 minutes before cooking. The surface of the products will appear slightly moist when cooking is complete. Allow 10-12 minutes standing time for layer cakes so that some cooking will continue for a short time. Lining the container with waxed paper will reduce the tendency for sogginess on the bottom of the cake. Biscuits, yeast bread, cookies (other than bar cookies), and cakes without shortening are less satisfactory when cooked by microwaves than when baked conventionally.

Fats and Oils

Fats and oils heat rapidly when exposed to microwaves. However, they do not heat uniformly, which can result in very dangerous spattering of hot fat and uneven cooking. Therefore, deep fat frying in a microwave is not recommended.

Baby Food

A 4 1/2 ounce (128 g) jar of baby food may be heated with the lid off, for 45-90 seconds To heat a baby bottle, place bottle and 1/2 cup (125 ml) of room temperature water in oven. Heat on high for 15 seconds. Refrigerated milk or formula requires 30-40 seconds on high. Allow at least one minute standing time before stirring or shaking well to help avoid having some of the formula dangerously hot. Check temperature before serving to prevent possible burning of baby.

PREPARATION OF MEALS BY MICROWAVES

Heat long-cooking foods and those which hold heat well first. Allow for continued cooking (particularly in large masses of food) after the microwave heating has stopped. If more than one food is cooked at one time, extend the length of time. Cooking time must be adjusted according to the amount of food cooked at one time. Use a microwave oven for partial cooking of some foods. Take advantage of this appliance for fast defrosting and for fast reheating of foods.

Plan meals for the characteristics of microwave heating, such as less evaporation of liquid, greater expansion of leavened products, rapid evolution of steam, and continued heating after oven is turned off, particularly in dense foods.

Remember that casseroles and entrees will require only about one-fourth to one-third as long for microwave as for conventional cooking. An interruption for testing doneness will not be detrimental to the finished quality of any product.

Adapting Conventional Recipes

Use successful microwave recipes as a guide to modify conventional recipes. Consider the major ingredients and their suitability for microwave cooking. Use small recipes first, as they are easier to convert than large recipes.

Recipes with a large amount of moisture may need adjusting as the microwave does not evaporate as much liquid. A general rule is to reduce the liquid in the conventional recipe by one-fourth. To determine cooking time, consider that 1 cup (250 ml) of tap water boils and 1 cup of food heats in 1 1/2 to 3 minutes on high. If your oven takes longer, add additional time to recipes. To be more accurate, weigh food and estimate 6-7 minutes/pound (0.5 kg) on high, depending on oven wattage. Increase cooking time as the amount of food increases. Other considerations are shape, volume, weight, density, initial temperature, oven wattage, peak electric use hours and the cooking container. Undercook when experimenting with new foods and recipes and then continue to cook if more time is judged to be needed.

High Altitude

Adjust conventional recipes by increasing flour 1/4 cup (60 ml) and liquid by 1/3 cup (80 ml). Since boiling occurs at a lower temperature, it may take longer (1-2 minutes) to cook dense foods.

Choosing Utensils

Choose utensils that are transparent to microwaves, such as glass, paper, dishwasher-safe plastics, china (without metal rim), earthenware, or straw. Do not use metal, aluminum foil, paper goods made from recycled paper, or Melamine ware. Plastic containers may deform from heat if used for syrups or high fat foods. Plastic film should be vented when used as a cover. Slit boil-in-bag containers to permit steam to escape.

Test dishes for microwave use by placing one cup (250 ml) of tap water and an empty dish in oven. Heat on high for one minute. If water gets hot and dish does not, it can be used. Use only glass-ceramic· dishes if oven has infrared browner. Metal reflects microwaves; if recommended by manufacturer, foil may be used for shielding.

Use only thermometers designed for microwave ovens. However, conventional thermometers can be used to test the temperature of food when the oven is turned off.

As covers, use casserole lids, plastic film, paper plates, waxed paper, paper towels, or napkins. Covering food traps heat and speeds up the cooking time. Choose porous materials, such as paper towels, if the surface of the food is dry. If possible, use round containers for cooking instead of those with square corners. A heatproof glass may be used in the center of casseroles to achieve the doughnut shape. Special microwave browning dishes are heated empty in the microwave to absorb energy. The bottom of the dish absorbs energy instead of transmitting it, thus causing the food to brown when placed on the very hot surface.

Reducing the Speed of Cooking

To retard the rate of cooking, utilize oven controls for reducing power, cycle energy on and off manually, or introduce an additional load, such as a container of water to absorb part of the energy.

Safety

Do not melt paraffin; it does not have any moisture to absorb energy. Home canning is not recommended because there is no way of knowing how much pressure is building inside the sealed jar. Home canned vegetables should be processed conventionally to ensure destruction of all *Clostridium botulinum* spores.

Cooking sponge cakes, deep fried foods, popovers, hard- and soft-cooked eggs in the shell are not recommended. Follow manufacturer's recommendations for cooking popcorn.

Do not operate a microwave oven empty. If the cavity does not have enough food mass, the microwaves may bounce back to the magnetron tube and shorten the life of the oven. Cooking containers will become hot to the level of food in the container as heat in the food transfers to the container. Use hot pads as a precaution. Transfer frozen, prepackaged convenience and frozen prepared food to non-metal containers for cooking.

To clean a microwave oven, heat 1 cup (250 ml) water until it steams. Wipe inside of cavity with soft cloth after steam softens food. Microwave ovens are always being updated, hence the need to follow manufacturer's direction for use and care of oven. To remove food odors, add lemon juice or baking soda to warm water, close oven door and let mixture sit for a short time.

Enhancing Appearance of Food

The speed of microwave cooking and the tendency for food to give up heat to the surrounding atmosphere are not conducive to browning and crusting of the surfaces of food. Browning occurs if the food requires cooking for 20 minutes or more. Many foods are acceptable without a brown crust. Browning ingredients and sauces may be used to advantage on other foods.

To Enhance Food Appearance

Biscuits   Brown in browning utensil. Top with toasted sesame seeds, poppy seeds, cinnamon and sugar, or dry onion mix.

Cakes   Sprinkle brown sugar and cinnamon in container before pouring batter, or sprinkle on top after cooking. Use topping for upside down cakes. Cool baked cake and then ice it.

Casseroles   Top with toasted bread crumbs, crushed chips, cereals, toasted nuts, grated cheese, chopped bacon. Brown under broiler before or after cooking by microwave.

Meat, Poultry   Brush with brown sauce or gravy mix. Sprinkle with paprika or dry onion soup.

Fish   Top, or coat, with toasted bread crumbs, nuts or grated cheese. Cover with sauce. Glaze with brown sugar or other ingredients. Brown on grill or broil and complete cooking by microwave. Use browning utensil.

Muffins   Include bran as an ingredient.

Pastry   Prepare with milk instead of water. Add a few drops of food coloring.

SLOW-COOKER COOKING

The slow cooker is an electrical appliance, specifically designed to cook foods slowly, generally taking 4 to 12 hours. There are at least two general types of slow cookers. One has a stoneware or crockery container in an electrical heating base. Heating elements often wrap around the sides of the stoneware and control settings may include low and high. Another type of slow cooker consists of a metal container that is heated from the bottom. The temperature control may include a variety of temperature settings, but a range for slow-cooking will be specifically noted. Variations of these two types, such as a crockery bowl in a metal cooking pot with an adjustable thermostat, are also available.

Check the manufacturer's instructions for

information on using a specific slow cooker, and note the recommended cooking times and settings. Always cook for the suggested time on the proper setting and with the cover on.

The slow cooker is helpful in cooking less tender cuts of meat, soups, and stews. A variety of other dishes, including casseroles, vegetables, beans, hot drinks and cereals can also be prepared in a slow cooker. For cooks who wish to adapt favorite recipes to the slow-cooker, this information provides a guide.

Adapting Recipes

■ Look for steps that may be omitted (for example, browning aspects). Most ingredients can be added at the beginning of the cooking period.

■ For most recipes, one cup of liquid is sufficient, but a general rule of thumb is to use only one-half as much as in a standard recipe. Additional amounts may be needed if cooking a product such as pasta or rice, which absorbs liquid.

■ Crushed or ground seasonings should be added near the end of cooking because they become too mild during the long cooking period. Whole seasonings may withstand the long cooking, and their flavor may intensify, so use about one-half as much as usual.

■ Rice and pasta become gummy with long cooking; add them during the last hour of cooking. If pasta is to be cooked before adding to the slow cooker, cook the pasta just until al dente.

■ Sour cream and milk curdle during long cooking and should be added during the last 30 minutes. Condensed soups are satisfactory for the longer cooking times and may be substituted for milk or cream.

Food Placement

Placement of foods in the cooker may determine the success or failure of the dish. Vegetables such as potatoes, carrots, and onions cook very slowly and should be kept small to medium in size and placed in the bottom of the pot. This also allows the meat juices to drip over the vegetables, enhancing their flavor. Unless the meat is very fatty, a rack usually is not necessary. If a sauce is used over meat or vegetables, it should be poured evenly over the food.

Timing Factors

■ Allow plenty of cooking time, especially on Low. Remember that timing is generally not critical and an extra hour will not greatly affect the food. Always cook the food until it is completely done and tender.

■ The temperature of the food when placed in the cooker will affect the cooking time. Most cooking times are based on using refrigerated foods. Frozen foods require a longer cooking time than refrigerated foods. In some slow cookers, frozen foods are not recommended or specific instructions must be followed; check the use and care manual for information on frozen foods in a specific slow cooker.

■ The volume of food will affect the cooking time. Refer to the use and care manual as a guide for the amount of food suited to the size of cooker you are using. Generally the cooking times are based on units one-half to three-fourths full. Do not overfill slow cookers. If cooking a very small amount of food in a cooker with a wrap-around heating element, the cooking time may be shortened, and the cooking progress should be checked.

- If there is much fat present, the meat should first be trimmed, browned or broiled to eliminate as much fat as possible.

- Minerals and acids increase the cooking time in dried legumes and may affect other foods in hard-water areas. Sugars and acid foods such as tomatoes should be added only after the legumes have been softened completely.

- Some foods that should be added during the last 1 to 2 hours of cooking include seafood, canned or frozen vegetables, and fresh mushrooms. Frozen vegetables and seafood should be thawed before being added to the cooker.

The following chart provides guidelines for cooking adapted recipes in a slow cooker.

TIME GUIDE FOR SLOW COOKER[a]

IF RECIPE SAYS:	TIME IN SLOW COOKER	
	High Setting	Low Setting
15 to 30 min.	1.5 to 2.5 hrs	4 to 8 hrs
35 to 45 min.	3 to 4 hrs	6 to 10 hrs
50 min. to 3 hrs.	4 to 6 hrs	8 to 18 hrs

[a] Courtesy of Rival Manufacturing Company

CONVECTION OVEN COOKING

A convection oven uses forced hot air to speed the baking/roasting process, thus saving time in the oven.

Types of Ovens

Convection ovens are available as countertop, wall, or range ovens. The three different convection modes are: convection with heating element located around the fan and outside the oven cavity; convection bake with heating elements on inside oven cavity and a fan to circulate the hot air; and microwave/convection — a combination of microwave power and heating element and fan located outside the oven cavity.

Factors to consider when adapting conventional recipes to the convection oven include time, temperature settings and type of bakeware. Check the appliance manual for specific suggestions.

Baking

Temperature— Oven Temperature is decreased by 25-50°F (15-30°C). Bakes items with sufficiently brown surface but undercooked centers may need the temperature lowered an additional 25°F (15°C) with increased baking time.

Time — Baking time varies with moisture content, richness and depth of product. Check times in appliance manual. Generally for convection or convection bake modes, times can be reduced as follows: thin items — about 1-2 minutes; cakes — 5 minutes; and large turkeys — up to 30 percent. Preheating is necessary only for food baked less than 20 minutes and products such as popovers where browning and rising are important.

Size — Large items may not cook fully in the center. Divide these into small units such as two or three loaves instead of one.

Roasting:

Temperature — Use the same temperature as conventional recipes. Preheating is not necessary. Roast meats uncovered except turkey, which should be covered once it is golden brown.

Time — Reduce the time by one-third depending on the size of product. If meat is too rare in the center, lower the temperature and increase the time.

Drying — Baste roasts with glaze or barbecue sauce only during the last 10 to 20 minutes; use a drip pan with 1/4 inch (0.8 cm) water. Frozen meat can be roasted in the same time as thawed meat in a conventional oven.

Quantity Cooking

A major benefit of convection ovens is quantity cooking. It is possible to bake three racks of cookies, biscuits, pizzas or similar items at the same time.

Bakeware

Metal bakeware such as aluminum and heavy-duty aluminum foil gives the greatest time savings, followed by cast iron and black steel. Ceramic and glass dishes require conventional baking time. Baking sheets should have only one edge. Shallow pans that allow at least 1 to 1 1/2 inches (2.5 to 3.7 cm) of space between the bakeware and the oven wall are recommended for roasting. Covered casseroles can be used in the convection oven, but the convection benefit of reduced time is mini-mized. Cookware should be centered in front of the fan with 1 inch (2.5 cm) air space on all sides.

FOOD LABELING

Federal laws governing food labeling are the concern of the following agencies:

FDA — Food and Drug Administration. A federal agency empowered to enforce five specific laws relating to checking all foods and food additives for safety, purity, and wholesomeness (Federal Food, Drug and Cosmetic Act; Fair Packaging and Labeling Act; Radiation Control and Health and Safety Act; Public Health Service Act; and Nutrition Labeling and Education Act of 1990). FDA officers inspect plants were food is processed. The agency is also responsible for the accuracy and correctness of information on packages and labels on the majority of foods.

USDA — U. S. Department of Agriculture. This department is responsible for meat and poultry safety, quality, and labeling (see FSIS). The Research Service of this agency conducts food and nutrition research. Areas investigated include effects of processing and cooking on nutrient content of food and food preferences and habits of individuals and groups.

FSIS — Food Safety and Inspection Service. This agency of the USDA inspects all red meats and poultry for purity, wholesomeness, and truthful labeling. This agency monitors meat and poultry for hazardous residues above EPA levels.

AMS — Agricultural Marketing Service. It is an agency within the USDA which grades fresh, frozen, canned and dehydrated vegetables into levels of quality. It also establishes grade standards for most fresh and processed fruits.

USDC NMFS — U. S. Department of Commerce - National Marine Fisheries. This agency provides voluntary inspection of fish and fish products. The service develops standards and specifications for quality, conditions, quantity, grade and packaging of fish, processing plants and fish products.

USPHS — U. S. Public Health Service. This agency safeguards the purity of dairy products. Evidence of contamination is monitored according to standards stated in the Grade A Pasteurized Milk Ordinance. This agency assists with enforcement of standards relating to sanitation, taste, odor, and milkfat content. The federal code defines milk fat standards for various milk products. This agency works with the USDA in monitoring processing at milk plants.

Ingredient Labeling

For nonmeat and nondairy products, the ingredient label is regulated by the FDA. Meat and dairy product labels are regulated by the USDA. The ingredient label must tell the name of a product, the form it is in, and identify anything which has been added to it. Ingredients must be listed by weight, from highest weight to lowest content.

The Nutrition Labeling and Education Act of 1990 established requirements for the declaration of all ingredients in standardized foods, declaration of certified color additives in foods, declaration of sources of protein hydrolysates, and declaration on the nutrition label of percentage of a fruit or vegetable juice in a beverage claiming to contain such a juice. The effective date for total percentage juice labeling, and ingredient labeling of standardized foods and certified colors was May 8, 1993.

Nutrition Labeling

The Nutrition Labeling and Education Act of 1990 brought about a great many changes to the labeling practices monitored by the Food and Drug Administration. Proposed rules for implementing the act were reviewed throughout 1992, with final rules published in the Federal Register on January 6, 1993. Effective date for mandatory nutrition labeling using the specified format will be May 8, 1994.

The purpose of the label is to allow comparison of foods for nutritional content. The 1990 law requires mandatory nutritional labeling of most foods offered for sale and regulated by FDA. The nutrition label is required to include information on total calories and calories from fat and on amounts of total fat, saturated fat, cholesterol, sodium, total carbohydrates, dietary fiber, sugars, protein, vitamin A, vitamin C, calcium and iron — in that order. Manufacturers also may voluntarily declare information on calories from saturated fat and on amounts of polyunsaturated and monounsaturated fat, soluble and insoluble fiber, sugar alcohol, other carbohydrate, potassium, additional vitamins and minerals for which Reference Daily Intakes (RDIs) have been established, and the percent of vitamin A present as beta-carotene. The information presented on the label is to represent the packaged product prior to consumer preparation.

The standard format for nutrition information on food labels consists of:

1. the quantitative amount per serving of each nutrient except vitamins and minerals;

2. the amount of each nutrient as a percent of the Daily Value for a 2,000 calorie diet;

3. a footnote with reference values for selected nutrients based on 2,000 calorie and 2,500 calorie diets; and

4. caloric conversion information.

Voluntary labeling applies to fresh produce and seafood unpackaged or packaged at retail. Nutrition information at point of purchase may be presented via large placards, brochures or videos. Unless claims are made about the following nutrients, these items are voluntary: calories from saturated and unsaturated fat, total carbohydrates, protein; unsaturated fat or amounts of polyunsaturated and monounsaturated fats (g); insoluble and soluble fiber; protein as percentage of RDI for foods other than infant foods; potassium (mg), thiamin, riboflavin, niacin and other vitamins and minerals as percentage of RDI unless added as a supplement. Nutrition information is given "as consumed" for raw fish and "as packaged" for raw fruits and vegetables. After a period of implementation, 60 percent of retailers surveyed must be in compliance for at least 90 percent of the 20 most frequently consumed raw fruits, raw vegetables and raw fish.

The USDA-Food Safety and Inspection Service (FSIS) also published in the January 6, 1993 issue of the *Federal Register* final rules amending the Federal meat and poultry products inspection regulations permitting voluntary nutrition labeling on single-ingredient, raw meat and poultry products, and mandatory nutrition labeling for all other meat and poultry products. The FSIS rules were an effort to parallel as much as possible the nutrition labeling regulations of the NLEA. The effective date for USDA nutrition labeling of meat and poultry products will be July 6, 1994.

Nutrition Profile

The FDA regulations established References Daily Intakes (RDIs) and Daily Reference Values (DRVs). The final rules published in 1993 retained the values established by FDA in 1973 for vitamins and minerals but changed the terms for those values from U.S. Recommended Daily Allowances (U.S.RDA) to Reference Daily Intake (RDI). The regulation also established label reference values for eight other nutrients, including fat, cholesterol, and fiber. The values were established as Daily Reference Values (DRVs). To avoid confusion, all reference values on food labels are referred to as Daily Values or DVs.

Reference Serving Sizes

Serving sizes are defined as the amount of food customarily consumed per eating occasion. Nutrient content values listed on product labels are then based on the standardized serving sizes. A total of 184 food product categories have been defined — 139 by FDA, 23 for meats by FSIS, and 22 for poultry by FSIS. Additionally, there are specific rules for single-serving containers and items that come in discrete units such as slices of bread or individual muffins or cookies.

Descriptive Terms

FDA has defined the terms "free," "low," "light" or "lite," "reduced," "less," and "high," as well as "good source," "very low" (for sodium only), "lean," "extra lean," "fewer," "more," and "added" (for "fortified" or "enriched").

Some of the specific definitions are as follows: Criteria for the term "**low**" are based on reference serving sizes or for products having reference amounts of less than 30 g or 2 tablespoons, per 50 g, and thus **low fat** is a food with not more than 3 g of fat, **low calorie** is a food with not more than 40 calories, and **low sodium** is a food with not more than 140 mg sodium; **light (lite)** can be used if the food has one-third fewer calories than a comparable product, if half of the calories are from fat the fat must be reduced by 50 percent; and **cholesterol-free** claims may be made only on foods that contain 2 g or less of saturated fat per reference serving.

The terms "**high**" and "**good source**" are based on a percentage of the Daily Value (DV) of the specific nutrients in a reference serving. "**High**" is defined as 20 percent or more of the DV, and "**good source**" as between 10 and 19 percent of the DV. See Table 1.2 for a more complete list of nutrient content labeling claims definitions.

Health Claims

Health claims are permitted on food labels only where they are supported by valid and substantial scientific evidence and only those that the FDA has specifically provided for by regulation. Those that are authorized include the following: calcium and osteoporosis; dietary saturated fat and cholesterol and risk of coronary heart disease; dietary

fat and cancer; sodium and hypertension; fiber-containing grain products, fruits and vegetables and cancer; fruits, vegetables, and grain products that contain fiber, particularly soluble fiber, and risk of coronary heart disease; and fruits and vegetables and cancer.

Nutrient Content Claims and Standardized Foods

The large number of substitute products now in the marketplace has created a need for standardization of these products. The product can not be nutritionally inferior to the original product. The product must also have similar performance characteristics to the original product, and if it does not, this must be clearly printed on the label. The product must contain the ingredients used in the original product, but may also contain certain safe and suitable ingredients, provided the product is not nutritionally and functionally inferior to the original food in its performance characteristics.

Exemptions from Mandatory Programs

Foods exempt from mandatory nutrition labeling requirements include:

1. foods offered for sale by small businesses;

2. food sold in restaurants or other establishments in which food is served for immediate human consumption;

3. foods similar to restaurant foods that are ready to eat but are not for immediate consumption, are primarily prepared on site, and are not offered for sale outside of that location;

4. foods that contain insignificant amounts

Table 1.2
NUTRIENT CONTENT LABELING CLAIMS DEFINITIONS

Descriptive Term	Definition by Food Energy/Nutrient Category						Comments
	Calories	Fat	Sat. Fat	Choles.	Sodium	Sugars	
Free	Contains no amount of, or only trivial amounts of, any one or more of the categories: calories, fat, saturated fat, cholesterol, sodium, and sugars.						Synonyms: "no," "without," "zero"
	<5 kcal/ serving	<0.5 g/ serving	<0.5 g/ serving	<2 mg/ serving	<5 mg/ serving	<0.5 g/ serving	
Low	40 kcal or less/ serving	3 g or less/ serving	1 g or less/ serving	20 mg or less/ serving	140 mg or less/ serving	Not defined	Synonyms: "little" ("few" for calories). Amount applies/50 g food if referenced amount 30 g or less (small serving)
Very Low					35 mg or less/ serving		
Lean		<10 g/ serving	<4 g/ serving	<95 mg/ serving			Amounts apply per 100 g also
Extra lean		<5 g/ serving	<2 g/ serving	<95 mg/ serving			Amounts apply per 100 g also
Light or Lite	contains 1/3 fewer calories than ref. food	contains 1/2 fat of ref. food			content reduced by 50% in low-calorie/ low-fat food		If food gets 50% or more of calories from fat, must have 50% reduction in fat
Reduced	Nutritionally altered product has at least 25% less of nutrient or calories than reference product. Claim can't be made if reference food meets requirement for "low" claim.						Synonyms: "lower" ("fewer'" for calories)
Less	Food, altered or not, has 25% less of a nutrient or calories per reference serving						Synonym: "fewer"
High	Contains 20% or more of DC for nutrient per reference serving.						
More	Food, altered or not, has 10% or more of DV of nutrient per reference serving.						
Good Source	10-19% of DV of a particular nutrient per reference serving.						
Fresh	May only be used on a food that is raw, never frozen or heated and contains no preservatives.						

of all nutrients subject to the law such as coffee and tea;

5. dietary supplements, except those in conventional food form;

6. infant formula;

7. medical foods;

8. custom-processed fish or game meats;

9. foods shipped in bulk form; and

10. donated foods. Otherwise-exempted foods that make a nutrient content claim or health claim forfeit the exemption.

FOOD ADDITIVES

By the broadest definition, a food additive is any substance that becomes a part of the food product when added directly or indirectly.

The 1906 Food and Drug Act and the more comprehensive Food, Drug and Cosmetic Act of 1938 gave the government authority to remove adulterated and obviously poisonous foods from the market. The 1958 Food Additives Amendment, The Delaney Clause, and the 1960 Color Additives Amendment are laws specifically set up to regulate additives in foods. In these laws, legislation shifted the burden from the government to the manufacturer to prove that a food additive is safe. The FDA was authorized to regulate additives only on the basis of safety. The agency has no power to limit the number of additives approved, or to judge whether an additive is really needed.

Under the Food Additives Amendment,

however, two major categories of additives were exempted initially from the testing and approval process. The first group of some 700 substances belongs to the "generally recognized as safe" (GRAS) list, which includes salt and other common ingredients as sugar and many herbs and spices, considered safe based on either a history of safe use before the Food Additives Amendment was passed in 1958 or the results of scientific studies. The GRAS list was designed to allow continued use of substances considered harmless because of past extensive use without known harmful effects. However, GRAS additives have been undergoing systematic testing for safety since 1971. Also exempted from testing were the "prior sanctioned substances," those that had been approved before 1958 for use in food by either FDA or USDA.

An additive is intentionally incorporated into foods for one or more of these four purposes:

■ to maintain or improve nutritional value

■ to maintain freshness

■ to help in processing or preparation

■ to make food more appealing

Some people's bodies have adverse reactions to foods and some food additives. When that happens, the body's reactions can range from headaches or hives to seizures or death. If you suspect you have had an allergic reaction to an additive, contact your physician for diagnosis and treatment.

The following Additives Index is a guide to some substances commonly added to foods:

ADDITIVES INDEX

KEY DEFINITIONS:

Nutrients: enrich (replace vitamins and minerals lost in processing) or fortify (add nutrients that may be lacking in the diet).

Preservatives (Antimicrobials): prevent food spoilage from bacteria, molds, fungi and yeast; extend shelf life; or protect natural color or flavor.

Antioxidants: delay/prevent rancidity or enzymatic browning.

Emulsifiers: help to distribute evenly tiny particles of one liquid into another; improve homogeneity, consistency, stability, or texture.

Stabilizers, Thickeners, Texturizers: impart body; improve consistency or texture; stabilize emulsions; affect mouth feel.

Leavening Agents: affect cooking results—texture and volume.

pH Control Agents: change/maintain acidity or alkalinity.

Humectants: cause moisture retention.

Maturing and Bleaching Agents, Dough Conditioners: accelerate the aging process; improve baking qualities.

Anticaking Agents: prevent caking, lumping or clustering of a finely powdered or crystalline substance.

Flavor Enhancers: supplement, magnify or modify the original taste and/or aroma of food without imparting a characteristic flavor of their own.

Flavors: heighten natural flavor; restore flavors lost in processing.

Colors: give desired, appetizing or characteristic color of food.

Sweeteners: make the taste of food more agreeable or pleasurable.

Alternative Sweeteners: make the taste of food sweeter with no or few added calories.

Fat Substitutes: affect the mouth feel of foods by replacing fat with fat substitutes.

Key to Abbreviations used in Following List:

stabil-thick-tex	=	stabilizers-thickeners texturizers
leavening	=	leavening agents
pH control	=	pH control agents
mat-bleach-condit	=	maturing & bleaching agents, dough conditioners
anticaking	=	anticaking agents

Acetic acid (vinegar)	pH control
Acetone peroxide	mat-bleach-condit
Acesulfame-K	sweetener
Agar	stabil-thick-tex
Alginate	stabil-thick-tex
Aluminum, sodium sulfate	pH control firming agent
Ammonium alginate	pH control
Annatto extract	color

Arabingalactan
(larch gum) — stabil-thick-tex

Ascorbic acid
(Vitamin C) — nutrient, antioxidant

Aspartame — sweetener

Beet powder — color

Benzoyl peroxide — mat-bleach-condit

Benzoic acid
(sodium
benzoate) — preservative

Beta carotene — nutrient, color

BHA (butylated
hydroxyanisole) — antioxidant

BHT (butylated
hydroxytoluene) — antioxidant

Calcium bromate — mat-bleach-condit

Calcium carbonate — anticaking

Calcium caseinate — stabil-thick-tex
nutrient (fortify)

Calcium phosphate — leavening
(monocalcium — pH control
phosphate) — nutrient

Calcium propionate — preservative

Carob bean gum — stabil-thick-tex

Caramel — color

Carrageenan — stabil-thick-tex

Carrot oil — color

Cellulose — stabil-thick-tex

Chlorine & chlorine
dioxide — mat-bleach-condit

Citric acid — pH control, antioxidant

Cyclamate — sweetener (legal in Canada, illegal in USA)

Diglycerides — emulsifier

DSG (disodium 5'-
Guanylate) — flavor enhancer

EDTA
(ethylene-
diaminetetra-
acetate) — antioxidant

Ethyl vanillin — flavor

Ferrous gluconate — nutrient, color

Ferrous sulfate
(iron) — nutrient

FD & C Colors — color
Blue 1
Blue 2
Green 3
Orange B
Citrus Red
Citrus Red 2
Red 3
(provisional)
Red 40
Yellow 5
Yellow 6

Gelatin — stabil-thick-tex

Glutamic acid — flavor

Glycerine — humectant

Grape skin extract — color

Guar gum — stabil-thick-tex

Gum arabic (acacia) — stabil-thick-tex

Heptyl paraben — preservative

Hydrogen peroxide — mat-bleach-condit

HVP (hydrolyzed
vegetable protein) — flavor enhancer

Iron-ammonium
citrate — anticaking

Iron, reduced — nutrient

Isopropyl citrate — antioxidant

Lactic acid — pH control
preservative

Lecithin — emulsifier

Limonene — antioxidant, flavor

Locust bean gum
(carob bean) — stabil-thick-tex

Magnesium silicate	anticaking	Sorbic acid	preservative
Mannitol	sweetener	Sorbitan	
Methyl cellulose	anticaking	monostearate	emulsifier
	stabil-thick-tex	Sorbitol	flavoring, humectant
	bulking	Stearyl lactylate	emulsifier
Methyl paraben	preservative		conditioner
Modified food starch	stabil-thick-tex		whipping agent
Monoammonium		Sugar (fructose,	
glutamate	flavor enhancer	invert sugar,	
Monoglyceride	emulsifier	glucose, sucrose,	
Monosodium		dextrose)	sweeteners
glutamate (MSG)	flavor enhancer	Sulfite salts	preservative
Niacinamide	nutrient	Sulfur dioxide	preservative
Nitrites	preservative	Tartaric acid	
Oleoresins	flavor	(cream of tartar)	pH control
Parabens	preservative	TBHQ	
Pectin	stabil-thick-tex	(tertiary butyl	
Phosphoric acid	pH control	hydro-quinone)	antioxidant
Polysorbates		Thiamin	nutrient
(60, 65, 80)	emulsifiers	Titanium dioxide	color
Potassium bromate	mat-bleach-condit	Tocopherols	
Potassium iodide		(Vitamin E)	nutrient, antioxidant
(iodine)	nutrient	Tragacanth gum	stabil-thick-tex
Propionic acid &		Trisodium phosphate	stabil-thick-tex
salts	preservative	Tumeric	color
Propylene glycol	stabil-thick-tex	Vanilla	flavor
Propyl gallate	antioxidant	Vanillin	flavor
Riboflavin	nutrient, color	Vitamin A	nutrient
Saccharin	sweetener		
Saffron	color		
Silicon dioxide	anticaking		
Simplesse®	fat substitute		
Sodium ascorbate			
(Vitamin C)	nutrient		
Sodium citrate	pH control		
Sodium erythorbate	antioxidant		
Sodium propionate	preservative		
Sodium stearyl			
fumarate	mat-bleach-condit		

SUPPLEMENTARY AIDS TO FOOD PREPARATION
BAKING TEMPERATURES AND TIMES

Type of Product	Oven Temperature*		Baking Time
	°F	(°C)	(minutes)
Breads			
Biscuits	425 - 450	(220 - 230)	10 - 15
Corn bread	400 - 425	(200 - 220)	30 - 40
Cream puffs, popovers	375	(190)	60
Muffins	400 - 425	(200 - 220)	20 - 25
Quick loaf breads	350 - 375	(180 - 190)	60 - 75
Yeast bread	400	(200)	30 - 40
Yeast rolls, plain	400 - 425	(200 - 220)	15 - 25
sweet	375	(190)	20 - 30
Cakes with fat			
Bundt	350	(180)	40 - 45
Cup, 12 cups	350 - 375	(180 - 190)	15 - 25
Layer, 9 inch	350 - 375	(180 - 190)	20 - 25
Loaf	350	(180)	45 - 60
Cakes without fat			
Angel food and sponge	350 - 375	(180 - 190)	30 - 45
Jelly roll	325	(160)	22 - 28
Cookies			
Drop	350 - 400	(180 - 190)	8 - 15
Rolled	375	(190)	8 - 15
Meringues	200	(100)	60 + 120 after oven off
Egg, meat, milk, and cheese dishes			
Cheese soufflé, custards (baked in a pan of hot water)	350	(180)	45 - 60
Macaroni and cheese	350	(180)	25 - 30
Meat loaf	300	(150)	60 - 90
Meat pie	400	(200)	25 - 30
Rice pudding (raw rice)	300	(150)	120 - 180
Scalloped potatoes	350	(180)	60 - 75
Pastry			
One-crust pie (custard type), unbaked shell	400 - 425	(200 - 220)	30 - 40
Meringue on cooked filling in prebaked shell	350 or 425	(180) or (220)	12 - 15 or 4 - 4 1/2
Shell only	450	(230)	10 - 12
Two-crust pies			
with uncooked filling	400 - 425	(200 - 220)	45 - 55
with cooked filling	425 - 450	(220 - 230)	30 - 45

* When baking in ovenproof glassware, reduce oven temperature by 25°F or by 10°C.
NOTE: For packaged mixes, follow direction on package.

SOLUBILITY OF SALT (Sodium Chloride)

Temperature	Amount of salt to saturate 100 g water	
	grams	%
-4°F (-20°C)	30.9	23.6
68°F (20°C)	36.0	26.4
212°F (100°C)	39.8	28.2

SUBSTITUTION OF INGREDIENTS

For: Substitute:

1 Tbsp flour (15 ml) (used as thickener)
0.5 Tbsp (7 ml) cornstarch, potato starch, rice starch, or arrowroot starch; 1 Tbsp (15 ml) quick-cooking tapioca; 2 tsp (10 ml) tapioca

1 c (250 ml) sifted all-purpose flour
1 c (250 ml) unsifted all-purpose flour minus 2 Tbsp (30 ml)

1 c (250 ml) sifted cake flour
7/8 c (225 ml) sifted all-purpose flour, or 1 c minus 2 Tbsp (225 ml) sifted all-purpose flour

1 c (250 ml) sifted self-rising flour
1 c (250 ml) sifted all-purpose flour plus 1.5 tsp (7 ml) baking powder and 1/2 tsp (2 ml) salt

1 c (250 ml) dark corn syrup
3/4 c (175 ml) light corn syrup and 1/4 c (50 ml) light molasses

For: Substitute:

1 c (250 ml) corn syrup
1 c (250 ml) sugar plus 1/4 c (50 ml) liquid*

1 c (250 ml) light brown sugar
1/2 c (125 ml) dark brown sugar plus 1/2 c (125 ml) granulated sugar

1 c (250 ml) honey
1 1/4 c (300 ml) sugar plus 1/4 c (50 ml) liquid*

1 ounce (28 g) semisweet chocolate
1/2 ounce (14 g) baking chocolate plus 1 Tbsp (15 ml) sugar

1 ounce (28 g) unsweetened chocolate
3 Tbsp (50 ml) cocoa plus 1 Tbsp (15 ml) fat

* Use whatever liquid is called for in the recipe.

NOTE: The amounts of corn syrup and honey are based on the way these products function in recipes and not on the sweetness equivalence with sugar.

For:	Substitute:

1 c (250 ml) coffee cream (20 per cent)
> 3 Tbsp (50 ml) butter plus about 7/8 c (225 ml) milk

1 c (250 ml) heavy cream (40 per cent)
> 1/3 c (75 ml) butter plus about 3/4 c (175 ml) milk

1 c (250 ml) whole milk
> 1 c (250 ml) reconstituted nonfat dry milk plus 2-1/2 tsp (12 ml) butter or margarine, or 1/2 c (125 ml) evaporated milk plus 1/2 c (125 ml) water

1 c (250 ml) milk
> 3 Tbsp (50 ml) sifted regular nonfat dry milk plus 1 c (250 ml) minus 1 Tbsp (15 ml) water, or 1/3 c (75 ml) instant nonfat dry milk plus 1 c (250 ml) minus 1 Tbsp water

1 c (250 ml) buttermilk or sour milk
> 1 Tbsp (15 ml) vinegar or lemon juice plus enough sweet milk to make 1 c (250 ml), let stand 5 minutes, or 1 3/4 tsp (8 ml) cream of tartar plus 1 c (250 ml) sweet milk

1 c (250 ml) sour cream
> 1 c (250 ml) plain yogurt or 7/8 c (225 ml) sour milk plus 1/3 c (75 ml) butter

For:	Substitute:

1 c (250 ml) buttermilk
> 1 c (250 ml) plain yogurt

1 c (250 ml) milk
> 1 c (250 ml) buttermilk and omit 1 tsp (5 ml) baking powder, replacing with 1/2 tsp (2 ml) soda and 1 tsp (5 ml) shortening

1 c (250 ml) butter
> 7/8 c (225 ml) oil

1 tsp (5 ml) baking powder
> 1/4 tsp (1 ml) baking soda plus 5/8 tsp (3 ml) cream of tartar; or 1/4 tsp (1 ml) baking soda plus 1/2 cup (125 ml) fully soured milk or buttermilk; or 1/4 tsp (1 ml) baking soda plus 1/2 Tbsp (7 ml) vinegar or lemon juice used with sweet milk to make 1/2 c (125 ml); or 1/4 tsp (1 ml) baking soda plus 1/4 to 1/2 c (50 ml to 125 ml) molasses; or 1/4 tsp (1 ml) baking soda plus 1/2 c (125 ml) yogurt

1 Tbsp (15 ml) active dry yeast
> 1 package active dry yeast, or 1 compressed yeast cake

(continued on the next page)

For:	Substitute:
1 whole egg	2 egg yolks, or 3 Tbsp (50 ml) plus 1 tsp thawed frozen egg, or 2 Tbsp (30 ml) and 2 tsp dry whole egg powder plus an equal amount of water
1 egg yolk	3 1/2 tsp (17 ml) thawed frozen egg yolk, or 2 tsp (10 ml) dry egg yolk plus 2 tsp (10 ml) water
1 egg white	2 Tbsp (30 ml) thawed frozen egg white, or 2 tsp (10 ml) dry egg white plus 2 Tbsp (30 ml) water
1 c (250 ml) bread crumbs	3/4 c (175 ml) cracker crumbs
1 c (250 ml) tomato juice	1/2 c (125 ml) tomato sauce plus 1/2 c (125 ml) water
1 medium clove garlic	1/8 tsp (0.5 ml) garlic powder or 3/4 tsp (3 ml) garlic salt
1 tsp (5 ml) lemon juice	1/2 tsp (2 ml) vinegar
1 tsp (5 ml) lemon peel	1/2 tsp (2 ml) lemon extract
1 small onion	1 tsp (5 ml) onion powder or 1 tsp (5 ml) minced dry onion

Table 1.3
TEMPERATURE CONVERSION TABLE

The numbers in the body of the table give in degrees F the temperature indicated in degrees C at the top and side. To convert 178°C to Farenheit scale, find 17 in the column headed degrees C. Proceed in a horizontal line to the column headed 8 which shows 352°F as corresponding to 178°C.

To convert 352°F to Celsius scale, find 352 in the Farenheit readings, then in the column headed degrees C, find the number which is on the same horizontal line, i.e., 17. Next, fill in the last number from the heading of the column in which 352 was found, i.e., 8, resulting in 178°C which is equivalent to 352°F.

Range:
-29°C (-20°F) to 309°C (588°F)

Conversion Formulae:
$T°C = 5/9 (T°F - 32)$ $T°F = 9/5 \ T°C + 32$

Degrees C	0	1	2	3	4	5	6	7	8	9
- 2	-4°F	-6°F	-8°F	-9°F	-11°F	-13°F	-15°F	-17°F	-18°F	-20°F
- 1	14°F	12°F	10°F	9°F	7°F	5°F	3°F	1°F	0°F	-2°F
- 0	32°F	30°F	28°F	27°F	25°F	23°F	21°F	19°F	18°F	16°F
0	32°F	34°F	36°F	37°F	39°F	41°F	43°F	45°F	46°F	48°F
1	50°F	52°F	54°F	55°F	57°F	59°F	61°F	63°F	64°F	66°F
2	68°F	70°F	72°F	73°F	75°F	77°F	79°F	81°F	82°F	84°F
3	86°F	88°F	90°F	91°F	93°F	95°F	97°F	99°F	100°F	102°F
4	104°F	106°F	108°F	109°F	111°F	113°F	115°F	117°F	118°F	120°F
5	122°F	124°F	126°F	127°F	129°F	131°F	133°F	135°F	136°F	138°F
6	140°F	142°F	144°F	145°F	147°F	149°F	151°F	153°F	154°F	156°F
7	158°F	160°F	162°F	163°F	165°F	167°F	169°F	171°F	172°F	174°F
8	176°F	178°F	180°F	181°F	183°F	185°F	187°F	189°F	190°F	192°F
9	194°F	196°F	198°F	199°F	201°F	203°F	205°F	207°F	208°F	210°F
10	212°F	214°F	216°F	217°F	219°F	221°F	223°F	225°F	226°F	228°F
11	230°F	232°F	234°F	235°F	237°F	239°F	241°F	243°F	244°F	246°F
12	248°F	250°F	252°F	253°F	255°F	257°F	259°F	261°F	262°F	264°F
13	266°F	268°F	270°F	271°F	273°F	275°F	277°F	279°F	280°F	282°F
14	284°F	286°F	288°F	289°F	291°F	293°F	295°F	297°F	298°F	300°F
15	302°F	304°F	306°F	307°F	309°F	311°F	313°F	315°F	316°F	318°F
16	320°F	322°F	324°F	325°F	327°F	329°F	331°F	333°F	334°F	336°F
17	338°F	340°F	342°F	343°F	345°F	347°F	349°F	351°F	352°F	354°F
18	356°F	358°F	360°F	361°F	363°F	365°F	367°F	369°F	370°F	372°F
19	374°F	376°F	378°F	379°F	381°F	383°F	385°F	387°F	388°F	390°F
20	392°F	394°F	396°F	397°F	399°F	401°F	403°F	405°F	406°F	408°F
21	410°F	412°F	414°F	415°F	417°F	419°F	421°F	423°F	424°F	426°F
22	428°F	430°F	432°F	433°F	435°F	437°F	439°F	441°F	442°F	444°F
23	446°F	448°F	450°F	451°F	453°F	455°F	457°F	459°F	460°F	462°F
24	464°F	466°F	468°F	469°F	471°F	473°F	475°F	477°F	478°F	480°F
25	482°F	484°F	486°F	487°F	489°F	491°F	493°F	495°F	496°F	498°F
26	500°F	502°F	504°F	505°F	507°F	509°F	511°F	513°F	514°F	516°F
27	518°F	520°F	522°F	523°F	525°F	527°F	529°F	531°F	532°F	534°F
28	536°F	538°F	540°F	541°F	543°F	545°F	547°F	549°F	550°F	552°F
29	554°F	556°F	558°F	559°F	561°F	563°F	565°F	567°F	568°F	570°F
30	572°F	574°F	576°F	577°F	579°F	581°F	583°F	585°F	586°F	588°F

Table 1.4
BASIC RECIPE PROPORTIONS

The following table shows proportions of ingredients to one another in certain basic recipes. The amounts of ingredients do not constitute full-size recipes and are not intended for family meal preparation. Weights are given for situations where ingredients are being weighed. Metric conversions can be done on the basis of 1 cup equals 236.6 milliliters and 1 teaspoon equals 5 milliliters.

Product	Flour*	Liquid	Fat	Eggs	Sugar	Salt	Baking Powder†	Other Ingredients
BEVERAGES								
Cocoa and chocolate		1 c milk 242 g			2 tsp to 1 Tbsp 8.3 - 12.5 g	Few grains		1 Tbsp cocoa 7 g or 1/2 oz chocolate 14.2 g
Coffee		3/4 c water 178 g						1 Tbsp coffee 5.3 g
instant		3/4 c water 178 g						1 to 2 tsp instant coffee 0.8 to 1.6 g
freeze dried		3/4 c water 178 g						2/3 tsp 0.5 g
Tea		3/4 c water 178 g						1/2 to 1 tsp tea 0.75 - 1.5 g
BREADS								
Biscuits	1 c 115 g	1/3 to 1/2 c milk 80.7 - 121 g	2 to 4 Tbsp 23.6 to 47.2 g			1/2 tsp 3 g	1 1/4 or 2 tsp 4.5 or 5.8 g	
Griddle cakes	1 c 115 g	3/4 to 7/8 c milk 181.5 - 211.8 g	1 Tbsp 11.8 g	1/2 25 g	0 to 1 Tbsp 0 - 12.5 g	1/2 tsp 3 g	1 1/2 or 2 tsp 5.4 or 5.8 g	
Muffins	1 c 115 g	1/2 c milk 121 g	2 to 3 Tbsp 23.6 - 35.4 g	1/2 25 g	1 to 2 Tbsp 12.5 - 25 g	1/2 tsp 3 g	1 1/4 or 2 tsp 4.5 or 5.8 g	
Popovers	1 c 115 g	1 c milk 242 g	1 to 2 Tbsp 11.8 - 23.6 g	2 to 3 50-150 g		1/4-3/4 tsp 1.5-4.5 g		

Product	Flour*	Liquid	Fat	Eggs	Sugar	Salt	Baking Powder†	Other Ingredients
Waffles	1 c 115 g	3/4 to 1 c milk 181.5 - 242 g	1 to 3 Tbsp 11.8 - 35.4 g	1 to 2 50-100 g		1/2 tsp 3 g	1 1/4 or 2 tsp 4.5 or 5.8 g	
Yeast Bread	1 c 115 g	1/3 c milk 80.7 g	0 to 1 Tbsp 0 to 11.8 g		1 tsp to 1 Tbsp 4.2 - 12.5 g	1/4 tsp 1.5 g		1/4 compressed yeast cake 12.8 g or 1/4 small package active dry yeast 1.7 g
CAKE AND PASTRY Cake with fat	1 c cake or all-purpose 96 or 115 g	1/4 to 1/2 c milk 60.5 - 121 g	2 to 4 Tbsp 23.6 - 47 g	1/2 to 1 25 - 50 g	1/2 to 3/4 c 100 - 150 g	1/8 to 1/4 tsp 0.75-1.5 g	1 or 2 tsp 3.6 - 5.8 g	Flavoring
Chiffon	1 c cake 96 g	1/3 c water 79 g	1/4 c (salad oil) 52.5 g	3 150 g	2/3 c 134 g	1/2 tsp 3 g	1 1/4 or 1 1/2 tsp 4.5 - 5.4 g	1/4 tsp cream of tartar 0.8 g Flavoring
Cake without fat Angel food	1 c cake 96 g			1-1 1/2 c whites 246-369 g	1 1/4 to 1 1/2 c 250 - 300 g	1/2 tsp 3 g		3/4 to 1 1/2 tsp cream of tartar 2.3 to 4.6 g Flavoring
Sponge	1 c cake 96 g	0 - 3 Tbsp water 0 - 44.4 g		5 to 6 250-300 g	1 c 200 g	1/2 tsp 3 g		0 to 3/4 tsp cream of tartar 0 - 2.3 g Flavoring
Cream Puffs	1 c 115 g	1 c water 237 g	1/2 c 144 g	4 200 g		1/4 tsp 1.5 g		
Doughnuts	1 c 115 g	1/4 c milk 60.5 g	1 to 1/2 tsp 3.9 - 5.9 g	1/2 25 g	1/4 c 50 g	1/4 tsp 1.5 g	1 or 2 tsp 3.6 - 5.8 g	Flavoring
Pastry	1 c 115 g	2 Tbsp water 29.6 g	4 to 5 Tbsp 47 - 58.8 g			1/2 tsp 3 g		*(continued)*

BASIC RECIPE PROPORTIONS (continued)

Product	Flour*	Liquid	Fat	Eggs	Sugar	Salt	Baking Powder†	Other Ingredients
EGG DISHES Custards		1 c milk 242 g		1 to 1 2/3 50-83.5 g	1 1/2 to 3 Tbsp 18.8 - 37.5 g	1/8 tsp 0.75 g		Flavoring
Omelets		1 Tbsp 15.1 g		1 50 g		1/8 tsp 0.75 g		Seasonings
Soufflés entree	3-4 Tbsp 21.6-28.8 g	1 c milk 242 g	3 to 4 Tbsp 35.2 - 47 g	3 150 g		1/4-1/2 tsp 1.5 - 3 g		Seasonings
PUDDINGS Cornstarch		1 c milk 242 g		0 to 1 0 to 50 g	2 to 3 Tbsp 25 to 37.5 g	1/8 tsp 0.75 g		1 to 1 1/2 Tbsp cornstarch 8 to 12 g Flavoring
Gelatin, Jellies Plain		2 c milk, water, fruit juices or other liquid 494 g			2 Tbsp 25 g			1 envelop gelatin 1 Tbsp 7 - 10 g
Fruit or vegetable		3 c liquid 741 g			1/4 c 50 g	Few grains		2 envelopes gelatin-2 Tbsp 14-20 g
Bavarian Creams		2 c milk 242 g		4 200 g	1/4 c 50 g			2 envelopes gelatin - 2 Tbsp 14 - 20 g 2 c fruit pulp 484 g 1 c whipping cream - 242 g Flavoring

Product	Flour*	Liquid	Fat	Eggs	Sugar	Salt	Baking Powder†	Other Ingredients
Tapioca		1 c milk 242 g		1/2 to 1 25 50 g	2 Tbsp 25 g	1/8 tsp 0.75 g		1 1/2 Tbsp quick cooking tapioca 14.25 g Flavoring
Rice (steamed)		1 c milk 242 g			1 to 2 Tbsp 12.5 g	1/8 tsp 0.75 g		2 to 4 Tbsp raw rice 22.8 - 45.5 g Flavoring
Rice (baked)		1 c milk 242 g	1 Tbsp 11.8 g		1 Tbsp 12.5 g	Few grains		1 Tbsp raw rice 11.4 g Flavoring
SAUCES								
White sauce thin	1 Tbsp 7.8 g	1 c milk 242 g	2 Tbsp 23.6 g			1/4 tsp 1.5 g		Pepper, if desired
medium	2 Tbsp 15.6 g	1 c milk 242 g	3 Tbsp 35.4 g			1/4 tsp 1.5 g		Pepper, if desired
thick	3-4 Tbsp 23.4 - 31.2 g	1 c milk 242 g				1/4 tsp 1.5 g		Pepper, if desired
Fruit sauce		1 c fruit juice 247 g			2 to 4 Tbsp 25 - 50 g	Few grains		3/4 to 1 Tbsp cornstarch 6 to 8 g Fruit, if desired
SOUPS								
Cream with nonstarchy vegetables	1 Tbsp 7.8 g	1 c milk 242 g	1 Tbsp 11.8 g			1/4 tsp 1.5 g		Seasonings, vegetables
Cream with starch vegetables	1 1/2 tsp 3.7 g	1 c milk 242 g	1 Tbsp 11.8 g			1/4 tsp 1.5 g		Seasonings, vegetables

* All-purpose flour unless cake flour is specified.
† Use the smaller amount with SAS-phosphate powder and the larger amount with quick acting powder.

Table 1.5
TABLE OF EQUIVALENTS

ABBREVIATIONS AND SYMBOLS*

CAPACITY
Cup (c)
Deciliter (dl)
Fluid ounce (fl oz)
Gallon (gal)
Liter (l)
Milliliter (ml)
Pint (pt)
Quart (qt)
Peck (pk)
Bushel (bu)
Gill (gi)
Tablespoon (Tbsp)
Teaspoon (tsp)

TIME
Hour (hr)
Minute (min)
Second (sec)

TEMPERATURE
Degrees Celsius (°C)
Degrees Fahrenheit (°F)

LENGTH
Centimeter (cm)
Foot (ft)
Inch (in)
Meter (m)
Millimeter (mm)
Millimicron (mμ)

WEIGHT
Gram (g)
Kilogram (kg)
Microgram (μg)
Milligram (mg)
Ounce (oz)
Pound (lb)

* Note that abbreviations are used in the singular form regardless of whether the item is singular or plural. For metric units a symbol is used, as g for grams.

WEIGHT AND VOLUME EQUIVALENTS

COMMON UNITS OF WEIGHT

1 gram	=	0.035 ounces
1 kilogram	=	2.21 pounds
1 ounce	=	28.35 grams
1 pound	=	453.59 grams

COMMON UNITS OF VOLUME

1 bushel	=	4 pecks
1 peck	=	8 quarts
1 gallon	=	4 quarts
1 quart	=	2 pints
	=	946.4 milliliters
1 pint	=	2 cups
1 cup	=	16 tablespoons
	=	2 gills
	=	8 fluid ounces
	=	236.6 milliliters
1 Tablespoon	=	3 teaspoons
	=	1/2 fluid ounce
	=	14.8 milliliters
1 teaspoon	=	4.9 milliliters
1 liter	=	1000 milliliters
	=	1.06 quarts

EQUIVALENTS FOR ONE UNIT AND FRACTIONS OF A UNIT

TABLESPOON

1 Tbsp	=	3 tsp
7/8 Tbsp	=	2 1/2 tsp
3/4 Tbsp	=	2 1/4 tsp
2/3 Tbsp	=	2 tsp
5/8 Tbsp	=	1 7/8 tsp
1/2 Tbsp	=	1 1/2 tsp
3/8 Tbsp	=	1 1/8 tsp
1/3 Tbsp	=	1 tsp
1/4 Tbsp	=	3/4 tsp

CUP

1 c	=	16 Tbsp
7/8 c	=	14 Tbsp
3/4 c	=	12 Tbsp
2/3 c	=	10 2/3 Tbsp
5/8 c	=	10 Tbsp
1/2 c	=	8 Tbsp
3/8 c	=	6 Tbsp
1/3 c	=	5 1/3 Tbsp
1/4 c	=	4 Tbsp
1/8 c	=	2 Tbsp
1/16 c	=	1 Tbsp

PINT

1 pt	=	2 c
7/8 pt	=	1 3/4 c
3/4 pt	=	1 1/2 c
2/3 pt	=	1 1/3 c
5/8 pt	=	1 1/4 c
1/2 pt	=	1 c
3/8 pt	=	3/4 c
1/3 pt	=	2/3 c
1/4 pt	=	1/2 c
1/8 pt	=	1/4 c
1/16 pt	=	2 Tbsp

QUART

1 qt	=	2 pt
7/8 qt	=	3 1/2 c
3/4 qt	=	3 c
2/3 qt	=	2 2/3 c
5/8 qt	=	2 1/2 c
1/2 qt	=	1 pt
3/8 qt	=	1 1/2 c
1/3 qt	=	1 1/3 c
1/4 qt	=	1 c
1/8 qt	=	1/2 c
1/16 qt	=	1/4 c

GALLON

1 gal	=	4 qt
7/8 gal	=	3 1/2 qt
3/4 gal	=	3 qt
2/3 gal	=	10 2/3 c
5/8 gal	=	5 pt
1/2 gal	=	2 qt
3/8 gal	=	3 pt
1/3 gal	=	5 1/3 c
1/4 gal	=	1 qt
1/8 gal	=	1 pt
1/16 gal	=	1 c

POUND

1 lb	=	16 oz
7/8 lb	=	14 oz
3/4 lb	=	12 oz
2/3 lb	=	10 2/3 oz
5/8 lb	=	10 oz
1/2 lb	=	8 oz
3/8 lb	=	6 oz
1/3 lb	=	5 1/3 oz
1/4 lb	=	4 oz
1/8 lb	=	2 oz
1/16 lb	=	1 oz

Table 1.6
CONVERSION TO METRIC UNITS

Comparison of Avoirdupois and Metric Units of Weight

1 oz	=	0.06 lb	=	28.35 g	=	(30 g)*
2 oz	=	0.12 lb	=	56.70 g		
3 oz	=	0.19 lb	=	85.05 g		
4 oz	=	0.25 lb	=	113.40 g	=	(125 g)
5 oz	=	0.31lb	=	141.75 g		
6 oz	=	0.38 lb	=	170.10 g		
7 oz	=	0.44 lb	=	198.45 g		
8 oz	=	0.50 lb	=	226.80 g	=	(250 g)
9 oz	=	0.56 lb	=	255.15 g		
10 oz	=	0.62 lb	=	283.50 g		
11 oz	=	0.69 lb	=	311.85 g		
12 oz	=	0.75 lb	=	340.20 g	=	(350 g)
13 oz	=	0.81 lb	=	368.55 g		
14 oz	=	0.88 lb	=	396.90 g		
15 oz	=	0.94 lb	=	425.25 g		
16 oz	=	1.00 lb	=	453.59 g	=	(500 g)

1 g	=	0.035 oz
2 g	=	0.07 oz
3 g	=	0.11 oz
4 g	=	0.14 oz
5 g	=	0.18 oz
6 g	=	0.21 oz
7 g	=	0.25 oz
8 g	=	0.28 oz
9 g	=	0.32 oz
10 g	=	0.35 oz
11 g	=	0.39 oz
12 g	=	0.42 oz
13 g	=	0.46 oz
14 g	=	0.49 oz
15 g	=	0.53 oz
16 g	=	0.56 oz

* Figures in parentheses indicate common use.

Comparison of U.S. and Metric Units of Liquid Measure

1 fl oz	=	29.573 ml	1 qt	=	0.946 l	1 gal	=	3.785 l
2 fl oz	=	59.15 ml	2 qt	=	1.89 l	2 gal	=	7.57 l
3 fl oz	=	88.72 ml	3 qt	=	2.84 l	3 gal	=	11.36 l
4 fl oz	=	118.30 ml	4 qt	=	3.79 l	4 gal	=	15.14 l
5 fl oz	=	147.87 ml	5 qt	=	4.73 l	5 gal	=	18.93 l
6 fl oz	=	177.44 ml	6 qt	=	5.68 l	6 gal	=	22.71 l
7 fl oz	=	207.02 ml	7 qt	=	6.62 l	7 gal	=	26.50 l
8 fl oz	=	236.59 ml	8 qt	=	7.57 l	8 gal	=	30.28 l
9 fl oz	=	266.16 ml	9 qt	=	8.52 l	9 gal	=	34.07 l
10 fl oz	=	295.73 ml	10 qt	=	9.46 l	10 gal	=	37.85 l

1 ml	=	0.034 fl oz	1 l	=	1.056 qt	1 l	=	0.264 gal
2 ml	=	0.07 fl oz	2 l	=	2.11 qt	2 l	=	0.53 gal
3 ml	=	0.10 fl oz	3 l	=	3.17 qt	3 l	=	0.79 gal
4 ml	=	0.14 fl oz	4 l	=	4.23 qt	4 l	=	1.06 gal
5 ml	=	0.17 fl oz	5 l	=	5.28 qt	5 l	=	1.32 gal
6 ml	=	0.20 fl oz	6 l	=	6.34 qt	6 l	=	1.59 gal
7 ml	=	0.24 fl oz	7 l	=	7.40 qt	7 l	=	1.85 gal
8 ml	=	0.27 fl oz	8 l	=	8.45 qt	8 l	=	2.11 gal
9 ml	=	0.30 fl oz	9 l	=	9.51 qt	9 l	=	2.38 gal
10 ml	=	0.34 fl oz	10 l	=	10.57 qt	10 l	=	2.64 gal

Table 1.7
HYDROGEN ION CONCENTRATION AND pH OF SOME COMMON FOODS

Common Indicator Changes*	Hydrogen Ion Concentration	pH	Average Values for Common Foods
R at pH 1.2	1.0×10^{-2}	2.0	Limes
	8.0×10^{-3}	2.1	
	6.3×10^{-3}	2.2	Lemons
	5.0×10^{-3}	2.3	
Thymol blue	4.0×10^{-3}	2.4	
	3.2×10^{-3}	2.5	
	2.5×10^{-3}	2.6	
	2.0×10^{-3}	2.7	
	1.6×10^{-3}	2.8	
Y	1.3×10^{-3}	2.9	Vinegar, plums
Y	1.0×10^{-3}	3.0	Gooseberries
		3.1	Prunes, apples, grapefruit (3.0 to 3.3)
		3.2	Rhubarb, dill pickles
		3.3	Apricots, blackberries
		3.4	Strawberries, lowest acidity for jelly
		3.5	Peaches
Y		3.6	Raspberries, sauerkraut
Bromphenol blue		3.7	Blueberries, oranges (3.1 to 4.1)
		3.8	Sweet cherries
		3.9	Pears
	1.0×10^{-4}	4.0	Acid fondant, acidophilus milk
R		4.1	
		4.2	Tomatoes (4.0 to 4.6)
		4.3	
Bromcresol green R		4.4	Lowest acidity for processing at 100°C
		4.5	Buttermilk
Y B		4.6	Bananas, egg albumin, figs, isoelectric point for casein, pimentos
		4.7	
		4.8	
		4.9	
	1.0×10^{-5}	5.0	Pumpkins, carrots
		5.1	Cucumbers
Methyl red Y		5.2	Turnips, cabbage, squash
Chlorophenol red		5.3	Parsnips, beets, green peppers, string beans
		5.4	Sweet potatoes, bread
B		5.5	Spinach
		5.6	Asparagus, cauliflower
		5.7	Red kidney beans, lima beans
		5.8	Meat, ripened, poultry, succotash
		5.9	
Bromcresol purple Y	1.0×10^{-6}	6.0	Tuna
		6.1	Potatoes
		6.2	Peas
Y		6.3	Corn, oysters, dates
R		6.4	Egg yolks
		6.5	
		6.6	
Litmus Y		6.7	Milk (6.5 to 6.7)
P		6.8	
		6.9	Shrimp, wet packed
Bromthymol blue	1.0×10^{-7}	7.0	Meat, unripened
		7.1	Lye, hominy
		7.2	
		7.3	
		7.4	
		7.5	
Phenol red		7.6	
B		7.7	
		7.8	
		7.9	
	1.0×10^{-8}	8.0	Egg white (7.0 to 9.0)
		8.1	
B		8.2	
R		8.3	
		8.4	

* COMMON INDICATOR CHANGES:
B = Blue
P = Purple
R = Red
Y = Yellow

Table 1.8
TEMPERATURE OF FOOD FOR CONTROL OF BACTERIA

°C	°F	
121	250	121°C to 116°C — Canning temperature for low-acid vegetables, meat, fish and poultry in pressure canner.
116	240	
		106°C to 102°C — Jam-jelly stage
100	212	**Boiling Point** 100°C temperature of boiling water at sea level. Temperature to can fruits, tomatoes, and pickles in a water-bath canner.
85		
80	180	100°C to 85°C — Simmering 80°C — Scalding Cooking temperatures destroy most bacteria. The time required to kill bacteria is less as temperature increases. 83° to 60°C — Pasteurizing
74	165	Warming temperatures prevent bacterial growth, but allow the survival of some bacteria.
60	140	Some bacterial growth may occur at this temperature. Many bacteria survive.
	125	**DANGER ZONE: Temperatures in this zone allow rapid growth of bacteria and production of toxins by some bacteria.** (Do not keep foods in this temperature zone for more than 2-3 hours.)
35	95	35°C — Lukewarm
30	86	26°C to 32°C — yeast dough rises. 15°C to 60°C — rennin, an enzyme, is active
	60	
10	50	60 to 4°C — These temperatures allow the growth of bacteria and mold that cause food-borne illness.
4	40	
2	36	4°C — optimum refrigerator storage. Temperature for thawing frozen foods. Cold temperatures permit slow growth of some bacteria that cause spoilage.
0	32	**Freezing Point** Freezing temperatures stop growth of bacteria, but may not kill them.
-18	0	-18°C to -29°C — Optimum freezer storage
-29	-20	

Adapted from *You Can Prevent Food Poisoning.* Pacific Northwest Publication No. 250, Coop. Ext. WSU, Pullman, WA, 1989.

Table 1.9

THICKENING AND GELLING AGENTS

Thickening Agent	Uses and Quantity Required	Precautions in Mixing	Effect of Temperature	Other Factors that Affect Thickening	Characteristics of the Gel
AGAR	**Salad and dessert jellies:** 4 to 6 g (about 2 tsp) per pt of liquid (500 ml).	Soak in 3 to 6 times the weight of cold liquid, then dissolve by bringing to a boil.	Gel forms on cooling to 40°C to 45°C (104°F to 113°F); softens at 80°C to 85°C (176°F to 185°F).	Gel strength not easily destroyed by heat or acid.	Gel rigid, short, crumbly; transparent; may have weedy odor if sample not highly purified.
EGG	**Custard puddings and sauces:** 2 to 3 medium eggs per pt (500 ml) of milk or 4 to 6 yolks.	Blend well with sugar and milk. Coagulate by slow heating.	Overcooking causes syneresis (weeping) and curdling.	Sugar and dilution raise coagulation temperature; acid lowers it. Use of water instead of milk results in a flocculent precipitate rather than a gel.	Baked custard forms firm, continuous clot. Stirred custard is soft, thickened but not set.
FLOUR	**Thin soup or sauce:** 2 Tbsp (16 g) per pt (500 ml) of liquid. **Medium sauces:** 4 to 5 Tbsp (32 to 40 g) per pt (500 ml) of liquid. **Soufflés, molded pastes:** 1/2 c per pt of liquid (125 ml/500 ml).	Disperse in cold liquid or in fat or mix with sugar before adding hot liquid. Stir while cooking.	Heat to 90°C (194°F) or above to obtain maximum thickening. Viscosity increases on cooling.	Heating with acid causes thinning. High sugar concentrations retard gelatinization and reduce thickening power.	Opaque paste

Thickening Agent	Uses and Quantity Required	Precautions in Mixing	Effect of Temperature	Other Facotrs that Affect Thickening	Characteristics of the Gel
WAXY RICE FLOUR (mochiko, sweet rice flour)	**Frozen sauces and gravies:** to prevent curdling and liquid separation 4 to 5 Tbsp per pt (32 to 40 g/500 ml) liquid. Also prevents gelatinization of thickened canned products.	Same as flour, but waxy rice is less likely to lump.	Maximum thickening at 70°C to 80°C (158°F to 176°F); little difference between hot and cold viscosity.	Heating with acid and homogenization cause thinning.	Does not gel. Forms flour short opaque paste.
GELATIN	**Molded desserts and salads:** 7 to 12 g (about 1 Tbsp or 1 envelope) per pt (500 ml) of liquid according to grade.	Soak in 3 to 6 times the weight of cold liquid, then dissolve by heating to 40°C (104°F) or by adding hot liquid, and then add sugar.	Gel forms after a few hours of chilling. Softens at 26.5°C (80°F) and higher.	Heating with acid causes reduction of gel strength. Raw pineapple prevents setting because of enzyme action.	Gel firm but springy and quivery; transparent in appearance.
GUM TRAGACANTH	**Salad dressings, sauces:** 2 to 3 g per pt (500 ml) of liquid give thin paste; 6 to 8 g per pt (500 ml) give thick gel.	Dissolve either in hot or cold water (dissolves much more rapidly in hot).	Little change in viscosity over a wide temperature range.	Acid, alkali or salt plus heat causes thinning.	Gel thick and mucilaginous but not rigid even at high concentrations.
IRISH MOSS	**Puddings, sauces:** 4 to 6 g per pt (500 ml) liquid give a thick paste; 15 to 25 g per pt (500 ml) of liquid give a stiff gel.	Soak in cold water, then heat to 60°C (140°F) or above to dissolve.	Gel melts at 27°C to 41°C (81°F to 106°F) depending on concentration.	Acid plus heat causes thinning. Heat alone has no effect.	Gel thick and mucilaginous; becomes rigid only at high concentrations; may have weedy odor if not highly purified.

(continued on the next page)

THICKENING AND GEL AGENTS continued

Thickening Agent	Uses and Quantity Required	Precautions in Mixing	Effect of Temperature	Other Factors that Affect Thickening	Characteristics of the Gel
CORNSTARCH AND RICE STARCH	1 Tbsp cornstarch or rice starch = 2 Tbsp flour.	Same as flour.	Same as flour.	Same as flour.	Pastes more translucent than flour paste.
POTATO STARCH and ARROWROOT STARCH	1 Tbsp potato or arrowroot starch = 2 Tbsp flour (*See Effect of Temperature column*). Suitable for starch-egg mixtures or fruit sauces where higher temperatures are not desired.	Same as flour.	Reaches maximum thickening at 70°C to 80°C (158°F to 176°F); higher temperature or further heating causes very marked thinning.	Same as flour, thinning also brought about by excessive stirring.	Pastes very transparent.
WAXY CEREAL STARCHES	Prevent gelation and syneresis of canned products during storage— may be used in combination with flour.	Same as flour.	Similar to waxy rice flour.	Thinned by heating with acid.	Waxy starches give somewhat ropy translucent pastes.
TAPIOCA, PEARL	About twice as much as quick-cooking tapioca.	Soak several hours before cooking.	Cook until tapioca is transparent.	Same as quick-cooking tapioca.	Same as quick-cooking tapioca.
TAPIOCA, QUICK-COOKING	**Puddings:** 3 Tbsp per pt (500ml) of liquid. **Fruit pie fillings:** 1 1/2 to 3 Tbsp for 8- or 9- inch pie. **Soup:** 1 1/2 to 3 Tbsp per qt (1000ml) of liquid.	Mix in cold or hot liquid; no soaking necessary.	Bring only to a boil. Mixture thickens as tapioca particles swell and become transparent. It continues to thicken while cooling.	Stir while cooking. Over-stirring while cooling tends to disrupt tapioca particles, resulting in a sticky, gelatinous mixture.	Pastes transparent, nonhomogeneous (particles remain distinct). Mixture thickens as it cools. Especially satisfactory for fruit pie fillings.

FOOD-BORNE ILLNESSES AND THEIR PREVENTION

Food handlers and cooks must constantly give attention to food sanitation and safety. Temperature of food plays a primary role in prevention of microbial growth and food-borne illnesses and in the maintenance of food quality. The length of time foods are held at a specific temperature also plays a primary role in food safety as well as food quality. The selection of storage, cooking and holding temperatures and times must be controlled rigidly. Food-borne illnesses are a major problem in home and food service preparation. The following table (Table 1.10), presents some of the common microorganisms involved in illnesses.

Table 1.10
FOOD-BORNE ILLNESSES

	SALMONELLOSIS and CAMPYLOBACTEROSIS	PERFRINGENS POISONING
Cause	*Salmonella* and *Campylobacter*. Bacteria widespread in nature; live and grow in intestinal tracts of humans and animals.	*Clostridium perfringens.* Spore-forming bacteria that grow in the absence of oxygen. Temperatures reached in thorough cooking of most foods are sufficient to destroy vegetative cells, but heat-resistant spores can survive.
Examples of foods involved	Poultry, red meat, eggs, and dairy products.	Cooked meat and poultry, stews, soups, gravies left at 60-125°F (16-52°C) several hours or cooled slowly.
Transmission	Eating contaminated food, or contact with infected persons or carriers of the infection. Also transmitted by insects, rodents and pets.	Eating food contaminated with large numbers of the bacteria.
Symptoms	Severe headache, followed by vomiting, diarrhea, abdominal cramps and fever. Infants, elderly people, persons with low resistance are most susceptible. Severe infections cause high fever and may even cause death.	Diarrhea, abdominal cramps, and flatulence.
Onset	Usually within 12-36 hours	Usually within 8-20 hours
Duration	2 - 7 days	May persist for 24 hours
Prevention	Cook foods thoroughly. The bacteria are destroyed by heating the food to 140°F (60°C) for 10 minutes or to higher temperatures for less time — for instance,	Cool food rapidly and refrigerate promptly at 40°F (4°C) or below, or above 140°F (60°C) to prevent growth of surviving bacteria in cooked meats, gra-

(continued on the next page)

	SALMONELLOSIS and CAMPYLOBACTEREROSIS	PERFRINGENS POISONING
Prevention (continued)	155°F (69°C) for a few seconds. Chill foods rapidly in small quantities. Refrigerate at 40°F (4°C). Wash hands, work surfaces and equipment after touching raw meat or poultry.	vies, and meat casseroles to be eaten later. Reheat leftover foods to 165°F (74°C).

	STAPHYLOCOCCAL POISONING	BOTULISM
Cause	*Staphylococcus aureus.* Bacteria growing in food produce a toxin that is extremely resistant to heat.	*Clostridium botulinum.* Spore-forming organisms that grow and produce toxin in the absence of oxygen, such as in a sealed container or below the surface of food.
Examples of foods involved	Custards, egg salad, potato salad, chicken salad, macaroni salad, ham, salami, cheese, cooked poultry, and dressing.	Improperly canned low-acid food (vegetables, fish, meat. poultry), smoked fish, and improperly handled low-acid cooked foods.
Transmission	Eating food containing the toxin. Food handlers can carry the bacteria in infected cuts and wounds.	Eating food containing the toxin.
Symptoms	Vomiting, diarrhea, prostration, abdominal cramps, retching, weakness. Onset usually sudden.	Headache, double vision, inability to swallow, speech difficulty, and progressive respiratory paralysis. Fatality rate is about 20%.
Onset	Usually within 2-8 hours.	Usually 12-36 hours or longer.
Duration	1-2 days.	Recovery is prolonged.
Prevention	Growth of bacteria that produce toxin is stopped by keeping hot foods above 140°F (60°C) and cold foods at or below 40°F (4°C). Chill food rapidly in small quantities. Once the toxin is formed, it is not easily destroyed by heat. Mishandled foods cannot be made safe by reheating.	Follow reliable instructions for time and temperature for home canning low-acid vegetables, meat, fish and poultry. Bacterial spores in these foods are destroyed only by high temperatures obtained in the pressure canner. Toxin is destroyed by boiling 10 minutes or heating in the oven to 185°F (85°C). Refrigerate cooked low-acid foods promptly.

FOOD-BORNE ILLNESSES continued

	LISTERIOSIS	VIBRIOSIS
Cause	*Listeria monocytogenes.* Bacteria widespread in nature that can live in soil as well as intestinal tracts of humans and animals.	*Vibrio parahaemolyticus.* Bacteria common in seawater. Other *Vibrio* species found in seawater (including *Vibrio cholera*) also cause food-borne disease.
Examples of foods involved	Raw milk, unripened and other soft cheese, undercooked meat and poultry.	Raw seafood such as oysters, shrimp, crabs and clams.
Transmission	Eating food contaminated with the large numbers of bacteria.	Eating seafood contaminated with bacteria.
Symptoms	Headache, fever and nausea. Can lead to meningitis. Can result in miscarriage or stillbirth. Pregnant women, infants and persons with low resistance to infections (such as cancer patients) are most susceptible. Can result in death unless there is antibiotic therapy.	Diarrhea, cramps, weakness, nausea, chills and headache.
Onset	Usually within 24 hours but can occur up to 12 days after ingestion.	3-76 hours (an average of 17 hours).
Duration	2-7 days.	1-8 days.
Prevention	Cook foods of animal origin thoroughly. Buy pasteurized milk. Prevent recontamination of cooked foods by cleaning hands, surfaces, equipment that come into contact with raw animal foods. Do not use animal manure or sewage sludge in your vegetable garden.	Keep raw and cooked seafood refrigerated. Cook seafood thoroughly. Prevent cross-contamination between raw and cooked seafood.

Glossaries

FOOD SCIENCE TERMS

Acid Substances that furnish hydrogen ions.

Acidulate To make slightly sour or acidic by adding vinegar, lemon juice, or cream of tartar.

Alkali Substances that form hydroxyl ions which can neutralize an acid.

Anthocyanins Pigments (classified as flavonoids) which are responsible for the red/blue colors found in certain vegetables and fruits. They are red in the presence of acid; blue-green in the presence of alkali.

Anthoxanthins Pigments (classified as flavonoids) which are colorless in acid, but turn yellow in the presence of alkali.

Antioxidant A substance which inhibits the chemical reaction that causes oxidation of foods.

Ascorbic acid Vitamin C. A vitamin which can be used to inhibit enzymatic browning of light-colored fruit such as apples, pears and bananas.

Boiling point The temperature at which the atmospheric pressure just exceeds the vapor pressure of a liquid.

Browning reactions Darkening of foods caused by enzymes (light-colored cut fruit) or reactions of protein and sugar (baked goods).

Carotenoids Yellow-to-red pigments found in fruits and vegetables.

Cellulose A polysaccharide which provides structural rigidity in cell walls of plants, fruits, and vegetables. It can be softened by cooking, but is not digested by humans.

Chlorophyll The green pigment in vegetables which turns olive-green in the presence of acid and/or heat for a period of several minutes.

Coagulation The change from a fluid state to a thickened curd or clot due to denaturation of protein.

Colloidal dispersion A dispersion of very tiny particles of one substance in another substance; the particles are too large to form a true solution and too small to form a coarse suspension. An example is gelatin in water.

Controlled atmosphere A long-term storage technique where respiration of products such as apples is retarded by rigidly controlling temperature and humidity and adding carbon dioxide at a controlled level.

Crystallization The formation of crystals resulting from chemical elements or compounds solidifying in an orderly structure.

Dehydration A method of food preservation where water is removed from food by drying in air, in a vacuum, in inert gas, or by direct application of heat.

Denaturation A change in the physical structure of protein molecules which alters their characteristics. Heat, for example, denatures the protein in an egg.

Emulsify To suspend small drops of an immiscible liquid in another, forming an emulsion such as mayonnaise.

Enzymes Proteins which catalyze chemical reactions that change the color, texture, and flavor of foods.

Enzymatic browning Discoloration of foods, such as cut fruit, due to oxidation catalyzed by enzymes.

Foam A type of colloidal dispersion in which bubbles of gas are surrounded by liquid.

Food Standards Specifications for certain foods such as identity, quality, fill of container and enrichment level which are regulated by governmental agencies.

Freeze drying A method of preserving food by first freezing and then drying under a vacuum. The freeze-dried product may be stored without refrigeration and is much lighter in weight than frozen products.

Freezing A method of preserving food by chilling it rapidly at a low temperature.

Gel A liquid-in-solid colloidal system that does not flow. It can be formed by gelatin, pectin, starch, soured milk, and egg.

Gelatinization The absorption of liquid by starch, which results in swelling of the granules and thickening of the liquid. Heat is required to accomplish this physical change.

Gluten The elastic substance formed from manipulating (kneading) the insoluble proteins of wheat flour with some liquid.

Homogenize To break up into tiny particles of the same size, such as fat in milk.

Hydration The process of absorbing water.

Hydrogenation The process of adding hydrogen ions to unsaturated (liquid) fat to form a solid or semi-solid fat such as margarine.

Hydrolysis The process of splitting compounds into simpler components by adding a molecule of water, a reaction that can be facilitated by acid, heat, or enzymes.

Irradiation A process in which foods can be exposed to ionizing radiation to lengthen storage life. Depending on dose, irradiation can kill insects, inhibit sprouting, and kill microorganisms.

Kilocalorie The amount of heat required to raise the temperature of 1 kilogram of water (1000 g) 1 degree Celsius.

Kosher Food produced in accordance with Jewish rabbinical law.

Leavening agent A substance which increases the volume of a baked product (air, steam, and microbiological or chemical agents capable of producing carbon dioxide).

Osmosis Movement of water through a semi-permeable membrane from an area of low concentration of solute to an area of higher concentration to equalize the osmotic pressure created by differences in concentration.

Pasteurization The process of destroying harmful microorganisms by heating food (such milk or fruit juice) to a specific temperature and holding for a specific length of time.

pH A measure of acidity/alkalinity based on the hydrogen ion concentration. On the scale of 1 to 14, 1 is most acidic and 14 is most alkaline.

Pickling The processing of preserving food by using acid and salt to inhibit microbial growth.

Proteolytic enzymes Enzymes capable of effecting a chemical reaction that splits proteins into simpler components. Examples are papain (from papaya) and bromelin (from pineapple).

Rancidity Flavor and odor deterioration due to either hydrolysis or oxidation of fats.

Rennet A substance from calves' stomachs which contains rennin, an enzyme used in cheese making.

Retrogradation Formation of crystalline areas in gelatinized starch mixtures (such as bread products and starch pastes) as they age.

Smoke point The temperature at which a fat begins to smoke and emit irritating vapors.

Sol A fluid colloidal system in which the continuous phase is liquid.

Solution A uniform liquid blend containing a solvent (liquid) and a solute (such as salt) dissolved in the liquid.

Specific gravity The weight of a specific volume of a substance in relation to the weight of an equal volume of water. (At 4^0 Celsius, 1 milliliter of water weighs 1 gram.)

Specific heat The heat or thermal capacity of a substance in relation to that of water.

Sterilize To destroy microorganisms by using a high temperature.

Supersaturated solution A solution which contains more solute than an unheated liquid could hold at a given temperature. It is unstable and prone to crystallization.

Suspension A dry substance suspended in a liquid (such as starch in cold water) which will only remain combined if stirred.

Syneresis Drainage of liquid from a gel when cut or disturbed.

Viscosity The degree to which a fluid flows readily or resists flow.

COOKING TERMS

Bake To cook in an oven or oven-type appliance. When applied to meats in uncovered containers, it is generally called roasting.

Barbecue To roast slowly on a rack or spit over coals or under free flame or an electric heat unit. The food is often brushed with a sauce during cooking.

Baste To moisten meat or other foods during cooking to add flavor and to prevent drying of the surface. The liquid is usually melted fat, meat drippings, fruit juice, sauce, or water.

Batter A mixture made of flour, liquid, and other ingredients that can be stirred or poured.

Beat To make a mixture smooth by incorporating air with rapid, regular motions using a wire whisk, spoon, hand beater or mixer.

Blanch To briefly heat vegetables or fruit in steam or boiling water to loosen or remove skins or to inactivate enzymes prior to freezing or drying.

Blend To mix two or more ingredients thoroughly.

Boil To cook in water that is at boiling temperature. Bubbles will rise continually and break on the surface.

Braise To cook meat or poultry over low heat in a covered utensil in a small amount of liquid or in steam.

Bread To coat a food with bread or cracker crumbs or other food. The surface may first be coated with beaten egg or other liquid.

Brine To soak pickled, fermented, or cured foods in a strong salt solution to add flavor and inhibit microbial growth.

Broil To cook by direct heat on a rack or spit.

Brown To cook food with moderate or high heat until it browns in color.

Candy To cook fruit or vegetables in sugar or syrup.

Caramelize To heat sugar or foods containing sugar until a brown color and characteristic flavor develop.

Chop To cut into pieces with a knife or other sharp tool, blender, or food processor.

Coat To spread food with or dip it into a substance such as flour or a sauce until it is covered.

Combine To stir two or more ingredients together to form a mixture of uniform consistency.

Cream To mix one or more foods (usually fat and sugar) with a spoon or mixer until soft and smooth.

Cube To cut food into small cubes; to cut the surface of meat in a checkered pattern to increase tenderness.

Curdle To form clots in a smooth liquid (such as milk) by precipitating the protein with heat or acid.

Cure To preserve beef or poultry with a combination of salt or brine, sodium nitrate and/or nitrite, seasonings, and sometimes smoking. Cured products such as corned beef and ham develop a distinctive pink/red color.

Cut To divide food materials with a knife or scissors.

Cut In To distribute solid fat throughout dry ingredients using two knives or a pastry blender until flour-coated fat particles are the desired size.

Deep fry To cook food in enough hot fat for submersion or floating.

Dice To cut into small cubes.

Dilute To make less strong by adding liquid.

Dissolve To make a solution such as sugar in water; to melt or liquefy.

Dough A mixture of flour and water (and usually other ingredients), which is stiff enough to be rolled or kneaded.

Dredge To cover or coat with flour or other fine substances such as bread crumbs or corn meal.

Dust To sprinkle lightly with flour or sugar.

Flake To break into small pieces, usually with a fork.

Fold To combine one ingredient with another by gently turning the mixture with a spoon or spatula to minimize loss of air. Two motions are used: cutting vertically through the mixture; sliding across the bottom of the bowl and up the other side.

Fricassee To cook cut pieces of food such as fowl, rabbit, or veal by braising in a sauce.

Fry To cook in fat. A small amount of fat is used for pan-frying or sauteing; deep-fat fried foods are submerged in fat.

Garnish To add decorative touches (usually edible) to food that is served.

Glaze To coat with a glossy mixture that enhances both flavor and appearance of food (such as meats, vegetables, and desserts).

Grate To produce particles of a specific size by rubbing food (such as carrots or cheese) on a grater (or chopping in a blender or food processor).

Grease To rub the surface of a pan or dish with fat to prevent food from sticking.

Grill To cook food on a rack with direct heat.

Grind To reduce food to small particles by cutting or crushing mechanically in a grinder, blender, or food processor.

Julienne To cut meat, fruit, or vegetables into long, thin strips.

Knead To work dough by hand or mechanically to develop the gluten needed for bread structure.

Lard To place strips of fat on top of or into gashes in the side of uncooked lean meat or fish to give flavor and prevent drying.

Lukewarm A temperature of about 95°F (35°C). Lukewarm liquids and foods feel neither hot nor cold when in contact with the inside of the wrist.

Macerate To soak foods in a liquid to soften them and to absorb flavor.

Marinate To let food stand in a liquid which is usually a mixture of oil, lemon juice or vinegar and seasonings.

Meringue A foam of beaten egg whites and sugar which is baked. A soft meringue may be baked on a one-crust pie; a baked hard meringue is used as a shell for berries or other dessert fillings.

Mince To chop or cut into very small pieces.

Mix To combine two or more ingredients into a uniform mixture.

Pan-broil To cook uncovered over high heat on a hot surface (usually a fry pan), pouring off accumulating fat.

Pan-fry To cook over high heat in a small amount of fat.

Panning Cooking vegetables in their own juices and a small amount of fat in a tightly covered pan.

Parboil To boil until partially cooked. Cooking is usually completed by another method.

Pare To cut off the outside covering such as skins of vegetables or fruits.

Peel To remove the outer covering of foods such as oranges or bananas.

Pinch The amount of a substance that can be held between the thumb and forefinger.

Pit To remove the seed from whole fruit.

Poach To cook in a hot liquid, being careful to retain shape of the food (poached eggs or fish, for example).

Punch down To deflate a risen yeast dough by pushing it down with the fist.

Puree To press food through a fine sieve or food mill; to blend in a blender or food processor to a smooth, thick mixture; also a thick sauce made from pureed vegetables.

Reconstitute To restore concentrated foods such as nonfat dry milk or frozen orange juice to their original form by adding water.

Reduce To decrease volume of liquid by rapidly boiling.

Rehydrate To restore water lost during drying by soaking or cooking dehydrated foods.

Roast To cook uncovered in an oven.

Saute To brown or cook in a small amount of fat.

Scald To heat liquid to just below the boiling point; to pour boiling water over food or dip food briefly in boiling water.

Scallop To bake food (usually cut into pieces) with a sauce or other liquid.

Score To cut shallow slits on the surface of meat or food to increase tenderness or to prevent the fat covering from curling.

Sear To brown the surface of foods quickly with high heat.

Simmer To cook food over low heat in a liquid just below the boiling point (about 180 to 210°F or 80 to 99°C). Bubbles will form slowly and break apart just below the surface.

Steam To cook food in steam over boiling water in a closed container.

Steep To let a food stand in liquid below the boiling point of water to extract flavor or color.

Stew To simmer food in a liquid.

Stir To mix ingredients with a circular motion.

Stir fry To fry thinly sliced food quickly in only a little oil, stirring with a tossing motion.

Strain To remove liquid from food using a strainer.

Toast To brown by direct heat or in a hot oven.

Toss To mix foods lightly with a lifting motion.

Warm A temperature of 105 to 115°F (40 to 46°C).

Whip To beat food such as cream, eggs, or gelatin rapidly to incorporate air and increase volume.

INTERNATIONAL CULINARY AND MENU TERMS

Áebleskiver Danish pancake, often filled with apple bits, baked in a special pan so it becomes a ball about two inches in diameter.

Á la carte Menu in which each dish is ordered and priced separately.

Á la king Style of presentation in which food is mixed with a seasoned cream sauce.

Á la lyonnaise Cooked with onions, in the style of Lyon, France.

Á la mode Made or served in a specific style, such as pie with ice cream.

Albóndiga (Spanish) meatball.

Al dente Cooking "to the tooth," a slightly firm but tender stage of cooking pasta.

Almandine Containing or topped with almonds.

Antipasto (Italian) Assorted relishes.

Au gratin Sprinkled with crumbs and/or cheese and baked until brown.

Au Jus Served with the natural juice or gravy.

Bagel Doughnut-shaped roll that is cooked in water before being baked.

Baklava Mid-Eastern confection made of multilayers of phyllo, honey, and chopped nuts.

Bannock Bread of oat or barley flour, frequently unleavened, and baked in flat loaves; common in the northern British Isles. In New England it is a thin corn bread, baked on a griddle.

Bar-le-duc Sugar syrup containing whole white or red currants and named for the town in Lorraine, France where it originated. It is used as a topping for desserts or pastry filling.

Béarnaise sauce Sauce made with egg yolks and butter.

Béchamel (French) A basic white sauce usually made with milk and sometimes with stock.

Beignet (French) Variety of fritters fried in deep fat.

Bisque (French) A thick, rich, creamy soup made from fish.

Blanquette (French) A stew of light-colored

meat or poultry in which the meat is cooked in water without browning.

Bleu or Au bleu (French) Method of quickly cooking fish while still alive to guarantee maximum flavor and freshness; results in curled tail and bluish skin color.

Blini (Russian, Polish) Small buckwheat crêpe usually served with caviar or sour cream.

Blintz (Jewish) Thin crêpe with fruit or cheese filling, rolled and sauteed in butter.

Bombé (French) Rich elaborate dessert made of ices, whipped cream, custard, and/or fruit frozen in a melon mold.

Borscht (Russian, Polish) Thick soup made with a beet base, which may contain other vegetables, meat, and a topping of sour cream.

Bouillabaisse (French) Thick, hearty soup made from an assortment of fish; originally made in the Mediterranean region of France.

Bouillon (French) Broth or clear soup made from various meats, fish, poultry or vegetables.

Bouquet garni (French) Combination of herbs, usually thyme, bay leaf, and parsley, tied together and used as flavoring.

Bratwurst Mild German sausage, usually light gray in color.

Braunschweiger (German) Smoked liver sausage.

Brioche Rich classic French yeast dough, usually shaped with a topknot.

Bulgur Cracked wheat originating in the Middle East; available as fine, medium, or coarse.

Buñuelos Spanish or Mexican fried doughnut.

Café au lait Beverage composed of equal parts of strong coffee and heated milk poured simultaneously into the cup; served at breakfast in Europe.

Café noir (French) Black coffee.

Caldo In Spanish literally a broth or gravy. In Mexico the term is broader and is used to describe soups or stews with meat and vegetables.

Canapés Toasted, buttered bread spread or topped with appetizers, flavored spreads, vegetables or seafood.

Cannelloni (Italian) Pasta dish made of squares of dough with meat or cheese filling, filled and baked in a sauce; crêpes sometimes are used instead of pasta.

Cannoli (Italian) Cream-filled tubular pastry.

Capers Pickled buds of a Mediterranean shrub with a sharp gherkin taste used as seasoning.

Cappuccino (Italian) After-dinner coffee made from hot milk and espresso coffee, flavored with cinnamon and/or brandy.

Cassoulet (French) Stew made from dried beans, assorted meats, and sausages.

Caviar Black caviar is the eggs, or roe, of the sturgeon and is imported from Russia and Iran; red caviar is the roe of salmon.

Ceviche Also Seviche. Raw fish marinated in lime juice.

Challah Braided Jewish Sabbath bread.

Chantilly (French) Containing whipped cream.

Chapati Flat bread made from whole wheat, baked on a griddle; from India.

Châteaubriand Thick piece of filet mignon, usually prepared for two and served with Béarnaise sauce.

Chili con carne Red beans, tomatoes, meat, and chili pepper seasoning; stew characteristic of southwestern United States.

Chili rellenos Omelet-type mixture containing green chili peppers stuffed with mild cheese.

Chitterlings Also chittlins. Well-cleaned small intestines of hogs, cut in pieces and boiled, then fried and seasoned.

Chorizo Hot Spanish or Mexican sausage.

Chutney Spicy-sweet relish originating in India, now popular in England.

Cilantro Pungent herb; also known as Chinese parsley or coriander leaves.

Compote Stewed fruit, often based on dried fruit.

Consommé Clarified double-strength brown stock.

Coq au vin (French) Chicken cooked in red wine sauce.

Crêpes (French) Very thin pancakes.

Croissants A rich, crescent-shaped roll or pastry.

Croutons Small cubes of toasted bread used to garnish soup or salad.

Curry Blend of many spices such as ginger, coriander, cardamom, cayenne, turmeric; originating in India.

Demitasse Small cup of strong, black, after-dinner coffee.

Du jour "Of the day" used as soup du jour or the soup specialty available that day.

En Brochette (French) Broiled and served on a skewer.

Enchilada (Mexican) Tortilla rolled around meat or cheese filling and covered with sauce.

Entrée In the Unites States, the main course; in France, the dish served before the main course.

Epice (French) Spice.

Espresso (Italian) Strong, black coffee made with steam.

Falaffel (Israeli, Middle Eastern) Croquettes made from mashed chick peas fried in deep fat.

Feijoada (Brazilian) Soup/stew of black beans, meat, and rice.

Fettucine (Italian) Narrow, flat noodles.

Fillet Strip of boneless lean meat, fish, or poultry.

Fines herbes Equal parts of freshly minced parsley, tarragon, chives, and chervil.

Fish sauce This is used in Southeast Asian cuisine. The sauce is made from one type of fish and is often salty. Finger foods are dipped into the sauce.

Flambé Served after flaming with brandy or other high-proof liqueur.

Flan Baked custard with caramel sauce also called crème caramel; also open-faced pastry tart with fruit toppings.

Florentine Served in the manner of Florence with spinach or a spinach base.

Foie gras (French) Specially fattened goose livers ground to a fine, smooth paste and seasoned.

Fondue Bourguignon Small pieces of meat deep fried at the table by each diner.

Fondue Suisse Melted cheese, white wine and kirsch into which cubes of dry French bread are swirled.

Foo yong Chinese omelet with bean sprouts, meat, and fish.

Frijoles refritos (Mexican) Cooked beans which have been mashed and fried.

Frittata (Italian) Omelet with flavorful filling or topping.

Fritter Batter-dipped food fried in deep fat or sauteed.

Gazpacho (Spanish) Chilled soup composed of finely chopped raw tomatoes, cucumbers, onions and other vegetables in spiced tomato juice.

Gefilte fish Also gefullete. German/Jewish stuffed or chopped fish.

Génoise (French) Rich light sponge cake; often used as a base for more elaborate desserts.

Ghee (India) A clarified butter.

Ginger root Spicy tropical root used for flavoring in many cuisines; available fresh, dried and powdered, candied or pickled.

Ginseng Thick root of plant highly prized in the Orient for its stimulating, refreshing qualities; plant originated in Korea.

Gnocchi (Italian) Small, tender dumplings made of potatoes, flour, or semolina.

Goulash (Hungarian) Beef stew liberally seasoned with paprika.

Guacamole (Mexican) Smooth paste of avocado, tomato, onion, and green chilies used as an appetizer and salad dressing.

Gumbo Thick soup/stew characteristic of Creole cooking in Louisiana; also means okra.

Hassenpfeffer (German) Spicy rabbit stew.

Hollandaise sauce Thick rich sauce made of egg yolks, butter, and lemon juice.

Hors d'oeuvres Attractive small appetizers.

Huevos (Spanish) Eggs.

Imbottite (Italian) Stuffed.

Kabob Also kebab (Middle Eastern) Skewered pieces of meat and vegetables roasted over the flames.

Kasha Russian buckwheat groats; also used in other East European cuisines as a staple.

Kim chee (Korean) Spicy pickled vegetables based on fermented cabbage.

Kippers Split, dried, salted, smoked herring; popular English breakfast food.

Kuchen (German) Cake or coffee cake; also specifically a flat round bread topped with cream cheese and sweetened fruit.

Kolachi Also Kolachy. (Middle European) Yeast roll filled with cheese or preserved fruit.

Kugelhopf (German) Yeast-raised dough usually baked in a Turk's head mold.

Lasagne (Italian) Broad noodles layered with meat, cheese, and sauce.

Limpa (Swedish) Rye bread flavored with orange rind.

Linguine A long, thin and narrow ribbon-like pasta.

Luau Hawaiian feast.

Lucia buns (Swedish) Sweet rolls served on St. Lucia Day, December 13.

Manicotti (Italian) Large tubular noodles stuffed with cheese, meat, or vegetables and served with sauce.

Matzos (Jewish) Thin flat pieces of unleavened bread eaten during Passover.

Menudo (Mexican) Soup/stew made of tripe, hominy and green chilies.

Minestrone (Italian) Thick vegetable soup.

Mocha Type of Arabian coffee; also coffee flavored.

Moussaka (Middle Eastern) Layers of eggplant alternated with chopped lamb or beef.

Mousse (French) Light delicate dish usually made with gelatin with sweet or savory fillings, depending on the use — sweet for dessert.

Nesselrode Dessert or sauce made of candied fruit and chestnuts.

Nicoise In the style of Nice, meaning use of tomatoes, onions, garlic, capers and olive oil.

Paella A rice casserole with chicken, vegetables, and seasonings.

Pannetone (Italian) Wine-flavored yeast bread filled with candied fruit, raisins, and nuts.

Pareve (Jewish) In kosher cuisine, foods such as fruits, vegetables, and eggs that may be eaten with either meat or dairy foods.

Pasta All forms of macaroni products.

Pâté Ground, seasoned meat or meats served with or without pastry covering.

Petits fours Small fancy iced cakes.

Phyllo Also Fila, brik, malsouka, yukka. A tissue-thin pastry which is used in the Near East.

Pilaf Also pilau (Middle Eastern) Browned rice, barley, or cracked wheat variously seasoned.

Pirozhki (Russian) Small meat-filled pastries used as appetizers.

Pita Flat bread with a pocket inside that may be stuffed with meat and/or salad.

Poi (Hawaii and South Pacific) Starchy, bland paste made from fermented taro root.

Polenta (Italian) Corn meal porridge.

Quesedilla (Mexican) Cheese wrapped in a tortilla and heated.

Quiche An unsweetened custard frequently containing cheese and usually baked in a pastry shell.

Ragôut (French) Highly seasoned stew made with meat, poultry, or fish, and sometimes vegetables.

Ravioli (Italian) Filled pasta dough that is boiled and served with a sauce.

Rigatoni Large fluted tubes of Italian pasta, often stuffed and covered with sauce.

Rijsttafel Literally "rice table"; Dutch-Indonesian dinner of rice and an assortment of spicy foods.

Risotto (Italian) Wide variety of rice dishes.

Roquefort (French) Blue-veined, pungent cheese; authentic Roquefort comes only from a certain area in France and bears the trademark of a small red outline of a sheep on the label.

Roux (French) Mixture of fat and flour used to thicken soups, sauces, and gravies.

Salsa Spanish for sauce. In Mexico a mixture of chopped fresh tomatoes, peppers, and onions.

Sashimi (Japanese) Raw fish served with dipping sauces, usually an appetizer.

Sauerbraten (German) Pot roast of beef that has been marinated several days in spicy vinegar sauce.

Smorgasbord (Scandinavian) Literally "sandwich table"; large assortment of hors d'oeuvres, cold salads, meats and desserts.

Smorrebrod (Danish) Open-face sandwiches, tastefully arranged and garnished.

Soufflé A delicate, baked dish with a base of firm white sauce and egg yolks blended with whipped egg whites.

Spätzle Also Spatzen. Small German egg dumplings.

Spumoni (Italian) Rich ice cream containing candied fruit and nuts.

Stollen (Germany) Pastry or yeast coffee cake containing dried and candied fruit and nuts; associated with Christmas.

Strudel (Austrian) Thin leaves of flaky pastry filled with fruit or cheese based on a stretched dough; characteristic of central Europe.

Stroganoff A casserole with noodles, onions, mushrooms, meat and a sauce with a sour cream base.

Subgum In Chinese cuisine, meaning mixture of vegetables.

Sukiyaki (Japanese) Sautéed beef and vegetables; usually cooked at the table.

Sushi (Japanese) Appetizer composed of vinegared rice topped with raw fish or wrapped in laver (seaweed).

Tàble d'Hôte (French) In restaurants a fixed price for all the courses of a meal; opposite of à la carte.

Taco (Mexican) Fried tortilla folded around various fillings.

Tahina (Middle Eastern) Oily paste prepared by grinding sesame seeds.

Tamale (Mexican) Ground corn paste shell wrapped around meat or poultry filling and steamed.

Tempura (Japanese) Batter dipped, deep-fried food of any type.

Teriyaki (Japanese) Soy sauce marinade used to flavor meat and fish.

Timbale A soufflé which is cooked in a drum-shaped mold; a pastry shell filled with a creamy mixture.

Tofu Soy bean curd used in oriental cooking.

Torte A rich cake usually made of eggs, chopped nuts, and crumbs.

Tortilla (Mexican) Thin, unleavened corn bread; in Spain an omelet.

Tostada (Mexican) Layered salad composed of tortilla, refried beans, shredded lettuce, ground meat, and grated cheese.

Vermicelli (Italian) Very narrow type of spaghetti.

Vichyssoise (French) Cream soup made with leeks and potatoes; usually served cold.

Vinaigrette (French) Marinade or salad dressing of oil, vinegar, pepper, and herbs.

Vol-au-vent (French) Flaky or puff pastry made into a shell.

Wiener schnitzel (Austrian) Vienna style breaded, sauteed veal cutlet.

Won ton Squares of noodle dough which are wrapped around meats and vegetables and cooked in boiling water.

Yorkshire pudding A batter pudding baked in the drippings of roasting meat.

Milk and Milk Products

Milk is ageless. It is the main food for young mammals and is used in countless ways as food in fresh, fluid form and food products. The term milk implies cow's milk. All milk and milk used in products should be pasteurized or ultra-pasteurized and meet local ordinances and state standards as well as federal specifications.

BUTTER

Butter is made from sweet or sour cream and contains not less than 80 percent milkfat. A lactic acid culture may be added to the cream for a short "ripening" period to develop desirable aroma and flavors before the cream is churned. The addition of annatto, a colorant derived from the annatto plant, and salt is optional.

Butter that has been officially graded by the U.S. Department of Agriculture for sale on the retail market bears a shield on the package with a letter grade that indicates the quality of the butter at the time of grading. Grades AA and A are available at the retail level. Grade B is usually used as an ingredient in manufac-

tured applications, rather than sold as a product. Occasionally the equivalent numerical flavor score of butter is shown under the grade shield. Grades for butter depend on quality factors of flavor, body, texture, color, and salt. The U. S. grade and score relationships are: AA or 93 score, A or 92 score, B or 90 score, and C or 89 score.

Whipped butter has been stirred or whipped to incorporate air or some inert gas and thereby increase the volume and make the butter easier to spread.

STORAGE AND USE

■ To store butter, leave it in its original package and keep it in the food compartment of the refrigerator or in the freezer.

■ Place partially used portions of butter in a covered dish, refrigerate, and use up within a few days.

■ Wrapped in moisture-vapor-proof packaging material, butter can be frozen for up to nine months at 0°F (-18°C).

- To measure unwhipped butter, press it firmly into individual measuring cups or spoons and level with the straight edge of a spatula. Or measure butter according to these equivalents: 1 pound = 2 cups = 4 sticks = 32 tablespoons (454 g = 473 ml).

- Whipped butter should not be substituted in most recipes for regular butter or margarine because the volumes are not equivalent.

- To substitute other fats in recipes that call for butter, allow for each cup of butter 1 cup (237 ml) margarine or 7/8 cup (207 ml) hydrogenated shortening or lard plus 1/2 teaspoon (2.5 ml) salt.

CHEESE

Cheese comes in many forms and in a wide variety of flavors and textures. Each one is best when used for its own particular purposes.

NATURAL CHEESE

Natural cheese is made from cow's, sheep's, or goat's milk or cream and is usually cured or aged for a specific period to develop flavor. It is prepared by coagulating milk and separating the curd or solid portion from the whey or watery portion. Natural cheese may be classified by texture or consistency and the degree or kind of ripening. Classifications include:

Very hard cheeses — Parmesan, Romano, Sap Sago, bacteria-ripened

Hard cheeses — Cheddar, Colby, Colby Jack, Swiss, and Provolone, bacteria-ripened

Semisoft to hard cheeses — Edam, Baby Swiss, Gouda, and Feta, bacteria-ripened; Gjetost, and Mysost, whey cheeses, unripened

Semisoft cheeses — Blue (Bleu), Gorgonzola Roquefort, and Stilton, mold-ripened; Brick, Monterey Jack, and Muenster, Port du Salut, bacteria-ripened; mozzarella, unripened

Soft cheeses — Brie and Camembert, mold-ripened; Limburger, Bel Paese, bacteria-ripened; cottage cheese, cream cheese, Neufchatel, and ricotta, unripened

Grades have been established for cheese such as Cheddar, Colby, Monterey and Swiss based on specifications for flavor, odor, body, texture, finish, appearance, and color with additional specifications applicable to cheese of different ages. The quality rating of cheese is seldom given in the retail market. Swiss cheese is rated for eye formation, as well as for flavor, body, and texture.

PROCESS CHEESE AND PRODUCTS

Process cheese is a blend of one or more natural cheeses that have been processed using heat to inactivate bacteria and enzymes. Included in this group are pasteurized process cheese, process cheese food, process cheese spread and coldpack cheese, which is not heated.

Pasteurized process cheese has up to three percent emulsifying salts such as sodium citrate or disodium phosphate and may contain milk, cream, or whey added to the natural cheese. The maximum moisture content is 40 percent, which is higher than natural cheese.

Cheese food is a product made from a mixture of one or more varieties of cheese with added solids, salt, and up to 3 percent of an emulsifier. All of which are mixed with the aid of heat. The moisture content of a pasteurized cheese food is about 4 percent higher than that permitted for process cheese; the milkfat content is lower. Fruit, vegetables and meats may be added.

Cheese spreads are similar to cheese foods except that a stabilizer is used, moisture content is about 8 percent more than in process cheese, and milkfat content is lower. Spreads may be flavored with pimiento, olives, pickles, onion, or other added ingredients. Fruit, other vegetables and meats may be added.

Cold pack cheese or club cheese is a blend of natural cheeses prepared without heat. Stabilizers, spices or smoke flavoring are often added. Softer in texture than natural cheese, cold pack cheese spreads readily.

REDUCED-FAT AND
LOW SODIUM CHEESES
Reduced-fat cheese may be a natural cheese or a processed cheese. Natural reduced-fat cheese is made from reduced-fat milk and contains less fat and fewer calories than its counterpart. A reduced-fat cheese generally contains more protein and calcium than its full-fat counterpart.

"Light" pasteurized process cheese is made by blending reduced-fat natural cheese with an emulsifier to increase keeping quality and improve melting consistency.

Fat-free cheeses are made from skim milk and cheese cultures. Fat-free ricotta, cottage cheese, and cheese are available. Other fat-free cheese products are currently under development.

Low sodium cheese contain 140 mg or less sodium per serving. Some varieties are available with two-thirds to one-half less sodium than their regular counterparts.

Imitation cheeses are made from cows' milk that does not meet Federal Standards of Identity for composition. These cheese may be made from filled milk or mixtures of sodium and calcium caseinate, emulsifying salts, flavorings and vitamins and minerals.

STORAGE AND USE
■ All cheese keeps best at refrigerator temperatures of 35 to 40°F (2-4°C). Store in the original wrap or container until opened, then rewrap cheese tightly in plastic wrap or place in a clean, airtight container.

■ Cheese should be used by the date listed on the container or wrapper.

■ Uncreamed dry curd cottage cheese may be frozen in appropriate freezer containers. It will keep well for about a month. Textural changes may occur.

■ Most hard cheeses can be frozen for six to eight weeks, but freezing results in a crumbly texture, which is difficult to slice. To freeze cheese, tightly wrap pieces of one pound (454 g) or less and about one inch (2.5 cm) thick in freezer wrap or in moisture-proof, air-tight packaging and freeze at 0°F (-18°C). Thaw cheese in the refrigerator and use within a few days after thawing.

- For full flavor and aroma serve cheese at room temperature or 20 to 60 minutes after removal from the refrigerator. The exceptions are soft, unripened cheeses such as cottage, cream or Neufchatel cheeses which should be served chilled unless being used as an ingredient in omelets, casseroles, and other hot dishes.

- Cooking temperatures for cheese should be low to prevent stringiness and toughness. High temperatures cause cheese to become leathery.

- Cheese that is thoroughly chilled grates or shreds more easily than cheese at room temperature.

- When mold is found on cheese, trim at least a 1-inch section of cheese away from the affected area and discard. Use the remaining cheese immediately.

- Reduced-fat cheeses can be added to casseroles, salads or sandwiches. The low-fat cheese does not "string" and melt as its fullfat counterpart.

CREAM

Cream is the fat portion of milk that rises to the surface when nonhomogenized milk is allowed to stand. Cream may be separated from milk by centrifugal force. To meet federal standards of identity, cream must have not less than 18 percent milkfat. Emulsifiers, stabilizers, sweeteners, flavorings or other optional ingredients may also be added.

Half-and-half is a mixture of milk and cream with 10.5 to 18 percent milkfat. Half-and-half is usually homogenized.

Light cream is coffee or table cream which is sometimes homogenized. It usually has 20 percent milkfat, but the fat content can range between 18 and 30 percent milkfat.

Light whipping cream contains between 30 and 36 percent milkfat and whips up satisfactorily but does not freeze successfully.

Heavy cream or whipping cream contains 36 to 40 percent milkfat and is not homogenized. As a foam it tends to be more stable than light whipping cream foams.

Pressurized whipped cream is whipping cream packed in aerosol cans under pressure. It is made from a mixture of cream, sugar, stabilizers, emulsifiers, flavors and a gas-forming substance such as nitrous oxide. State regulations specify kind of cream and minimum fat content.

Dairy sour cream is sweet cream to which a lactic acid culture has been added. Sour cream must comply with individual state requirements for minimum milkfat of the cream used (usually 18 to 20 percent).

Sour half-and-half is made with half-and-half rather than cream, and the acidity is not less than 0.5 percent. Products that resemble sour cream are sour half-and-half dressing and sour cream dressing in which butter or other dairy ingredients replace the cream or milk.

Reduced-fat sour cream is made like dairy

sour cream, but skim milk has been added to reduce the fat content.

Sour cream dressing or sour half-and-half dressing resemble sour cream and sour half-and-half except some of the cream and/or milk is replaced by other dairy ingredients such as butter.

STORAGE AND USE
- Cream should be kept in its original container and refrigerated at 40°F (4°C) or lower until used.

- Cream has a pull date on the package label. Ultra-pasteurized cream will keep several weeks in the refrigerator. Once opened, it should be treated like pasteurized cream and used within a few days.

- In recipes using sour cream, add the sour cream at the end of the cooking period or combine with flour or condensed soup to help prevent separation or curdling.

MILK

Pasteurized milk is raw milk that has been subjected to temperatures which ensure destruction of pathogenic microorganisms, some spoilage bacteria and natural milk enzymes. This results in a prolonged refrigerated shelf life. Milks pasteurized by vat, batch (LTLT, 145°F, 63°C 1800 seconds), high-temperature-short-time (HTST), higher-heat shorter-time (HHST), or ultra-pasteurization most be refrigerated. Milk pasteurized by ultra-high-temperature (UHT) (280-320°F, 138-150°C for 2-6 seconds) and packaged in aseptic con-

tainers is shelf stable for about three months. When opened, it must be refrigerated.

FLUID MILKS

Fluid Milks are classified primarily by the milkfat content, nonfat milk solids and added nutrients. Vitamin D is regularly used to fortify most fluid milks - 400 International Units (IU) per quart (946 ml). Fluid lowfat milk products also may be fortified with vitamin A which has been removed with the milkfat. The vitamin A is added at 2000 IU per quart (946 ml). Most fluid milks with fat are **homogenized** to stabilize the dispersion of milkfat globules throughout the milk, so the fat does not rise to form a cream layer. The milk is forced under pressure through small apertures, which break the fat globules into smaller ones.

	Milkfat %	Nonfat Milk Solids %	Nutrient Added
Whole milk	≥3.25	≥8.25	D
Lowfat milks			
skim/nonfat	≤0.5	+8.25	A, D
	1.0	+8.25	A, D
	1.5	+8.25	A, D
	2.0	+8.25	A, D

Flavored milk includes a variety of chocolate or cocoa flavored products. Other flavors such as strawberry, maple and coffee may be used for flavored milks or drinks. The caloric content of flavored milks or drinks vary according to the amount of milkfat and composition of other added ingredients.

	Kind of Milk	Flavor	Other Additives
Chocolate milk	whole	chocolate	sweetener
Chocolate-flavored milk	whole	cocoa syrup	sweetener
Chocolate drink	skim/lowfat	chocolate	sweetener
Chocolate-flavored drink	skim/lowfat	cocoa syrup	sweetener

CULTURED AND SOURED MILKS

Cultured buttermilk is obtained by treating pasteurized skim or part skim milk with a suitable culture of lactic acid bacteria. The lactic acid produced gives the characteristic acidity and increased thickness of the product. Buttermilk originally was a byproduct of butter making.

Sour milk is milk soured naturally or artificially by the action of lactic acid bacteria or artificially by the addition of vinegar or lemon juice. Milk that has soured to the stage that a firm curd has formed is called clabber. The whey and curds have not separated.

Acidophilus cultured milk is prepared by the addition of a *Lactobacillus acidophilus* concentrated culture to low-fat or skim milk that has been pasteurized, homogenized, and chilled. The rapid chilling halts bacteria growth retaining the sweet flavor and consistency of the milk.

Bifidobacteria milk, as produced and marketed in the United States, is a nonfermented, lowfat milk containing 1 percent acidophilus/bifidobacteria culture. Bifid-amended dairy products are in great demand in Japan and Europe. Products fermented with the *Bifidobacteria* culture have a mild, acidic flavor, similar to that of yogurt. The culture is added during fermentation or to the finished fermented or fresh product prior to shipment.

YOGURT

Yogurt is a creamy, custard-like cultured milk product made by fermenting whole, low-fat or skim milk with a bacterial culture such as *Streptococcus thermophilus* and *Lactobacillus bulgaricus*. The minimum milk solids is 8.25 percent with an average of 15 percent and 0.5 percent acid. The milkfat standards for lowfat yogurts range from 0.5 to 3 percent; nonfat yogurt contains 0.5 percent or less.

Nonfat milk solids, sweeteners, stabilizers (such as pectin, agar or gelatin), fruit, flavorings, colorings and vegetables may be added. Yogurts are pasteurized or ultra-pasteurized to kill pathogenic microorganisms.

Plain, flavored-containing-no-fruit and flavored-with-fruit yogurts are available. Coffee, vanilla, lemon are examples of flavored yogurt containing no fruit.

If yogurt contains a fruit it may be **sundae-style** with fruit on the bottom of the container topped with plain or flavored yogurt or **Swiss- or French-style** with fruit blended throughout plain or flavored yogurt.

Frozen yogurt is prepared by adding suitable

stabilizers, nonfat milk solids, sweeteners, fruits, and juices to cultured yogurt before freezing. It may be soft or hard. Federal standards have not been established for frozen yogurt.

Low-lactose yogurt has about 60 percent less lactose than milk, making this product suitable for lactose-intolerant people.

CONCENTRATED AND DRIED MILK PRODUCTS

Evaporated and evaporated skimmed milk has about 60 percent of the water removed. They may be fortified with Vitamins D and/or A. Whole milk concentrates are homogenized. The milk is then sealed in cans and sterilized. According to federal standards, evaporated milk must contain at least 7.5 percent milkfat and not less than 25.5 percent total milk solids. Evaporated skimmed milk must contain not less than 0.5 percent milk fat and a minimum of 20 percent total solids and fortified with 125 IU of vitamin A per fluid ounce (30 ml). The composition of evaporated milks mixed with an equal volume of water is slightly above the average of fresh milks.

Sweetened condensed milk and skimmed milk are the products resulting from the evaporation of about half the water from whole or skimmed milk, and the addition of refined cane and/or corn sugar in amounts (44%) sufficient for preservation. The high sugar adds to the browning of the milk when heated. The high concentration of milk protein allows thickening with the addition of acid or heat to make toppings or desserts.

Dried whole milk is similar to fresh whole milk but is specially packed in vacuum-packed or gas-pack containers to prevent deterioration. It contains not less than 26 percent milk fat and not more than four percent moisture. U.S. grades are Extra and Standard with dry whole milk also having a Premium grade.

Nonfat dry milk is the product resulting from the removal of fat and water from pasteurized milk. It contains not over five percent moisture and 1.5 percent milkfat by weight. Nonfat dry milk contains the same relative proportions of proteins, minerals and water soluble vitamins of fluid nonfat milk and is fortified with vitamins A and D. Most nonfat dry milk is instantized to form rather coarse, creamy-white, free-flowing particles that dissolve readily in water.

SPECIALTY MILKS

Multivitamin and multimineral milks are sold in some localities to which multivitamin and multimineral concentrates are added.

Lactase-treated milk is processed milk to which lactase, an enzyme, is added. The lactase hydrolyzes lactose to glucose and galactose giving the milk a sweeter taste. Lactose-intolerant individuals can use lactase-treated milk or purchase lactase tablets to add to milk.

Low Sodium Milk is a product which has about 95 percent of the sodium replaced with potassium by an ion-exchange method resulting in about 6 mg of sodium per cup (237 ml) as compared to 120 mg in regular milk. Both fresh or canned low sodium milk may be available.

Certified Milk is a costly and sanitary product produced according to American Association of Medical Milk Commissions' *Methods and Standards for the Production of Certified Milk.* Its sale is not permitted in all states. The milk may be raw, pasteurized, homogenized and/or fortified with vitamin D. Raw certified milk may cause food-borne illnesses.

Kefir and koumiss are fermented milk beverages commonly produced in Southwestern Asia and similar in taste to yogurt. They are prepared by the use of kefir grains which contain bacteria and a lactose-fermenting yeast held together by layers of coagulated protein. Acid production is controlled by the bacteria, while yeast produces alcohol and some carbon dioxide. The final concentration of lactic acid is 0.8 percent, and alcohol may be as high as 1 percent.

Eggnog is made from pasteurized milk or cream, pasteurized eggs, sugar and flavored with vanilla. It is available during the holiday season.

STORAGE AND USE
- Use milk in order of pull date found on container. The pull date indicates when the milk should be withdrawn from retail sale. This date allows for additional storage life when the consumer's refrigerator is maintained at 35-40°F (1-4°C). Yogurt keeps about 10 days after the pull date stamped on the carton.

- Unopened packages of any shelf-stable milk should be stored in a cool, dry place. After opening, the unused milk must be refrigerated.

- Evaporated milks may be substituted for other milks. Sweetened condensed milk, however, is not a satisfactory substitute because of the high sugar content that affects flavor and texture.

- To measure dry milk, pour from package or spoon lightly into individual measuring cup, heaping to the brim. Level with straight edge of spatula or knife. Shaking the cup to level the powder tends to pack it down and give an inaccurate measure.

- In recipes, dry milk may be added either to dry or liquid ingredients unless the recipe specifically calls for reconstitution.

- For best flavor, milk for drinking should be served icy cold from the refrigerator. Store milk in its original container.

- Use of acidophilus milk in cooking will destroy the culture.

FROZEN DAIRY PRODUCTS

Ice cream is made from a pasteurized mixture of milk, cream, sugar, stabilizers, flavorings, and sometimes eggs. Coloring may also be added. As the mixture is frozen, it is whipped to approximately 80 to 100 percent more than its original volume. The finished product usually weighs about 4.5 pounds per gallon (2 kg/3.7 l) and contains not less than 1.6 pounds (726 g) of food solids per gallon (3.7 l). The milkfat content ranges from 8 to 14 percent, usually 10 to 12 percent for plain ice cream, although some special ice creams may be as high as 20 percent. Federal standards require that plain ice cream contain at least 10 percent milkfat and 20 percent total milk solids by weight. Ice cream with chocolate, nuts, or fruits must contain at least 8 percent milkfat and 16 percent total milk solids.

Frozen custard and French custard ice cream are products with high levels of egg yolk solids cooked as a custard before freezing.

Ice Milk is a product made in the same manner and with the same ingredients as ice cream but in different proportions. The milkfat content ranges from two to about seven percent, and the total milk solids must be at least 11 percent according to the federal standard. It may be either soft- or hard-frozen drawn from the freezer.

Imitation ice cream and ice milk are currently available. Products which do not meet the definition of ice cream must be labeled imitation. Mellorine has the butterfat replaced by a suitable animal or vegetable fat. Parevine contains no dairy ingredients. Diabetic products may contain sorbitol instead of sugar to lower the freezing point and bind water. Low-calorie ice cream may use non-nutritive sweeteners or high-intensity nutritive sweeteners with bulking agents. Low-calorie or noncaloric fat substitutes can be used in products. One is a microparticulation of egg white and/or milk. This product, Simplesse®, is used in some ice cream, yogurt, sour cream and cream cheese.

Sherbet is a frozen product made of a pasteurized mixture of sugar, milk solids, stabilizer, flavorings such as fruit, fruit juices, or extract, and water. Milk fat content of sherbet is one to two percent, and the total milk solids content is two to five percent.

Refrigerated Puddings are made with whole or skim milk, packaged and held at refrigeration temperatures in the grocery store and at home.

STORAGE AND USE
■ Store ice cream in a tightly closed container at O°F (-18°C) for up two months.

■ For easy serving, frozen dairy products should be removed from freezer to refrigerator 10 to 20 minutes before serving time.

■ Ice crystals can be minimized by covering the product with plastic wrap before closing.

WHIPPING PROPERTIES
Cream — Cream increases two to three times in volume depending on the type of beater used. The fat content should be 20 to 40 percent. Pasteurization and homogenization decreases foam volume and stability. Cream chilled for 48 hours has increased foam volume and stability.

■ To whip cream, chill utensils (50°F, 10°C) before use. Keep utensils and cream cold during preparation. Choose a deep bowl just wide enough for beater. Add sugar after whipping, never before. Beat rapidly until stiff, but never over beat.

- Whipped cream should be kept chilled at 50°F (10°C) or below until used. The foam is stable for about one hour.

- Whipped cream freezes well, particularly in individual serving portions. Once the portions are frozen, wrap in moisture-proof, air-tight packaging and keep frozen until used.

Evaporated milk — Evaporated milk, when whipped, increases two to three times in volume depending on the type of beater used. The foam is less stable than whipped cream unless the milk is made acid or supplemented with gelatin.

- Undiluted evaporated milk will whip best if it is first chilled to 32°F (0°C) or lower until fine ice crystals form.

- To stabilize the foam, increase the acidity by adding 1 tablespoon (15 ml) lemon juice or vinegar for each cup (250 ml) of undiluted evaporated milk. Whip the milk and then fold in the juice or soften 1/2 teaspoon (2.5 ml) unflavored gelatin in 2 teaspoons (10 ml) cold water and dissolve in 1 cup (250 ml) scalded undiluted evaporated milk. Chill as above, whip, sprinkle with 1/4 cup (60 ml) powdered sugar and fold in.

Nonfat dry milk — Nonfat dry milk triples in volume when whipped and is stable for several hours.

- Use 1/3 cup (80 ml) cold water to 1/2 cup (125 ml) instant nonfat dry milk. Chill and whip until the mixture is thick enough to stand in soft peaks. Add 1 tablespoon (15 ml) lemon juice and continue to whip until stiff peaks form. Then beat in 2 to 4 tablespoons (30 to 60 ml) sugar.

- Whipped nonfat dry milk should be refrigerated and kept chilled until served.

Meat

Meat is generally defined as the edible portion of cattle, swine, and sheep. The major physical component of meat as it appears in the market is muscle tissue (lean). Depending on the cut of meat, adipose tissue (fat), connective tissue, and skeletal tissue (bone) may also be present.

The most abundant component of meat is water, which ranges from 45 percent to 75 percent. The amount of water in the tissues, which decreases as the animal ages and deposits fat, affects the texture, color, and flavor of the muscle.

Protein and fat are also present in abundant amounts. Meat proteins are grouped in three general classifications: (1) myofibrillar, (2) stromal, and (3) sarcoplasmic. Each class of proteins contributes different functional properties to meat.

The amount of adipose tissue differs widely among carcasses. As an animal grows, fat is first deposited around the kidney and heart and in the pelvic canal area. External or subcutaneous fat, located just beneath the skin, is the second site of deposition. The third site is between the muscles (intermuscular or seam fat). The fourth area is within the muscles (intramuscular fat or marbling).

Other important nutrients in meat that occur in significant amounts are the minerals iron, phosphorus, zinc, and most of the B vitamin complex (thiamin, riboflavin, niacin, B_6, and B_{12}). Vitamin B_{12}, essential for growth and the synthesis of DNA, occurs naturally only in animal foods.

Meat is marketed in many forms: fresh, frozen, freeze-dried, canned, cured, smoked, dried, and cured and smoked. Many meat items are available both raw and cooked.

FRESH MEAT

BEEF

The major sources of beef on the retail market are from:

Steers — male animals that have been castrated as calves: Steers (15 to 24 months old) account for more than 2/3 of the high grade beef on the market.

Heifers — young female animals that have not borne calves. Heifers produce high grade meat.

Cows — female bovines that have borne one or more calves.

Bullocks — young bulls under 2 years of age that have begun to develop secondary characteristics of a bull.

VEAL is from immature bovine animals under four months of age. It contains little fat and has a high water content.

CALF is meat from immature cattle, about four to nine months old. Calves weighing 400 to 800 pounds (181 to 363 kg) at the time of slaughter are classified as "baby beef."

LAMB

Meat from sheep under one year of age accounts for about 90 percent of the lamb on the market. Lamb is designated as:

Spring Lambs — lambs from three to seven months, weighing 70 to 120 pounds (32 to 54 kg).

Yearlings — ovines approximately one to two years of age.

Mutton — meat from sheep that are older than two years.

PORK

Most pork is from young swine of either sex under one year of age. Most of the pork on the retail market is from:

Pigs — porcine animals that are less than four months of age and/or weigh less than 120 pounds (54 kg).

Hogs — porcine animals that are more than four months of age and weigh more than 120 pounds (54 kg).

Barrows — male porcine animals castrated when young.

Gilts — female porcine animals that have not had offspring or have not reached an evident stage of pregnancy.

Although most beef, lamb, and veal cuts are sold fresh, much pork is also available in cured or cured and smoked forms. See Table 4.1 for the location and bone of various retail cuts of beef, veal, lamb, and pork.

VARIETY MEATS

Organ meats from beef, veal, pork, and lamb are excellent sources of many essential nutrients. They include: brains; heart; kidneys; liver; tongue; tripe (stomach tissue); and sweetbreads (thymus).

PROCESSED MEAT

Processed meat may be defined as meat that has been changed by any mechanical, chemical, or enzymatic treatment which alters the taste, appearance, or keeping quality of the product. It is made from wholesome meat that has been inspected at every stage of production. Major categories are:

SAUSAGE

Seasoned chopped meat may be sold in bulk or as stuffed links, with casings of natural or synthetic materials. Trimmings and some of the less popular meat cuts from pork, beef,

Table 4.1
IDENTIFICATION OF MEAT CUTS[1]

LOCATION	BEEF	VEAL	LAMB	PORK
BREAST	Brisket Shank Cross Cuts Short Plate	Breast Riblets Shank Cross Cuts	Breast Breast, rolled Riblets Spareribs Shanks	Spareribs Bacon Salt Pork

SHOULDER/
CHUCK
	Arm Steak or Pot
	  Roast
	Blade Steak or
	  Roast
	Chuck Eye Steak or
	  Roast
	7-bone Steak or Pot
	  Roast
	Short Ribs
	Shoulder Steak or
	  Pot Roast
		Arm Steak or Roast
		Blade Steak or
		  Roast
			Arm Chops or
			  Roast
			Blade Chops or
			  Roast
			Shoulder Roast
			Neck Slices
				Arm Steak or Arm
				  Picnic Roast
				Blade Steak
				Blade Boston

RIB	Rib Steak or Roast,
	  small end
	Rib Roast, large end
	Rib Eye Steak or
	  Roast
		Rib Chops or Roast
		Crown Roast
			Rib Chops or Roast
			Crown Roast
				Rib Chops
				Center Rib Roast

LOIN
(SHORT LOIN)
	Porterhouse Steak
	T-Bone Steak
	Tenderloin Steak or
	  Roast (Filet
	  Mignon)
	Top Loin Steak or
	  Roast
		Loin Chops or
		  Roast
		Loin Kidney Chops
		Top Loin Roast
			Double Loin Chops
			Loin Chops or
			  Roast
				Loin Blade Chops
				  or Roast
				Loin Chops
				Center Loin Roast
				Tenderloin
				Top Loin Chops or
				  Roast
				Canadian Bacon
				Country-Style Ribs
				Backribs

SIRLOIN	Sirloin Steak, flat,
	  pin, round or
	  wedge bone
	Sirloin Roast
	Top Sirloin Steak
		Sirloin Steak or
		  Roast
			Sirloin Chops or
			  Roast
				Sirloin Chops or
				  Roast
				Sirloin Cutlets

LEG
(HAM)/ROUND
	Bottom Round
	  Steak or Roast
	Eye Round Steak or
	  Roast
	Top Round Steak or
	  Roast
	Rump Steak
	Rump Roast
	Round Tip Steak or
	  Roast
		Round Steak
		Roast
		Rump Roast
		Cutlets
			Leg
			Leg Slice or Roast
				Ham Steak
				Leg (Fresh Ham)
				  Roast
				Leg (Fresh Ham)
				  Center Slice

FLANK	Flank Steak			

[1] *Location and bone of retail cuts of meat*
are often clues to identification

veal, lamb, poultry, or a combination of these meats may be used in the processing of sausage.

More than 200 varieties of sausages and cold cuts are marketed in the United States. Some sausages are made from meat that is cured, smoked, cooked, or treated by a combination of these processes. Others may be finely or coarsely textured, fermented, dried, or semi-dried. Sausages are classified as:

Fresh — sausages made from ground meat and not cured, smoked, or cooked. They must be cooked before serving. Examples are fresh pork sausage, fresh bratwurst, chorizo, and Italian-style sausage.

Uncooked and Smoked— sausages that are smoked after forming and must be cooked before serving. Examples are smoked pork sausage, kielbasa, and smoked country-style sausage.

Cooked— sausages that have been cured and cooked. They are ready-to-eat, but may be heated before serving. Blood sausage, pre-cooked bratwurst, liverwurst, and braunschweiger are some examples.

Cooked and Smoked — products made from meat that has been cured, formed into sausages, cooked, and lightly smoked. They are ready-to-eat, but may be heated before serving. Examples are cotto salami, bologna, frankfurters, and Vienna sausage.

Dry & Semi Dry — sausages that may be smoked or unsmoked. Processing always includes curing and generally involves cooking at the plant. Carefully controlled fermentation acts as a preservative and provides the distinctive flavors. Hard salami is usually a dry sausage, while summer sausage is semi-dry. Cervelat, thuringer, pepperoni, and mortedella are examples of these ready-to-eat sausages.

Specialty Meats — meats which are cured and fully cooked during processing and are ready-to-eat. Loaf examples are honey, minced ham, old-fashioned, olive, pepper, and pickle and pimiento.

CURED WHOLE MUSCLE CUTS

Curing and drying are among the oldest methods of preserving meats. Salt, sugar, nitrites, and nitrates may all be used in the curing process. Salt acts as a preservative and a flavor enhancer; sugar also improves the flavor. Today, nitrites are the primary curing ingredient used in meat products. Nitrites develop the characteristic red-pink color in the lean parts of meat, impart a typically cured flavor, and inhibit the growth of a number of food poisoning and spoilage microorganisms, including *Clostridium botulinum*. Cured whole muscle cuts include:

Ham — the hind leg of pork that has been cured and smoked or cured and canned. One of the most highly valued pork products, ham can be produced three ways: bone-in, semi-boneless, and boneless. There are also cooked and uncooked varieties. To be labeled "fully cooked," hams must be cooked to an internal temperature of 148°F (65°C) at the processing plant. No additional heating is necessary for fully cooked hams. To serve warm, however, ham should be cooked to 130°F to 140°F (55 to 60°C) for optimum palatability. Hams that are labeled "cook-before-eating" must be cooked to an internal temperature of 160°F to 170°F (71 to 77°C) before serving.

Country-style hams — specialty hams that have been dry-cured, smoked, and aged to provide a distinct flavor and texture. Before baking, these hams require soaking or simmering.

Corned (Cured) Beef — prepared from brisket or round. Formerly, "corning" referred to preserving meat by sprinkling it with grains ("corns") of salt. Today, corned beef is cured with a pickle solution of water, salt, sugar, nitrite, and spices.

Bacon — produced primarily from pork bellies. Beef bacon is made from the boneless beef short plate, which is similar to the belly in pork. Canadian-style bacon is made from the top loin muscle of pork, usually from heavier hogs. Both bacon and Canadian bacon are cured and smoked.

Dried Beef — made from the round that has been cured, lightly smoked, and dried.

Pastrami — made from beef brisket, plate, or top round. After dry-curing with salt, the beef is rubbed with a paste of garlic powder, ground cumin, red pepper, cinnamon, cloves, and allspice. It is then smoked and cooked.

Pork Shoulder — can be divided into two major cuts: Picnic (arm) and Boston (blade). They can be prepared by the same methods used for hams. Shoulder cuts are usually priced more economically than leg cuts, due to differences in palatability and yield of edible portion.

RESTRUCTURED MEAT

Restructured meat products are generally made from flaked, ground, or sectioned beef or pork, which is then shaped into roasts, steaks or loaves. The restructuring process consists of three steps: reducing or modifying the particle size, blending, and reforming into the desired shape. Examples of restructured meats are smoked sliced beef and most boneless hams.

INSPECTION PROGRAMS

The Federal Meat Inspection Act of 1906 made inspection mandatory for all meat that was transported across state lines. The Wholesome Meat Act of 1967 required that inspection of meat sold within a state meet requirements at least as stringent as those of the federal system. Federal meat inspection is the responsibility of the Food Safety and Inspection Service, a division of the United States Department of Agriculture (USDA). State inspection is the responsibility of each state government, with partial funding by the federal government.

These federal and state inspection programs assure that only healthy animals are used for meat and guarantee that facilities and equipment meet sanitation standards. The Meat Inspection Program also includes: inspection of meat at various stages of processing; temperature monitoring for both fresh and cooked meat; review of packaging and labels; control and monitoring use of additives; and control and monitoring of imported meat.

To be designated as Kosher ("fit and proper"), meat must be processed under the supervision of persons authorized by the Jewish faith and must meet the standards of the Mosaic and Talmudic laws.

MEAT GRADES

The USDA meat-grading system, established in 1927, sets standards of quality and yield of edible meat that are used in buying and selling most meat. The program is administered by the USDA, but participation is voluntary. There are federal grades for beef, veal, lamb, and pork; however, there are more grades for beef due to the greater variance in age and weight of the animals. The USDA quality grade is indicated by a shield-shaped purple stamp. In addition, individual packers and retailers may use their own brand names to designate different grades of meat, such as Armour "Star," Monfort "Gold," or Safeway "Lean." Federal designations are:

Beef—Prime, Choice, Select, Standard, Commercial, Utility, Cutter, and Canner. The last four grades are seldom sold in retail stores. Beef carcasses may also be yield graded according to the predicted percentage of edible meat. The range is from one (highest yield) to five (lowest yield).

Veal & Lamb — Prime, Choice, Good, Standard, Utility, and Cull. There is no Standard grade for lamb. Only lamb may be yield-graded from U.S. No. 1 (highest yield) to U.S. No. 5 (lowest yield).

Pork—U.S. No. 1, U.S. No. 2, U.S. No. 3, and U.S. No. 4. The basis for grading pork is the cutability of the carcass and the quality of the meat. The range is from U.S. No. 1 (highest yield) to U.S. No. 4 (lowest yield).

MEAT STORAGE AND USE

Proper storage is essential for maintaining food safety and quality. When meat spoils, the color, odor, and texture deteriorate. When food is contaminated it is invaded by microorganisms, which may not be detected by an off odor or color, but can cause food poisoning and infections in humans. Fortunately, most bacteria that can cause food poisoning cannot grow at low refrigerator temperatures. Recommended storage time for maximum quality of meats at refrigerator and freezer temperatures are shown in Table 4.2. Following are a few guidelines for safe meat storage.

- Fresh meat should be stored in the coldest part of the refrigerator and used within a few days. The temperature should be as low as possible, approximately $36^{\circ}F$ to $40^{\circ}F$ (2 to $4^{\circ}C$).

- Meat can be kept in the original supermarket wrap in the refrigerator for several days or in the freezer for up two weeks.

- For longer freezer storage, meat should be tightly rewrapped in moisture-vapor-proof material designed for freezer use (for example, foil, freezer paper, and some transparent wraps and food storage bags). Be sure to label and date the packages and store at $0^{\circ}F$ (-$18^{\circ}C$) or lower.

- Cured meats can be refrigerated in the original wrapper; but should be used within one or two weeks.

- Unopened canned hams can be refrigerated until ready to use, unless the label indicates otherwise.

- Cooked meats should be wrapped or placed in tightly covered dishes or containers and refrigerated within two hours after serving.

- To defrost frozen meat, keep it wrapped, and let it stand in the refrigerator. Thaw time will depend on size and thickness of the cut - approximately four to seven hours per pound (0.5 kg) for large roasts, three to five hours per pound (0.5 kg) for a small roast, and 12 to 14 hours for a 1-inch (2.5 cm) thick steak. Thawed meat can be refrozen if the temperature of the meat has not risen above 40°F (4°C).

Table 4.2

REFRIGERATOR AND FREEZER STORAGE TIMETABLE

MEAT	CUT	REFRIGERATOR 36° to 40°F 2-4°C	FREEZER* 0°F or Colder -18°C
FRESH	Beef Cuts	3 to 4 days	6 to 12 months
	Veal Cuts	1 to 2 days	6 to 9 months
	Pork Cuts	2 to 3 days	6 months
	Lamb Cuts	3 to 5 days	6 to 9 months
	Ground Beef, Veal and Lamb	1 to 2 days	3 to 4 months
	Ground Pork	1 to 2 days	1 to 3 months
	Variety Meats	1 to 2 days	3 to 4 months
	Leftover Cooked Meat	3 to 4 days	2 to 3 months
PROCESSED	Luncheon Meat**	3 to 5 days	1 to 2 months
	Sausage, fresh pork**	2 to 3 days	1 to 2 months
	Sausage, smoked**	1 week	1 to 2 months
	Sausage, dry and semi-dry (unsliced)	2 to 3 weeks	1 to 2 months
	Frankfurters*	3 to 5 days	1 to 2 months
	Bacon**	1 week	1 month
	Smoked Ham, whole	1 week	1 to 2 months
	Ham Slices**	3 to 4 days	

Meat in freezer wrapping.

**If vacuum packaged, check manufacturer's date*

COOKING METHODS

Heat affects the physical properties of meat by making it more tender, flavorful, and safe to eat. Different cooking methods are used to maximize the flavor and eating enjoyment of various cuts of meat. When heat is applied to meat, two changes occur: muscle fibers become tougher and connective tissue becomes more tender. The time required to cook a specific cut of meat by any method depends on the composition of the meat, size, weight, and shape of the cut.

Tender cuts of meat, cooked by dry-heat methods, result in tender juicy products. Less-tender cuts must be cooked for longer periods by moist-heat methods to soften connective tissue, prevent surface drying, and develop flavor. If using a marinade, refrigerate the meat at least six to eight hours in an acidic liquid, such as wine, vinegar, or lemon juice.

Timetables are guides to approximate cooking times required for meat cuts to reach the desired internal temperature, or desired tenderness.

DRY HEAT METHODS

Roasting — This cooking method is recommended for larger cuts of beef, veal, lamb, and pork. Season meat with herbs, spices, or other seasoning before, during, or after roasting. Place meat fat side up on rack in a shallow roasting pan. In some roasts, rib bones serve as a rack. Insert meat thermometer. Do not add water or cover. Roast in a slow oven, 300°F to 325°F (150 to 160°C), to the desired doneness. No basting is necessary. Remove roast 5°F (3°C) below desired doneness. The temperature of the meat will rise 5°F (3°C) during standing for 15 to 20 minutes, and the roast will be easier to carve. See Roasting Time-

table, Table 4.3, on pages 90-92.

Oven Broiling — Broiling is suitable for tender steaks and chops; kabobs; pork ribs; sliced ham; bacon; butterflied lamb leg; and ground meat patties or meatballs. Steaks and chops should be at least 3/4 inch (2 cm) thick, and ham should be at least 1/2 inch (1 cm) thick. Less tender cuts, such as beef flank or top round steak, and veal, lamb, and pork shoulder chops, may also be broiled, if they have been marinated.

Trim the outer edge of fat. Place thinner cuts of meat (3/4 inch to 1 inch or 2 to 2.5 cm thick) on rack of broiler pan 2 to 3 inches (5 to 7.5 cm) from heat. Allow 3 to 6 inches (7.5 to 15 cm) for thicker cuts. Broil until the top side is brown, then turn and brown the other side. To test steaks or chops for doneness, cut a small slit in the center or close to a bone and check the color of the meat. Season, if desired.

Grilling (Barbecuing) — Grilling is actually a method of broiling. Meat can be grilled on a grid or rack over coals or heated ceramic briquettes. While usually done outdoors, grilling can be done in the kitchen with special types of range tops or small appliances.

Start the fire as the manufacturer's instructions indicate. Spread coals in a single layer after they reach the gray ash stage. Low to medium cooking temperatures should be used. To lower the temperature, spread coals farther apart or raise the grid. To make the fire hotter, move the coals closer together and tap off ash. The temperature of the coals can be checked by cautiously holding your hand 4" (10 cm) above the coals. Count the number of seconds before the heat forces the removal of your hand. Check the following chart.

Charcoal Temperature For Grilling

Time	Temperature
2 seconds	hot (high)
3 seconds	medium-hot
4 seconds	medium*
5 seconds	low*
6 to 7 seconds	very low

Recommended cooking temperature for meat.

For direct cooking, arrange coals in a single layer directly under the food. Use this method for steaks, ham slices, chops, kabobs, and other quickly cooked foods. For larger roasts and steaks, which require longer cooking at lower temperatures, use indirect cooking. This method cooks food by reflecting heat, similar to the way in which a conventional oven cooks. Arrange an equal number of briquettes on each side of the grate, ignite, and make sure the coals are burning equally on both sides. If necessary, move the coals from one side to the other. Place an aluminum foil drip pan between the coals. Arrange the meat on the grid above the drip pan. Cover with damper open and cook as the recipe directs. Turning the meat during indirect cooking is not necessary.

Baste meat with marinade or sauce throughout cooking time, if desired. If the basting sauce contains a large amount of sugar or other ingredients which burn easily, limit basting to last 15 to 20 minutes. Cooking time can be affected by the type of equipment used, the cooking temperature maintained, the weather, wind velocity, and desired doneness.

PANBROILING
Panbroiling is a faster, more convenient method than oven broiling for cooking thinner steaks and chops. Place the meat in a preheated, heavy frying pan or on a griddle. Most meat cuts have enough fat to prevent sticking; however, the cooking surface may be lightly brushed or sprayed with oil when panbroiling very lean cuts. No oil is needed with a non-stick frying pan. Do not add water or cover.

For cuts thicker than 1/4 inch (0.6 cm), cook at medium heat, turning occasionally. Cuts less than 1/4 inch (0.6 cm) thick should be cooked at medium-high. Turn more than once to assure even cooking. Remove fat as it accumulates, so that meat does not fry. Cook until brown on both sides. Do not overcook. To test doneness, cut a small slit in the center or close to the bone and check color of the meat.

Panfrying — In panfrying, a small amount of fat is added to the frying pan and fat is allowed to accumulate during cooking. This method is suitable for small or thin cuts of lean meat; thin strips; and pounded, scored, or other tenderized cuts that do not need prolonged heating for tenderization.

Brown meat on both sides in small amount of oil. Some cuts will cook in the fat that comes from the meat. Lean cuts, such as cubed steak or cuts which are floured or breaded require additional oil on the surface of the pan to prevent sticking. If there is a coating, seasonings may be added to the coating ingredients. Otherwise, the meat may be seasoned after browning.

Do not cover the meat or the meat will lose its crisp texture. Cook at medium heat, turning occasionally to promote uniform cooking.

Stir-frying — Stir-frying is similar to panfrying except the food is stirred almost

Table 4.3

ROASTING TIMETABLE FOR MEAT

CUT	WEIGHT		OVEN TEMPERATURE		APPROXIMATE COOKING TIME — Minutes per Pound		
	Pounds	Kilograms	°F	°C	Rare	Medium	Well Done
BEEF							
Rib Roast	4 to 6	2 to 3	300 - 325	150 - 160	26 to 32	27 to 30	40 to 42
	6 to 8	3 to 4	300 - 325	150 - 160	23 to 25	34 to 38	32 to 35
Rib Eye Roast	4 to 6	2 to 3	350	180	18 to 20	20 to 22	22 to 24
Boneless Rump Roast	4 to 6	2 to 3	300 - 325	150 - 160		25 to 27	28 to 30
Round Tip Roast	3.5 to 4	1.6 to 2	300 - 325	150 - 160	30 to 35	35 to 38	38 to 40
	6 to 8	3 to 4	300 - 325	150 - 160	22 to 25	25 to 30	30 to 35
Top Round Roast	4 to 6	2 to 3	300 - 325	150 - 160	20 to 25	25 to 28	28 to 30
Tenderloin Roast — Half	2 to 3	1 to 1.5	425	220		35 to 45 total time	
Whole	4 to 6	2 to 3	425	220		45 to 60 total time	
Ground Beef Loaf (9" x 5"; 3.6 x 2 cm)	1.5 - 2.5	0.7 to 1	300 - 325	150 - 160		60 to 90 total time	
VEAL							
Loin Roast Boneless	2 to 3	1 to 1.5	300 - 325	150 - 160		18 to 20	22 to 24
Bone-In	3 to 4	1.5 to 2	300 - 325	150 - 160		34 to 36	38 to 40
Rib Roast	4 to 5	2 to 2.3	300 - 325	150 - 160		25 to 27	29 to 31
Crown Roast 12-14 ribs	7.5 to 9.5	3.4 to 4.3	300 - 325	150 - 160		19 to 21	21 to 23

| CUT | WEIGHT | | OVEN TEMPERATURE | | APPROXIMATE COOKING TIME — Minutes per Pound | | |
	Pounds	Kilograms	°F	°C	Rare	Medium	Well Done
VEAL							
Rib Eye Roast	2 to 3	1 to 1.5	300 - 325	150 - 160		26 to 28	30 to 33
Rump Roast — Boneless	2 to 3	1 to 1.5	300 - 325	150 - 160		33 to 35	37 to 40
Shoulder Roast — Boneless	2.5 to 3	1 to 1.5	300 - 325	150 - 160		31 to 34	34 to 37
PORK							
Loin Roast, Center — Bone-In	3 to 5	1.5 to 2.3	325	160		20 to 25	26 to 31
Top Loin, Double	3 to 4	1.5 to 2	325	160		29 to 34	33 to 38
Single	2 to 4	1 to 2	325	160		23 to 33	30 to 40
Crown Roast	6 to 10	3 to 4.5	325	160			20 to 25
Tenderloin Roast, Whole	0.5 to 1	0.2 to 0.5	425	220		27 to 29 total time	30 to 32 total time
Ribs Backribs			325	160	Cook until tender — 90 to 105 total time		
LAMB							
Leg Roast Whole — Bone-In	7 to 9	3 to 4	325	160	15 to 20	20 to 25	25 to 30
Boneless	4 to 7	2 to 3	325	160	25 to 30	30 to 35	35 to 40
Shank— Half	3 to 4	1.5 to 2	325	160	30 to 35	40 to 45	45 to 50

(continued on the next page)

ROASTING TIMETABLE FOR MEAT continued)

CUT	WEIGHT		OVEN TEMPERATURE		APPROXIMATE COOKING TIME — Minutes per Pound		
	Pounds	Kilograms	°F	°C	Rare	Medium	Well-Done
LAMB Sirloin — Half	3 to 4	1.5 to 2	325	160	25 to 30	35 to 40	45 to 50
Shoulder Roast — Boneless	3.5 to 5	1.6 to 2.3	325	160	30 to 35	35 to 40	40 to 45

CUT	WEIGHT		OVEN TEMPERATURE		FINAL THERMOMETER READING		COOKING TIME — Minutes per Pound
	Pounds	Kilograms	°F	°C	°F	°C	
PORK **Smoked** Ham (Fully cooked) Whole —							
Boneless*	8 to 12	4 to 5	300 - 325	150 - 160	140	60	13 to 17
Bone-In**	14 to 16	6 to 7	300 - 325	150 - 160	140	60	12 to 14
Half —							
Boneless*	6 to 8	3 to 3.6	300 - 325	150 - 160	140	60	17 to 20
Bone-In**	6 to 8	3 to 3.6	300 - 325	150 - 160	140	60	14 to 17
Portion —							
Boneless	3 to 4	1.5 to 2	300 - 325	150 - 160	140	60	20 to 23
Canadian-Style Bacon (Fully cooked)	2 to 4	1 to 2	300 - 350	150 - 160	140	60	20 to 30

NOTES: Cooking times are based on meat taken directly from the refrigerator.
Smaller roasts require more minutes per pound than larger roasts.
Cooking times are approximate.

*   Add 1/2 cup (125 ml) water, cover tightly, and cook as directed.
**   Cover tightly and cook as directed.

continuously. Cooking is done with high heat, using small or thin pieces of meat. Partially freeze meat to facilitate slicing. Slice meat across the grain into thin, uniform slices, strips, or pieces. If desired, marinate while other ingredients are prepared. Cook meat and vegetables separately and then combine. Place meat in a small amount of hot oil in wok or large frying pan. Stir-fry about a half pound (0.2 kg) at a time. Cook at a high temperature, sliding the spatula under the meat and turning continuously with a scooping motion.

MOIST HEAT METHODS

Braising — In some areas of the country, "fricassee" and "braising" are interchangeable terms. Two popular examples of braised meats are pot roast and Swiss steak. To braise, first dredge the meat with flour or coat with crumbs, if desired. Then, slowly brown the meat on all sides in a heavy pan in just enough oil to prevent sticking; drain the drippings; and season the meat with salt, herbs, and spices. Browning develops flavor and color. Cuts with sufficient fat do not require additional fat, unless they have been coated with flour or crumbs.

Next, add a small amount of liquid (2 tablespoons to 1/2 cup; 30 ml to 125 ml), such as water, tomato juice, wine, meat or vegetable stock. Cover tightly and simmer on low heat on top of the range or in a 300ºF to 325ºF (150 to 160º C) oven until meat is fork-tender. Sauce or gravy may be made from liquid in the pan. Braising times for various cuts of meat are:

Round Steak (3/4" to 1".; 2 to 2.5 cm)	1 to 1 1/2 hours
Beef Chuck and Pot Roasts	1 3/4 to 3 hours
Shortribs	1 1/2 to 2 1/2 hours
Beef Cubes (1 1/2"; 3.7 cm)	1 1/2 to 2 1/2 hours
Veal Shoulder Roast	2 to 2 1/2 hours
Spareribs and Backribs	1 1/2 hours
Pork Cubes (1" to 1 1/4"; 2.5 to 3 cm)	45 to 60 minutes
Lamb Breast	1 1/2 to 2 hours
Lamb Shanks	1 to 1 1/2 hours

Meat can also be braised in cooking bags designed specifically for oven use. The benefit is a reduction in cooking time for larger cuts of meat. No additional liquid is needed, as moisture is drawn from the meat as it cooks. Follow manufacturer's instructions for best results.

Cooking In Liquid — Less tender cuts of meat can be covered with liquid and gently simmered until tender. The temperature of the liquid should not rise above 195ºF (90ºC), since boiling (212ºF or 100ºC) toughens meat protein. The three ways to cook in liquid are simmering, stewing, and poaching. Simmering (for large cuts) and stewing (for small pieces) are used for less tender cuts of all meats. Poaching can be used for tender beef roasts, such as rib eye, and less tender cuts, like eye of round and boneless chuck shoulder.

To simmer or stew, brown meat on all sides in a large, heavy pan or Dutch oven; drain drippings. Corned beef and cured and smoked pork need not be browned. Completely cover the meat with water or stock and season as desired. Cover tightly and simmer (do not boil) until meat is fork-tender.

When vegetables are to be cooked with the meat, add them whole or in pieces near end of cooking period. When done, remove meat and vegetables to a platter or casserole and keep hot. The cooking liquid may be reduced or thickened for a sauce or gravy. Approximate cooking times are:

Beef for Stew (1" to 2"; 2.5 to 5 cm)	2 to 3 hours
Fresh or Corned Beef Brisket (2 1/2 to 3 1/2 lb; 1 to 1.5 kg)	2 1/2 to 3 1/2 hours
Beef Shank Cross cuts (1" to 1 1/2"; 2.5 to 3.7 cm)	2 1/2 to 3 1/2 hours
Boneless Breast of Veal	1 to 1 1/2 hours
Lamb and Pork for Stew (1 to 1 1/2 lb; 0.5 to 0.7 kg)	1 1/2 to 2 hours
Country-Style Pork Ribs	2 to 2 1/2 hours

To poach, rub meat with seasonings, if desired. Roasts should be tied with heavy string at two-inch (5 cm) intervals, if necessary. Brown all sides in a large heavy pan or Dutch oven in small amount of oil; drain drippings. Cover with liquid and season with additional ingredients, if desired. Bring to a boil. Reduce heat, cover, and simmer until internal temperature of roast reaches 10°F (6°C) below desired doneness. Remove roast to carving board. Cover tightly with transpar-ent wrap or aluminum foil; let stand 10 minutes before carving.

Appropriate beef cuts for poaching are tender roasts, such as beef rib eye or tenderloin, and less-tender cuts, like eye round and boneless chuck shoulder. Roasts should weigh approximately two pounds (1 kg). They can be poached to desired doneness — rare, medium, and well done. Poaching requires one-third less time than roasting (about 20 to 30 minutes for a rare beef roast) and will minimize shrinkage. A poached beef roast is just as tender, juicy, and flavorful as one that has been prepared conventionally.

INTERNAL TEMPERATURE

The degree of doneness for meat can be accurately determined by measuring internal temperature with a standard meat thermometer. The thermometer should be inserted into the roast surface at a slight angle or through the end of the roast so the tip of the thermometer is in the thickest portion of the cut, but is not resting in fat or against the bone. Following are internal temperatures for preparing meat:

BEEF AND LAMB		
Rare	140°F	60°C
Medium rare	150°F	65°C
Medium	160°F	70°C
Well done	170°F	80°C
VEAL		
Medium	160°F	70°C
Well done	170°F	80°C
PORK (fresh and cured)		
Medium	160°F	70°C
Well done	170°F	80°C
HAM (fully cooked)	140°F	60°C

COOKING FROZEN MEATS

Frozen meat may be defrosted in the original wrapper and cooked according to directions for meat that has not been frozen, or it may be unwrapped and cooked in the frozen state. Additional cooking time is needed when cooking frozen meat. Frozen roasts require 30 to 50 percent more cooking time than roasts started at refrigerator temperature. The additional time needed for cooking steaks and chops varies according to surface area and thickness of the meat and the cooking temperature.

Thick frozen steaks, chops, and meat patties must be broiled farther from the heat than those that have been defrosted. This allows the internal temperature to reach the desired level without excessive surface browning. When panbroiling frozen steaks or chops, a heated frying pan should be used for defrosting the surface rapidly and browning on all sides. The heat should be reduced after browning and the meat turned often, so it will cook evenly.

COOKING VARIETY MEATS

All variety meats may be simmered or braised. Some, such as calves' liver, and lamb or veal kidneys, may be broiled. Regardless of the method, variety meats are usually cooked until well done.

MICROWAVES AND FOOD SYSTEMS

MEAT

The best cuts of meat for microwave cooking are tender, high-quality, boneless, and uniform in shape. Bone tends to cause uneven cooking, due to the reflective effect on microwaves. Popular meat choices are ground beef; steaks; chops; small roasts; country style ribs or spareribs; smoked and cured meat; and precooked, skinless sausage.

As a general rule when microwaving meat dishes, use MEDIUM (50%) power (350 watts) or MEDIUM-LOW (30%) power (230 watts) to assure tender, flavorful, and evenly cooked meat. Use HIGH (100% power; 700 watts) for ground meat and for reheating cooked meat dishes.

Following are some additional tips for promoting even cooking:

- Cut meat into uniform pieces or form ground meat into donut-shaped patties, 1/2 " (1.2 cm) thick.

- Arrange uniform meat shapes, such as meatballs, in a circle on microwave safe dish, leaving center empty. For chops, place meatier portion to outside of dish, with the bone toward the center.

- Stir meat strips several times during cooking, moving the less cooked pieces to the outside and the more cooked pieces to the inside.

- Stir soups, stews, and other dishes with high liquid contents several times to distribute the heat.

- Turn meat over several times or rotate dish 1/4 to 1/2 turn at intervals.

- Meat dishes should be covered with a lid or heavy-duty plastic wrap, turned back at one corner. The steam created will help food cook more evenly. Be sure plastic wrap does not touch the food.

A standing period of 10 to 20 minutes may be needed for heat to penetrate the center of the meat after microwaving. When estimating cooking time, allow for a rise in internal temperature of $5^\circ F$ to $10^\circ F$ (3 to $6^\circ C$) during standing. The slower the cooking and the smaller the mass, the shorter the standing time required. The following internal temperatures are suggested as a guide for determinating microwave cooking:

BEEF
rare	$130^\circ F$ to $135^\circ F$	$55^\circ C$ to $57^\circ C$
medium	$150^\circ F$ to $155^\circ F$	$66^\circ C$ to $69^\circ C$
well done	$160^\circ F$ to $165^\circ F$	$71^\circ C$ to $74^\circ C$

LAMB
medium	$150^\circ F$ to $155^\circ F$	$66^\circ C$ to $69^\circ C$
well done	$160^\circ F$ to $165^\circ F$	$71^\circ C$ to $74^\circ C$

PORK
well done	$160^\circ F$ to $165^\circ F$	71° C to $74^\circ C$

HAM (fully cooked):
$130^\circ F$ to $135^\circ F$	$55^\circ C$ to $57^\circ C$

Fish and Shellfish

NUTRITIVE VALUE

The consumption of fish (finfish and shellfish) has risen dramatically within the last decade, primarily because consumers are increasingly aware that fish is one of the most nutritious foods.

Protein Content

Fish is a complete protein with little or no connective tissue that is easily digested and absorbed by the body. Most species have 17 to 20 percent protein.

Vitamin and Mineral Content

Fishery products are a good source of many vitamins, especially niacin, B_6 and B_{12}. Fish, particularly shellfish, is known for its mineral content, with certain species having substantial amounts of calcium, iron, copper, chromium and/or zinc and other trace minerals. The flesh of both saltwater and freshwater fish is quite low in sodium content, with finfish averaging about 50 mg sodium in a 3.5 ounces (100 g) raw portion. Shellfish are higher in sodium. Shrimp and oysters contain 235 and 250 mg of sodium per 3.5 ounces (100 g),

respectively. Pickled, canned and smoked fish and surimi seafood have added sodium.

Fat Content

The fat content of fish can range from as low as 1.6 g in ocean perch to 8.6 g in salmon per 3.5 ounces (100 g) portion of uncooked seafood and averages about two grams of fat and 85 kilocalories per 3.5 ounces (100 g).

The lipid in fish is high in polyunsaturated fat. Many fish contain omega-3 fatty acids. The cholesterol content of 3.5 ounces (100 g) portion of finfish average about 60 mg, similar to amounts found in pork, beef and the dark meat of chicken. Most shellfish have moderate levels of cholesterol ranging from 35 to 90 mg per 3.5 ounces (100 g) portion. Shrimp and squid are higher in cholesterol (about 150 and 200 mg, respectively) but, like all fish, both are low in total fat and saturated fat. Fish is classified as either "lower fat" or "higher fat" which affects the preferred cookery method. Species with less than five percent fat content are considered "lean" and are usually characterized by a mild flavor and lighter colored flesh. Species that have a fat content of five percent and higher are considered "fat" with a more distinctive flavor and a darker color to the flesh.

MARKET FORMS

There are over 500 species of fish and shellfish commercially available in the United States today. They are marketed fresh, frozen, canned, dried, salted, smoked and in many convenience forms.

Fresh and frozen fish are marketed in various forms. The following are the most common:

Whole or **round** fish are just as they came from the water. Before cooking they must be eviscerated.

Drawn fish have been eviscerated and, usually, scaled.

Dressed fish have been scaled and eviscerated and the head, tail and fins have been removed. A small dressed fish is called **pan-dressed.**

Fillets are the sides of a fish cut away from the backbone. They may be purchased with the skin on or off and may have small rib or pin bones.

Butterfly or **kited fillets** are both sides of a fish cut away from the backbone and left connected by the uncut flesh and skin of the back or belly.

Steaks are cross section slices of large dressed fish, typically 3/4 to 1 inch (2 to 3 cm) thick. Usually, the skin is left on, and a cross section of the backbone remains. In the case of very large fish (such as some tuna), the fish is cut into loins before steaking, and therefore has neither skin nor bone.

Chunks are cross section portions of large dressed fish, having a cross section of backbone as the only bone. They are cut much like a beef or pork roast and are ready to cook as purchased.

Raw breaded fish portions are cut from frozen fish blocks, coated with a batter, breaded, packaged and frozen. They are ready to cook as purchased.

Fried fish portions and **fried fish sticks** are cut from frozen fish blocks, coated with a batter, breaded, partially cooked, packaged and frozen. They are ready to heat and serve as purchased.

Canned fish have been dressed or filleted, mechanically sized and placed into a can which is then sealed and heated. Many species of fish are available canned. Among them are salmon, tuna, sardines, mackerel, shrimp, oysters and clams. They may be served as purchased.

Salmon, canned on the Pacific coast, is usually sold by the name of the species. These differ in fat content, color, texture and flavor. The higher priced varieties are deeper red in color and have a higher oil content than the less costly ones (in descending order: sockeye; chinook or king;

coho or silver; pink; and chum or keta).

Tuna canned in the United States is produced from several species of tuna. Albacore, a very light meat, is the only tuna to be labeled white-meat tuna. The other species (yellowfin, blackfin, bluefin and skipjack) are labeled light-meat tuna. Fancy or solid pack tuna usually contains three or four large pieces packed in oil or water. Chunk, flaked and grated-style packs contain mechanically sized pieces packed in oil or water.

Sardines are small, immature sea herrings that are packed in water, oil, mustard or tomato sauce.

Cured fish are either salted or smoked and include salt herring, salmon, salmon eggs, chubs, sablefish, sturgeon, whitefish, mackerel and mullet. Lox is a mildly-cured salmon.

Surimi seafood is an imitation shellfish product made from a mild-flavored finfish, usually Alaskan pollock. The freshly caught fish is made into a paste and then formed into the shape, texture and color of a shellfish, most commonly crab meat. The processing involves the addition of certain stabilizers, binders and flavorings, often including real shellfish or a shellfish extract. Surimi seafood is pre-cooked and may or may not be breaded. The nutrient value of unbreaded surimi seafood is similar to that of finfish, with the exception of a higher sodium content. It is generally lower in cost than the shellfish it imitates.

SIGNS OF FRESHNESS
Fresh Finfish

Good quality fresh (unfrozen) finfish have the following characteristics:

■ The flesh is firm, not separating or soft. It springs back when pressed gently.

■ The odor is fresh and mild. Do a "nasal appraisal" before purchasing.

■ The eyes are bright, clear and often protruding. As the fish loses freshness, the eyes become cloudy, pink and sunken.

■ The gills are bright red or pink and are free from slime. Avoid fish with dull colored gills that are gray, brown or green.

■ The skin is shiny, with scales that adhere tightly. Characteristic colors and markings may begin to fade soon after the fish is removed from the water.

■ The intestinal cavity is clean and pink.

Fresh Shellfish

Different species of shellfish vary greatly in terms of market forms and physical characteristics. Look for the following signs of freshness when buying fresh (unfrozen) shellfish:

■ The odor is fresh and mild.

■ The flesh of shrimp and spiny (southern) lobster is firm. The shell is free of black spots, called melanosis, which are a sign of aging.

- Oysters, clams and mussels in the shell are alive, as indicated by a tightly closed shell or one that closes upon handling. If a shell opens slightly, tap it with a knife, and it will close. Discard any that do not.

- Uncooked crabs and northern lobsters are alive, as indicated by leg movement. They will not be very active if they have been refrigerated, but they should move at least a little. Also, the tail of a live lobster curls under tightly when it is handled. Discard any uncooked crabs and northern lobsters that do not show these signs of life.

- Fresh shucked oysters are in a clear, slightly milky or light gray liquid, called liquor. Oysters are usually creamy white, but there are color variations depending on variety and diet.

- The smaller bay and calico scallops are usually creamy white, though there may be some normal light tan or pink coloration. The larger sea scallops are generally creamy white, though they may show some normal light orange or pink color.

- Crab meat has a fresh, mild odor.

Frozen Fish

Fishery products that are sold in the frozen form are usually packed during the seasons of abundance, at the peak of freshness, and are held in cold storage until ready for distribution. Thus, the consumer is given the opportunity to select varied species of fish throughout the year and at better prices. High quality frozen fish that are properly processed, packaged and held will remain in good condition for relatively long periods of time.

Frozen fish of good quality have the following characteristics:

- The fish is solidly frozen when purchased.

- The flesh has no discoloration or freezer burn (a dry, white or grayish "cottony" appearance).

- The fish has little or no odor. When thawed, it has a mild odor.

- The wrapping is intact and is of moisture-vapor proof material.

- There is little or no air space between the fish and the wrapping, and there are no ice crystals or frost in the package which indicate that a variation in temperature has occurred.

HOW MUCH TO BUY

The amount of fish to buy per serving varies with the market form, the recipe to be used and the yield of edible flesh for the species. Consider about 3 ounces (85 g) of cooked, edible flesh as a serving. The following list can help you determine how much fish to buy per serving.

Finfish

Whole	3/4 pound (350 g)
Dressed, pan-dressed	1/2 pound (250 g)
Fillets, steaks	1/3 pound (140 g)
Portions	1/3 pound (140 g)
Sticks	1/4 pound (125 g)
Canned	1/6 pound (75 g)

Shellfish

Crab, cooked meat	1 /4 pound (125 g)
Crabs, live	1 to 2 pounds (500 g to 1 kg)
Lobster, cooked meat	1/3 pound (140 g)
Lobster, whole	1 to 2 pounds (500 g to 1 kg)
Mussels, live	12
Oysters, clams, live	6
Oysters, clams, shucked	1/4 pint (125 ml)
Oysters, clams, breaded	4 to 6
Scallops, shucked	1 /4 pound (125 g)
Shrimp, unpeeled, headless	1/2 pound (250 g)
Shrimp, cooked, peeled	1/4 pound (125 g)
Shrimp, breaded	4 to 6
Squid, whole	1/2 pound (250 g)
Squid, cleaned	1/4 pound (125 g)

STORING AND THAWING

Fresh fishery products that are to be cooked the day of purchase should be stored immediately in the coldest part of the refrigerator in the original wrapper. Fish that is to be held up to two days before cooking should be rinsed, patted dry and rewrapped in clean wrapping before refrigerating. For optimum quality, do not hold fresh fish in the refrigerator longer than two days before cooking. A storage temperature of 32° to 40^oF (4^oC) is needed to maintain the quality of the product.

Fish that is purchased fresh may be successfully frozen at home. While there are a number of ways to properly freeze fish, the primary concern with all methods is to keep air away from the product. It should be wrapped in a moisture-vapor proof wrapping (paper, plastic and/or foil) or frozen in water.

Frozen fishery products should be placed in the freezer in their original moisture-vapor proof wrapping immediately after purchase, unless the fish is to be thawed for cooking. A storage temperature of 0^oF (-18^oC) or lower is necessary to maintain the quality. At higher temperatures, chemical changes cause the fish to lose color, flavor, texture, and nutritive value. Generally, higher fat species may be held in the freezer up to four months without significant loss of quality, and lean species may be frozen for up to one year. It is, however, best to use frozen products soon after purchase for optimal quality.

When thawing fish, take into consideration the following:

■ Schedule thawing so that the fish will be cooked soon after it is thawed. Do not hold thawed fish longer than a day before cooking.

■ Place frozen packages in the refrigerator to thaw, allowing 18 to 24 hours or longer for thawing a one pound (500 g) package.

■ If quicker thawing of unbreaded product is necessary, place the frozen package under cold running water or in cold water to thaw. Allow 1/2 to 1 hour per pound (500 g) of frozen product.

■ Thaw fish in the microwave on the defrost setting for four to five minutes per pound (500 g), just until it is pliable enough to handle.

■ Do not thaw fish at room temperature or in warm water.

■ Avoid refreezing fish, as it results in a poorer quality product with a higher bacteria count.

- For prepared products including fish sticks and portions, follow the manufacturer's instructions.

- Frozen fillets and steaks may be cooked without thawing if additional cooking time is allowed.

SAFE HANDLING

All raw foods, including finfish and shellfish, contain bacteria. Handle fish as you would any perishable food product: keep it properly refrigerated, cook it adequately, and handle it with safety in mind. To maintain wholesomeness and quality, always follow these guidelines:

- Know your fish retailer. Buy fishery products from approved, licensed stores and markets.

- Purchase raw shellfish carefully. Buy raw oysters, clams and mussels only from approved, licensed, reputable sources. If in doubt, ask to see the certified shipper's tag that accompanies all live mollusks; look for a shipper number on containers of shucked oysters.

- Keep fish cold.

- Refrigerate live shellfish properly. Live oysters, clams and mussels should be stored under well ventilated refrigeration, not in air-tight plastic bags or storage containers. Burlap, net or heavy paper bags work well, as do plastic bags that are left open. Live lobsters and crabs should be stored similarly, with a covering of damp paper towels.

- Keep live shellfish alive until cooking. Discard any that have died during storage.

- Do not cross-contaminate. Handle and store raw and cooked products separately. Once a cutting board or colander or platter has been in contact with raw finfish or shellfish, wash it thoroughly before using it for cooked products.

- Cook fish thoroughly.

- Harvest fish carefully. If you catch fish or shellfish from local waters, make sure the waters are approved for harvest. Check with your local state Department of Health. Always carry plenty of ice and do not catch more than you can chill immediately.

Eating Raw Fish and Shellfish

Many consumers enjoy raw fish. Just as the consumption of raw or undercooked beef, pork, chicken and eggs carries a degree of risk of food-borne gastrointestinal illness, so does the consumption of undercooked fish, raw fish (i.e. sashimi, sushi, ceviche) and raw oysters, clams and mussels. Here are some tips to reduce the risk:

- Buy only the highest quality fish and shellfish; keep it properly refrigerated, and use it the day of purchase.

- If not previously frozen, hard freeze fish intended for the preparation of sashimi, sushi or ceviche for seven days, to avoid the slight risk associated with parasites.

■ Be certain that oysters, clams, and mussels come from certified growing waters. Make certain they are kept well refrigerated.

■ Never eat raw or undercooked fishery products if you are seriously ill with a disease that compromises the immune system, such as cancer, AIDS, alcoholism, liver disease or kidney disease.

HOW TO COOK FISH

Fish is delicious if properly cooked. Cooking fish develops its flavor, softens the small amount of connective tissue present and makes the protein easier to digest. Over-cooking fish toughens it, dries it out, destroys the fine flavor and reduces the yield.

Raw fish has a watery, translucent look. During the cooking process, the moisture in fish becomes milky colored, giving the flesh an opaque, whitish tint. When this occurs at the center of the thickest part of the fish, the fish is properly cooked.

To estimate how long to cook a fish, use the "10-minute rule" as a guideline, unless the fish is to be microwaved or deep-fried. Follow these steps:

1. Measure the fish at its thickest point. If other ingredients are added, include them in the measurement.

2. Plan to cook the fish for approximately 10 minutes per inch (2.5 cm) of thickness.

3. Before the estimated cooking time is complete, use a fork or knife, check the fish for doneness at the thickest point. Remove the fish from the heat when finfish are flaky, and shellfish are tender; both should no longer be translucent in the center. An internal temperature of 145°F (60°C) insures the fish is safe to eat. The cooking time required will vary somewhat according to the temperature and cooking method used. Check for doneness early and often.

4. Double the estimated cooking time for frozen fish that has not been thawed.

Most fish are quite delicate and tend to break up easily, so handle as little and as gently as possible during and after cooking to preserve appearance.

When choosing a cooking method and recipe for fish, carefully consider the species to be used. Fat fish are usually distinctive in flavor and can therefore be used in recipes with other robust flavors; the higher fat content also helps maintain moisture in the cooked product. Lean species of fish and shellfish should be used with ingredients that will not overpower their milder flavors, and care should be taken to prevent the product from drying out.

One may substitute a different species for the one specified in a recipe as long as it has similar characteristics. Consider the texture, flavor and fat content.

COOKING METHODS
Baking

Whole fish lend themselves well to baking, as do fillets and steaks. Cut fish into serving-size portions. Arrange on a well-oiled baking dish, and baste with melted butter or margarine, oil or a marinade. If desired, sprinkle with herbs or spices, citrus juice, or wine. Bake at 375°F (190°C). Turning is not necessary.

Broiling

Choose pan-dressed fish, fillets, steaks or shellfish for broiling. Prepare the fish as for baking. Place under the broiler, about 3 or 4 inches (8 to 10 cm) from the source of heat. Place thicker cuts of fish farther from the heat than thin ones. Baste frequently; turn halfway through cooking time unless fish is very thin.

Deep-fat Frying

Choose fillets, shucked shellfish and small dressed fish for this method. In a deep-fat fryer, heat enough vegetable oil to float the fish but do not fill the fryer more than half full. Heat the oil to 375°F (190°C). Cut the fish into serving-size portions. Dip the fish into seasoned milk or beaten egg and then into seasoned crumbs, cornmeal or flour. Or coat with flour and then dip into a batter. Arrange in a fryer basket to be lowered into the fryer or drop gently into the oil and fry until golden brown, flaky and no longer translucent in the center. Drain on absorbent paper.

Pan-Frying

Pan-frying is an excellent way to cook pan-dressed fish, fillets and steaks. Prepare the fish as for deep-fat frying. Heat 1/4 to 1/2 inch (6 mm to 1 cm) oil or other fat in a heavy fry pan. Place one layer of fish in the hot fat, taking care not to overload the pan and thus cool the fat. Fry until golden brown on one side, then turn and brown the other side. Drain on absorbent paper.

Oven-Frying

Fillets are the preferred market form to use for oven-frying. Cut the fish into serving-size portions. Dip the pieces in seasoned milk or other liquid and coat with flour or crumbs such as crackers, bread or a snack food. Place the fish on a shallow, well-oiled baking pan, drizzle lightly with oil and bake at 450°F (240°C). Turning is not necessary.

Poaching

Any cut of fish may be poached. Often, shellfish is referred to as "boiled," when actually it is prepared by poaching or simmering. Place just enough liquid to cover the finfish into a shallow, wide pan, such as a large fry pan. A Dutch oven or stock pot may be used for shellfish. The liquid may be plain or lightly salted water, water seasoned with herbs and spices, milk, or a mixture of white wine and water. Cover the pan and heat until the liquid simmers. Gently add the fish, cover, and simmer. After the fish is removed, the liquid may then be reduced and thickened to make a sauce for the fish.

Steaming

Choose any market form of fish for steaming. A steam cooker or any deep pot with a tight cover may be used for steaming fish. If a steaming rack or basket is not available, use a plate or cake rack placed atop an inverted cup or bowl to hold the fish above the water. Pour about 2 inches (5 cm) of water into the pot and bring to a boil. The water may be plain or seasoned with herbs, spices or wine. Place the fish on a lightly-oiled rack, basket or plate over the boiling water. Cover the pot tightly and steam.

Charcoal Broiling

Fillets, steaks and shellfish are good choices for this cooking method. Before heating the grill, lightly brush the grill and the fish with oil. For fish that is 1 inch (3 cm) thick or less, place the grill 2 to 4 inches (5 to 10 cm) away from the coals; for thicker pieces, 5 to 6 inches (12 to 15 cm) away. For particularly delicate fish, use a hinged, wire fish or hamburger basket (oiled); wooden or metal skewers may be used for shrimp or scallops. Turn the fish halfway through the estimated cooking time, basting frequently with oil or sauce.

Microwave Cooking

Small whole fish, fillets and steaks are particularly good choices for microwave cookery. To achieve the best results when microwaving fish, special consideration should be given to the quantity and shape of the fish, the size, shape of the dish, and the wattage and power settings of the oven. Because there are no standard power settings among most oven brands, the cooking time suggested in recipes should be considered only as a guideline. Frequent checking for doneness is required, and notations should be made on actual cooking time for future reference. Use the following techniques when microwaving fish:

■ Use a shallow dish to allow the fish maximum exposure to the microwaves. Cover the dish with a paper towel, waxed paper or plastic wrap (vented).

■ Arrange fillets with the thicker parts toward the outside of the dish. The thinner parts, separated by plastic wrap, may be overlapped in the center.

■ Use the high power setting and plan to microwave the fish 3 to 5 minutes per pound (500 g). Rotate the dish halfway through the estimated cooking time; turning the fish is not necessary. Check the fish early and often for doneness. If needed, continue to microwave and check for doneness at one-minute intervals.

COOKING SHELLFISH

There are special considerations for cooking each species of shellfish, particularly regarding cooking times. Cook shellfish lightly, looking for the following signs of doneness.

■ When properly cooked, shrimp turn pink with an opaque rather than translucent center. One pound (500 g) of medium or large shrimp require only 3 to 5 minutes of cooking when being boiled or steamed.

■ Shucked mollusks, such as oysters, clams and mussels, become plump and opaque when cooked. The edges of oysters start to curl.

■ Mollusks in the shell open when they are done. Remove individual pieces from the heat as they open. Discard any that do not open.

■ Scallops turn milky white in the center when done. Depending on the size and the cooking method, scallops take from 2 to 5 minutes to cook.

■ "Boiled" northern lobster turns bright red. When properly cooked, the center of the meat is no longer translucent. Allow

5 to 6 minutes per pound (500 g) in simmering water.

■ Spiny lobster turns bright orange with an opaque rather than translucent center. Cooking time in simmering water varies from 8 to 15 minutes, depending on the size and market form.

AQUACULTURE

Aquaculture is the raising of fish or shellfish in tanks, ponds, waterways, or net pens and is one of the fastest growing sectors of the U. S. agricultural industry.

■ Worldwide consumer demand for fish continues to increase, while harvests of wild stocks remain static.

■ Cultured fish provide consumers with fresh fish year round.

■ The aquaculture industry is developing many species, such as hybrid striped bass and tilapia.

Among the species increasingly cultured are catfish, crawfish, shrimp, salmon, tilapia, oysters, clams, scallops, and lobster.

INSPECTION AND GRADING

By the authority of the federal Food, Drug, and Cosmetic Safety Act, the Food and Drug Administration (FDA) of the U. S. Department of Health and Human Services is primarily responsible for the regulation of fish and seafood. The FDA conducts inspections of seafood processing operations and evaluates fish handling procedures within each facility. Inspectors analyze and test the products produced in these plants for filth, decomposition and contaminants. Imported seafood is also overseen by the FDA, which is responsible for wharf examination and product testing.

The National Marine Fisheries Service of the U. S. Department of Commerce (USDC), the Environmental Protection Agency and coastal state governments all participate in seafood regulation programs which collectively and comprehensively monitor seafood safety.

Inspection and grading of fish and fishery products are voluntary services that the U. S. Department of Commerce makes available to the seafood industry on a fee-for-service basis. Labels of inspected and/or graded fishery products that meet federal standards then may carry U.S. grade and inspection marks with the grade of the product and a statement that the product was packed under federal inspection.

Quality grades include Grade A fishery products, which are top or best quality, uniform in size, practically free from blemishes or defects and of good flavor; Grade B, which is good quality but not as uniform in size or free from blemishes and defects as the top grade; and grade C, which is fairly good quality, considered wholesome and nutritious, but may not be as attractive in appearance as the other grades.

The USDC has issued standards for many frozen precooked and raw breaded fishery products to establish minimum percentages of flesh content. The following table (Table 5.1) lists the minimum percent flesh for breaded fishery products bearing the USDC Grade A and inspection marks.

Table 5.1
MINIMUM FLESH CONTENT REQUIREMENTS FOR USDC-INSPECTED PRODUCTS

PRODUCT	USDC GRADE MARKS	PUFI MARK[1]
	Min. % of Flesh by Weight	
FISH		
Raw Breaded Fillets	—	50%[2]
Precooked Breaded Fillets	—	50%
Precooked Crispy/Crunchy Fillets	—	50%
Precooked Battered Fillets	—	40%
Raw Breaded Portions	75%	50%
Precooked Breaded Portions	65%	50%
Precooked Battered Portions	—	40%
Raw Breaded Sticks	72%	50%
Precooked Breaded Sticks	60%	50%
Precooked Battered Sticks	—	40%
SCALLOPS		
Raw Breaded Scallops	50%	50%
Precooked Breaded Scallops	50%	50%
Precooked Crispy/Crunchy Scallops	—	50%
Precooked Battered Scallops	—	40%
SHRIMP		
Lightly Breaded Shrimp	65%	65%[3]
Raw Breaded Shrimp	50%	50%[3]
Precooked Crispy/Crunchy Shrimp	—	50%
Precooked Battered Shrimp	—	40%
Imitation Breaded Shrimp	—	NO MINIMUM. Encouraged to put percent on label [4]
OYSTERS		
Raw Breaded Oysters	—	50%[5]
Precooked Breaded Oysters	—	50%[5]
Precooked Crispy/Crunchy Oysters	—	50%[5]
Precooked Battered Oysters	—	40%[5]
MISCELLANEOUS		
Fish and Seafood Cakes	—	35%
Extruded and Breaded Products	—	35%

[1] PUFI: nonstandardized breaded and battered products.

[2] No USDC grading standard currently exists.

[3] FDA Standard of Identity requires any product to have 50% shrimp flesh by weight. If a product is labeled "lightly" breaded it must contain 65% shrimp flesh.

[4] Any product with a Standard of Identity which contains less flesh than the standard requires must be labeled imitation.

[5] Flesh content on oyster products can only be determined on an input weight basis during production.

Poultry and Eggs

POULTRY

Poultry is marketed as ready-to-cook raw poultry and ready-to-eat forms. More poultry is sold as parts, often skinless and boneless, and as further processed products than as whole birds. Many further processed food products include poultry meat as a main ingredient. New packaging techniques, such as modified atmosphere packaging, shelf-stable products and sous vide products (dishes with fresh ingredients which are vacuum-packed, cooked under vacuum and chilled), have expanded the variety of refrigerated, canned, and frozen items available.

FEDERAL POULTRY PROGRAMS

All poultry slaughtered in the United States is inspected for wholesomeness by the federal government (USDA) or by an equivalent state system. Federal inspection is mandatory for slaughtered poultry moving in interstate commerce. Poultry moving in intrastate commerce is subject to state inspection.

Birds are examined inside and out by an official inspector. Poultry may also be graded for quality by an official grader through a voluntary program. Officially inspected and graded poultry is prepared in processing plants that meet USDA sanitary requirements. The inspection mark (a circle stating "Inspected for Wholesomeness by the U.S. Department of Agriculture") and the grade mark (a shield stating USDA Grade A, B, or C) appear on the package label.

Grades for poultry have been established by USDA. Most poultry identified with a grade mark will be Grade A. It will be fully fleshed, meaty, well formed, have a uniform fat covering, a good, clean appearance, and be free from defects such as skin cuts and tears, pinfeathers, bruises, and missing or broken bones.

For each kind of poultry, USDA has also established classes, essentially based on the age of the bird. Unless specified, the birds may be of either sex. The age of the bird affects its tenderness and dictates the cooking method to use. Young birds are tender-meated and can be cooked by any method but are best roasted, broiled, or fried. Mature birds are less tender and need to be braised or stewed.

SAFE HANDLING

Poultry, like many other foods, may contain *salmonella* bacteria, but proper cooking and handling methods can eliminate any threat to health. Thorough washing under cool running water prior to cooking greatly reduces bacterial hazards. Since *salmonella* are easily destroyed by heat, all poultry should be cooked to the well-done stage, 170°F (80°C). Juices from the cooked meat should be clear, not pink.

Always thaw poultry in the refrigerator or in cold water, **NOT** on the counter. Bacteria multiply rapidly at room temperature.

Wash hands, counter tops and utensils in hot soapy water between each step of poultry preparation. Bacteria present on raw meat or poultry can get into other food if exposed to the same utensils. For instance, do not cut up raw poultry and then use the same knife or cutting board to prepare other foods unless the knife and board have been washed thoroughly. Be sure the platter that carries the cooked meat to the table is not the same platter that carried the raw meat to the grill.

Cooked poultry that is not eaten immediately should be kept either hot, 140°F (60°C) or hotter, OR cold, 40°F (4°C) or colder. Thoroughly reheat leftovers before eating. Bring gravies to a rolling boil before serving.

Store poultry for picnics or lunches in an insulated container until ready to eat.

In the refrigerator

Store chilled raw poultry in its transparent wrap for one or two days in the coldest part of the refrigerator. If wrapped only in market paper, unwrap, place on a tray, cover with waxed paper and refrigerate. Wrap and store giblets separately.

Cool cooked poultry quickly by wrapping loosely and setting it in the coldest part of the refrigerator.

Remove stuffing from cooked stuffed birds and store in a separate covered container in the refrigerator. Refrigerate broth or gravy promptly.

Use cooked poultry within three to four days. Use stuffing, broth or gravy within one or two days.

In the freezer

Both uncooked and cooked poultry may be frozen and stored for several months at 0°F

Table 6.1
FREEZER STORAGE TIMETABLE

POULTRY FORM	MONTHS
Uncooked poultry	
Chicken	
Cut-up	9
Giblets	3
Whole	12
Duck, whole	6
Goose, whole	6
Turkey	
Cut-up	6
Whole	12
Cooked poultry **(slices or pieces)**	
Covered with broth	6
Not covered with broth	1
Cooked poultry dishes	4 to 6
Fried chicken	4
Poultry gravy or broth	2 to 3

(-18ºC) or colder. (See Table 6.1 for recommended storage times for maximum quality). Do not stuff uncooked poultry before freezing. Remove stuffing from cooked poultry and freeze meat and stuffing separately.

Thawing

Keep poultry frozen until ready to thaw or cook. Thaw in the refrigerator in original wrapping (see Table 6.2) OR in cold water, changing the water every 30 minutes OR in the microwave following manufacturer's directions. Cook promptly after thawing. Do **not**

Table 6.2
THAWING TIMETABLE IN REFRIGERATOR FOR POULTRY

POULTRY TYPE AND SIZE	TIME REQUIRED
Chickens	
4 pounds (2 kg) or more	1 to 1 1/2 days
Less than 4 pounds (2 kg)	12 to 16 hours
Ducks	
3 to 7 pounds (1 to 3 kg)	1 to 1 1/2 days
Geese	
6 to 12 pounds (3 to 5 kg)	1 to 2 days
Turkeys	
4 to 12 pounds (2 to 5 kg)	1 to 2 days
12 to 20 pounds (5 to 9 kg)	2 to 3 days
20 to 24 pounds (9 to 10 kg)	3 to 4 days
Pieces of large turkey (half, quarter, half breast)	1 to 2 days
Cut-up pieces	3 to 9 hours
Boneless roasts	12 to 18 hours

thaw poultry at room temperature.

COOKING METHODS

All poultry should be washed in cold water before cooking and cooked to the well-done stage. Juices should run clear. Whole birds or parts may be roasted, fried, braised or stewed.

Dry Heat Methods
Roasting:

Allowing about 1 cup (250 ml) stuffing per pound (0.5 kg) of bird, stuff poultry lightly just before roasting. Do **not** stuff the day before.

Roast on rack in uncovered shallow pan. Do not add water.

Do **not** partly roast poultry one day and complete roasting the next day.

Roast stuffed or unstuffed poultry in preheated 325ºF (160ºC) oven. Do **not** cook at low temperatures over night.

You can use a meat thermometer to determine doneness of medium to large birds. Temperature in the inner thigh (not touching the bone) should reach 180 to 185ºF (80 to 85ºC) or for turkey roasts, 170ºF (77ºC). Stuffing should reach 165ºF (75ºC). For approximate total roasting times of various poultry products see Table 6.3.

To roast commercially stuffed poultry, follow directions on the package. Frozen commercially stuffed poultry is ready for the oven and must not be thawed before cooking.

Table 6.3
ROASTING TIME FOR POULTRY

KIND	PURCHASED WEIGHT[1]		APPROXIMATE TOTAL ROASTING TIME AT 325°(160°C)	
	Pounds	Kilograms	Fresh or Thawed Poultry 32 to 40°F, 4°C Hours	Frozen Poultry 0°F, -18°C or below Hours
Chickens				
Whole				
Broiler-Fryer	2 1/4 - 3 1/4	1 - 1.5	1 3/4 - 2 1/2	2 - 3
Roaster	3 1/4 - 4 1/2	1.5 - 2	2 - 3	2 1/2 - 3 1/2
Capon	5 - 8 1/2	2 - 4	3 - 4	
Rock Cornish game hen	1 - 2	0.5 - 1	1 1/2 - 2	
Pieces	1/4 - 3/4	0.1 - 0.3	1 - 2 1/2	1 - 2 3/4
Ducks	4 - 6	2 - 3	2 1/2 - 4	3 1/2 - 4 1/2
Geese	6 - 8	3 - 4	3 - 3 1/2	
Turkeys				
Whole	6 - 8	3 - 4	3 - 3 1/2	
	8 - 12	4 - 5	3 1/2 - 4 1/2	
	12 - 16	5 - 7	4 1/2 - 5 1/2	5 1/2 - 6 1/2
	16 - 20	7 - 9	5 1/2 - 6 1/2	
	20 - 24	9 - 10	6 1/2 - 7	7 - 8 1/2
Halves, Whole Breast	5 - 11	2 - 5	3 - 5 1/2	4 1/2 - 6 1/4
Quarters — thighs, drumsticks	1 - 3	0.5 - 1.5	2 - 3 1/2	2 - 3 3/4
Boneless roasts	3 - 10	1.5 - 5	3 - 4	

[1] *Weight of giblets and neck included for whole poultry.*

Table 6.4
BRAISING TIMETABLE FOR POULTRY

KIND	READY-TO-COOK WEIGHT[1]		APPROXIMATE TOTAL BRAISING TIME AT 400° F (200°C)	
	Pounds	Kilograms	Fresh or thawed poultry 32 to 40° F, 4° C Hours	Frozen Poultry 0°F, - 18° C or below Hours
Chickens				
Whole				
Broiler-				
Fryer	2 1/4 - 3 1/4	1 - 1.5	1 1/2 - 2 1/4	2 - 2 1/2
Roaster	3 1/4 - 4 1/2	1.5 - 2	1 3/4 - 2 1/2	2 1/2 - 3 1/2
Pieces	1/4 - 3/4	0.1 - 0.3	1/2 - 1	3/4 - 1 1/2
Wings	1/4 - less	0.1	1	1 1/4
Turkeys				
Whole	12 - 16	5 - 7	3 1/2 - 5	4 1/2 - 6
	16 - 20	7 - 9	4 1/2 - 6 1/2	5 1/2 - 7 1/2
	20 - 24	9 - 10	6 - 8	7 - 9
Half, breast	5 - 11	2 - 5	2 - 3 1/4	3 - 4 1/2
Quarters, thighs, drumsticks	1 - 3	0.5 - 1.5	1 - 2	1 1/4 - 2 1/4
Wings	3/4 - 1 1/4	0.3 - 0.5	2 - 2 1/2	2 - 2 1/2
Boneless roast	3 - 10	1.5 - 5	1 1/2 - 5	

[1] *Weight of giblets and neck included for whole poultry.*

Broiling

Chicken, small fryer-roaster turkeys and ducklings can be broiled satisfactorily. Cut into halves, quarters or pieces. Place cut chicken pieces on rack of broiler pan 5 to 6 inches (7.5 to 15 cm) from heat. Broil on one side until browned, turn and broil until done.

Chicken will require 20 to 30 minutes on the first side and 15 to 20 minutes after turning. Turkey and duck pieces, being thicker, require longer broiler time. Allow 60 to 75 minutes total.

Outdoor broiling

Set broiler racks 6 to 8 inches (15 to 20

cm) from the coals. If meat cooks too fast, raise rack or spread coals farther apart. Broil, turning occasionally, about one hour for chicken, longer for turkey.

Rotisserie cooking

Whole poultry or large pieces can be cooked on rotisserie equipment. Follow manufacturer's directions.

Frying

Young chickens, capons, Rock Cornish game hens and small turkeys can be fried. Serving size pieces are easiest to handle and may be coated or uncoated.

To avoid excess fat in the diet, it is wise to prepare fried poultry with a minimum of fat. Removing skin before cooking also reduces fat.

To panfry, heat enough fat or oil, about 2 or 3 tablespoons (30 to 45 ml), to cover the bottom of a heavy frying pan. Place meatier pieces in center of pan, smaller pieces at edges. Brown over medium heat on one side, turn and brown other side. For chicken, continue to cook slowly, uncovered, until tender, 30 to 45 minutes, or cook in 350°F (180°C) oven until done. For turkey, cover tightly after browning and cook slowly 45 to 60 minutes or until done, turning occasionally. Uncover for last few minutes to re-crisp, if desired.

To oven fry, place poultry pieces in a well-greased baking pan. Cook, skin side down, in 400°F (200°C) oven for 30 minutes. Turn and cook 20 to 30 minutes longer or until done. Turkey pieces will need a longer cooking time.

Deep-fat frying, while it produces a desirable crisp coating, also results in a cooked product very high in fat content. To cook by this method, coat poultry pieces with a thin batter, flour, or crumbs. Use a deep kettle, filled no more than half full with melted fat (deep enough to cover chicken pieces). Heat fat to 365°F (180°C). Check temperature with a deep-fat thermometer. Fry a few pieces at a time for 10 to 15 minutes. Drain on paper towels to remove excess fat.

Smoking

In some areas, smoking is a popular method for cooking turkeys. Smoking may be done in equipment designed for the purpose or in a covered backyard grill, following manufacturer's directions.

Prepare thawed or fresh unstuffed turkey as for roasting. Soaking in a brine solution before cooking lends a characteristic flavor but is not essential.

Allow the bed of coals to become hot. Add water to the drip pan under the turkey. Temperature of the smoker should be kept between 225 and 300°F (107 and 150°C) throughout cooking. To maintain this temperature, add coals every one to two hours. Cook until meat thermometer registers 180°F (80°C) in thigh and 170°F (75°C) in the breast meat, and juices run clear. Cooking time will vary depending on outside temperature, wind, and altitude and may take as long as eight hours.

Smoking methods may also be used for preparing geese, ducks and pheasants.

Moist Heat Methods

Braising

Mature, less tender poultry often requires braising (cooking slowly in a tightly covered pan with a small amount of moisture). Braising of young, tender poultry and boneless turkey roasts is faster than roasting. (See Table 6.4 for braising timetable.)

Place whole or cut up poultry on a rack in roaster or heavy pan and cover tightly. Cook in 400°F (200°C) oven until leg joints move easily and flesh on leg is soft and pliable. To brown, uncover for last 30 minutes of cooking of whole large turkeys or a shorter time for smaller sizes of poultry. Poultry may also be braised on top of the range. Use a heavy, covered pan, add 1/3 cup of water, and follow oven directions. Cook slowly over low to medium heat for 1 1/2 to 2 1/2 hours.

Simmering or stewing

Mature chickens or turkeys need to be simmered or stewed to become tender. Simmer or stew poultry in enough water to barely cover. Add vegetables such as onion and celery if desired. Cover pot and cook over low heat until tender when pierced with a fork. Mature chickens require 1 1/2 to 2 hours; young chickens, 3/4 to 1 hour; and young large turkeys, 3 to 3 1/2 hours.

To shorten cooking time, you can cook in a pressure cooker or pressure saucepan, following the manufacturer's directions.

EGGS

Eggs discussed in this section refer to chicken eggs unless otherwise noted.

Eggs are a nutrient-dense food with a low calorie count. A large egg contains 213 milligrams of cholesterol, but only about 1.5 grams of saturated fat. Egg protein is of exceptionally high quality. The yolk contains almost half the egg's protein and, except for riboflavin and niacin, a higher proportion of the egg's total vitamins and minerals. There is no difference in nutrition, taste or functional properties between brown and white-shelled eggs.

Shell Eggs

Chicken eggs are marketed according to grade and size standards established by the USDA or by equivalent standards set by state departments of agriculture. The USDA shield on the egg carton means that the eggs have been federally inspected. Most state laws require that the grade, size, date of pack and/or expiration date appear on the carton label. Plants not under USDA inspection are governed by laws of their states.

Size and grade are two entirely different factors bearing no relationship to one another. Grade is determined by the interior and exterior quality of the egg at the time the egg is packed.

Grades are AA, A and B. Most Grade B eggs go to egg breakers for use in egg products. As the egg ages, the white becomes thinner, allowing the egg to spread more when broken out. This characteristic makes the freshest eggs most desirable when appearance is im-

Table 6.5
PRICE PER DOZEN EGGS

SMALL (18 oz.)	MEDIUM (21 oz.)	LARGE (24 oz.)	X-LARGE (27 oz.)	JUMBO (30 oz.)	PRICE/LB (16 oz.)
(510 g)	(595 g)	(680 g)	(765 g)	(850 g)	(454 g)
$ 0.41	$ 0.48	$ 0.55	$ 0.62	$ 0.68	$ 0.36 1/2
0.45	0.53	0.60	0.68	0.75	0.40
0.48	0.56	0.65	0.73	0.81	0.43
0.52	0.61	0.70	0.78	0.87	0.46 1/2
0.56	0.66	0.75	0.84	0.94	0.50
0.60	0.70	0.80	0.89	0.99	0.53
0.64	0.74	0.85	0.95	1.06	0.56 1/2
0.68	0.79	0.90	1.01	1.13	0.60
0.71	0.83	0.95	1.06	1.18	0.63
0.75	0.87	1.00	1.12	1.25	0.66 1/2
0.79	0.92	1.05	1.18	1.31	0.70
0.82	0.96	1.10	1.23	1.37	0.73
0.86	1.00	1.15	1.29	1.43	0.76 1/2
0.90	1.05	1.20	1.35	1.50	0.80
0.93	1.09	1.25	1.40	1.56	0.83
0.97	1.14	1.30	1.46	1.62	0.86 1/2
1.01	1.18	1.35	1.52	1.69	0.90
1.05	1.22	1.40	1.57	1.74	0.93
1.09	1.27	1.45	1.63	1.81	0.96 1/2
1.13	1.31	1.50	1.69	1.88	1.00

portant, as for poaching or frying. Eggs a week or two old are best for hard-cooking, because they can be peeled more easily.

Size is classified according to minimum weight per dozen:

WEIGHT PER DOZEN

Jumbo	30 oz.	(850 g)
Extra large	27 oz.	(765 g)
Large	24 oz.	(680 g)
Medium	21 oz.	(595 g)
Small	18 oz.	(510 g)
Peewee	15 oz.	(425 g)

Although eggs are sold by number of eggs per carton, it is easier to determine which size is the best buy by comparing the price per pound, as shown in Table 6.5, on page 115.

Size Equivalents

Any size egg may be used for frying, scrambling, cooking in the shell or poaching, but other recipes are usually based on the use of large eggs. To substitute another size, use the following charts:

LARGE	JUMBO	X-LARGE	MEDIUM	SMALL
1	1	1	1	1
2	2	2	2	3
3	2	3	3	4
4	3	4	5	5
5	4	4	6	7
6	5	5	7	8

TO MAKE 1 CUP

EGG SIZE	WHOLE	WHITES	YOLKS
Jumbo	4	5	11
X-Large	4	6	12
Large	5	7	14
Medium	5	8	16
Small	6	9	18

Care and Handling

Although a small percentage of shell eggs may contain *Salmonellae*, eggs are a safe food when handled like other perishable foods. Refrigeration is of prime importance in preserving egg quality and safety.

- Buy eggs at retail from refrigerated cases only. For food service, use only eggs delivered under refrigeration.

- Refrigerate with large end up in cartons or cases, at 40°F (4°C) or colder. Properly refrigerated eggs keep 4 to 5 weeks past the pack date without significant loss of quality.

- Use only clean, uncracked eggs.

- Wash cutting boards and all utensils used in egg preparation before using for other foods.

- Do not leave broken-out eggs or egg dishes at room temperature more than two hours including preparation and service. If not served immediately, keep egg dishes below 40°F (4°C) or above 140°F (60°C).

- To store unbroken yolks, cover with water in a tightly covered container, refrigerate, and use in one to two days, or hard cook them, drain well and refrigerate in a tightly sealed container up to four or five days.

- Refrigerate raw whites in a tightly covered container for up to four days.

- Refrigerate hard-cooked unpeeled eggs and use within a week.

Freezing Eggs

Broken-out eggs can be frozen successfully. Label containers with date, number of eggs, and whether you have added salt or sugar.

Whites — pour into freezer containers and seal tightly.

Table 6.6
LARGE SHELL EGG EQUIVALENCY TO FROZEN OR REFRIGERATED LIQUID EGG PRODUCTS

	WEIGHT		MEASURE	
WHOLE EGGS				
1	1 3/4 oz.	50 g	3 Tbsp	45 ml
10	1 lb. 1 3/4 oz.	503 g	2 cups	473 ml
12	1 lb. 5 1/2 oz	610 g	2 1/2 cups	592 ml
25	2 lbs. 13 oz.	1276 g	1 qt. 1 1/4 cups	1242 ml
50	5 lbs. 8 oz.	2495 g	2 qts. 2 1/2 cups	2483 ml
YOLKS				
10	7 1/4 oz.	206 g	3/4 cup	177 ml
12	8 1/2 oz.	241 g	3/4 cup 2 Tbsp.	207 ml
22	1 lb.	454 g	2 cups less 2 Tbsp.	443 ml
WHITES				
10	11 1/2 oz	326 g	1 1/4 cups 2 Tbsp.	326 ml
12	14 oz.	397 g	1 1/2 cups 2 Tbsp.	385 ml
14	1 lb.	454 g	2 cups less 1 Tbsp.	458 ml

Yolks— the gelation property of frozen yolks makes them almost impossible to use in a recipe unless 1/8 teaspoon salt (0.5 ml) or 1 1/2 teaspoons (7 ml) sugar or corn syrup per 1/4 cup (60 ml) or 4 yolks is added before freezing.

Whole eggs — Beat just until blended and pour into freezer containers. Salt, sugar, or corn syrup needs to be added because of the presence of the yolks.

To Use Frozen Eggs

Thaw under running cold water or overnight in the refrigerator. Use immediately.

Whites will beat to a greater volume if allowed to stand at room temperature about 30 minutes.

2 tbsp (30 ml) thawed egg white = 1 large fresh white.

1 tbsp (15 ml) thawed egg yolk = 1 large fresh yolk.

3 tbsp (45 ml) thawed whole egg = 1 large fresh egg.

Use thawed frozen eggs only in dishes that are thoroughly cooked.

Table 6.7
SHELL EGG EQUIVALENCY
TO DRIED WHOLE EGG PRODUCTS

SHELL EGG (Large size)		DRIED WHOLE SIFTED		WATER	
6	3 oz.	85 g	1 cup	237 ml	1 cup
12	6 oz.	170 g	2 cups	473 ml	2 cups
24	12 oz.	340 g	1 qt.	946 ml	1 qt.
50	1 lb. 9 oz.	709 g	2 qt. 1/3 cup	1971 ml	2 qt. 1/3 cup
100	3 lb. 2 oz.	1418 g	1 gal. 2/3 cup	3942 ml	1 gal. 2/3 cup
150	4 lb. 11 oz.	2126 g	6 qt. 1 cup	5915 ml	6 qt. 1 cup
200	6 lb. 4 oz.	2835 g	2 gal. 1 1/3 cups	7886 ml	2 gal. 1 1/3 cups

MICROWAVE COOKING

Because few foods are as heat-sensitive as eggs, a reduced power level of 200 to 300 watts is recommended for all egg dishes except omelets, poached eggs with water added, and scrambled eggs.

Do not cook raw eggs in their shells or reheat peeled or unpeeled hard-cooked eggs. They will explode. Rapid build-up of steam can cause yolks of broken-out eggs to explode. Always prick yolks of unbeaten eggs and cover container with waxed paper or plastic wrap to avoid splattering.

Microwave cooking is not recommended for souffles and puffy omelets.

For quick hard-cooked eggs, separate yolks and whites into two small bowls. Stir yolks. Cover and cook separately on reduced power (200 to 300 watts), stirring once or twice. Allow 20 to 30 seconds per yolk and about 30 seconds to 1 minute per white. Let stand, covered, about 2 minutes. Cool long enough to handle, then chop or chill until ready to use.

Safety of Egg-containing Dishes

Salmonellae will not survive in dishes cooked to 140°F (60°C) for at least 3 1/2 minutes or in those cooked to 160°F (80°C). Cook poached, fried, soft-cooked, and scrambled eggs until whites are completely coagulated and yolks begin to thicken. Cook omelets, frittatas, and French toast until no visible liquid egg remains. When serving infants, the elderly, or the ill, cook all egg dishes thoroughly or use pasteurized egg product.

WHIPPING PROPERTIES

Beaten egg white provide the volume and texture of many baked products, puffy omelets, souffles and chiffon cakes. The volume of beaten egg whites can increases 6 to 8 times. Maximum volume is obtained with whites brought to room temperature (72°F, 22°C) about 30 minutes.

Fat inhibits foam formation, therefore

separate yolks and whites carefully to avoid the presence of any yolk in the white. Use metal or glass bowls for beating whites. Plastic bowls cannot be rendered completely fat-free.

Egg white foams should be beaten just until whites no longer slip when the bowl is tilted. Underbeaten whites result in poor volume of the finished product. Overbeaten whites have lost their elasticity and break apart when combined with other ingredients.

Drainage occurs fairly rapidly so whites should not be beaten more than a few minutes before they are needed.

Adding 1/8 teaspoon (0.5 ml) cream of tartar per egg white helps to stabilize the foam.

Sugar should be beaten in 1 or 2 teaspoons (5 or 10 ml) at a time after foaming has begun.

Beaten whole egg or egg yolk will increase about four times in volume. Beat until eggs become lemon-colored and form ribbons when beater is lifted, about three to five minutes.

EGG PRODUCTS

Processed and convenience forms of eggs available to food service include: refrigerated liquid, frozen, dried (egg solids), and specialty products. All egg products are produced in federally inspected plants and are pasteurized so they are salmonella negative.

Retail markets carry egg substitutes, in which yolks are replaced with oil, dried milk, gums or other ingredients. Dried whole eggs usually are available at camping goods stores, and meringue powder, based on dried egg white, is available at craft stores since it is frequently used to frost baked goods. Equiva-

lency of large shell eggs to frozen, refrigerated liquid, and dried egg products are shown in Table 6.6 (page 117) and Table 6.7 (page 118).

HANDLING EGG PRODUCTS

Do not accept frozen egg products which are beginning to thaw. Transfer frozen products to the freezer immediately after delivery.

Do not thaw at room temperature. Thaw in the refrigerator or under cold running water in sealed containers. Use defrosted egg products promptly. Cover and refrigerate unused portion and use within three days.

Refrigerate liquid egg products immediately upon delivery. Liquid product will keep, refrigerated at 40°F (4°C) or below and unopened, up to six days. Once opened, use immediately.

Store dried egg products in a dark cool (below 70°F, 20°C) place, preferably in the refrigerator.

Reconstitute only the amount of dried eggs which will be used immediately. Sift before measuring.

After opening dried eggs, seal tightly for re-storage and keep below 50°F (10°C).

Keep specialty egg products refrigerated or frozen according to their requirements.

DUCK EGGS

Duck eggs are available in a few markets. They are somewhat larger than chicken eggs, have a tougher membrane, a thicker shell, a stronger flavor, and poor foaming qualities.

Fruits

FRESH FRUITS

Many varieties of fresh fruits are available all year round in almost every part of the United States because of excellent transportation and storage facilities.

Kinds of Fruits

Fruits may be classified as following:

BERRIES — Those commonly marketed are blackberries, blueberries, boysenberries, cranberries, currants, elderberries, gooseberries, grapes, raspberries and strawberries.

CITRUS — These are the grapefruits, kumquats, lemons, limes, mandarins, oranges, tangerines and tangelos.

DRUPES — This is the botanical name given to apricots, cherries, nectarines, peaches, plums and prunes; also known as stonefruits.

MELONS — These vine-grown fruits include cantaloupe, casaba, Crenshaw, honeydew, Persian and watermelon.

POMES — Fruits include apples, pears, prickly pears and quinces.

TROPICAL AND SEMI-TROPICAL FRUITS — There are many species of tropical and semi-tropical fruits but those that are marketed commonly throughout the United States are avocados, bananas, coconuts, dates, figs, guavas, mangoes, papayas, persimmons, pineapples and pomegranates. More exotic fruits are Asian pear, atemoya, breadfruit, canistel, carambola (star fruit), cherimoya (custard apple), feijoa, jaboticaba, longans, lychees, mamey, monstera, passion fruit (granadilla), quince, sapodilla, sapote, tamarinds and ugli fruit.

Grades

Grades of fresh fruits are established by the USDA's Agricultural Marketing Service (AMS) and used primarily in wholesale channels of distribution. They have been widely used by growers, shippers and car lot receivers for domestic and foreign shipment but have not been so extensively used in the retail trade as those for canned products which are packed in consumer-size containers. However, homemakers have made considerable use of U.S. grades in the purchase of such commodities as apples, grapefruit, oranges and peaches. These voluntary grades frequently are found on boxes of fresh fruit.

In the U.S., the principal factors used as standards for grades of fresh fruit are maturity; decay, if any; shipping quality; appearance; and waste caused by various defects. The U.S. No. 1 grade is designed to include a fairly good proportion of the commercial crop. Standards for some commodities provide a Fancy or Extra No.1 grade for use of packers of superior fruits for which a premium is obtained. Apples, for example, may be graded U.S. Extra Fancy, U.S. Fancy, U.S. No. 1, or combination of these grades. There are also lower U.S. grades for fresh fruits, such as No. 2, No. 1 Cookers, and Combination. Tropical fruits currently are not marketed under U.S. grades.

Sizes

Fruits sold in quantity are usually sold by weight or count rather than size. Medium sizes tend to be more desirable than very large, which often lack quality, or very small, which have little edible portion compared to wasted parts. At retail, many fruits that used to be sold by number may now be sold by weight. With the development in biotechnology, some fruits have been downsized to create miniatures, such as melons.

A Few Reminders

■ Apple variations for eating out of hand or in salads or fruit cups include Delicious, Gala, Golden Delicious, Jonathan, McIntosh, Spartans, Stayman and Winesap. The tart and slightly acid apples — Granny Smith, Gravenstein, Grimes Golden, Jonathan, and Newton — are excellent for pies and sauces. Firm-fleshed apples that hold shape well in baking include Northern Spy, Rhode Island Greening, Rome Beauty, Winesap, and York Imperial.

■ Cherries may be of the sweet variety for eating out of hand or they may be tart, sometimes called sour cherries, and used in cooking and baking. These are lighter red in color than the sweet cherries and have a softer flesh. Most of the commercial crop of tart cherries goes to processors.

■ Figs may be black, yellow or green. For eating fresh, the black figs are popular.

■ The European varieties of grapes include Cardinal (early bright red), Emperor (late deep red), and Ribier (late black), Thompson seedless (early green) and Tokay (late red). The American varieties include Catawba, Concord (blue-black), Delaware and Niagara. Varietal groups include: table, raisin, wine, juice and canning.

■ Grapefruit may be white- or pink-fleshed, with or without seeds.

■ Limes may be acid varieties grown in the U.S., called Tahiti and Mexican. Tahiti includes Bearss and Persian. Mexican group includes the Key lime of Florida with a leathery, thin rind with light lemon-yellow color of fruit, round to oval and small size.

- Of the melon family, the mature cantaloupe has no stem but a slight indentation at the stem end and a yellow to light green netting. Casaba melon is pumpkin-shaped and has no netting but does have shallow, irregular, lengthwise furrows. Honeydew melon is large, bluntly oval, and smooth. Persian melon resembles cantaloupe but is nearly round, has a finer netting and is similar in size to the honeydew. Santa Claus or Christmas melon looks like a small watermelon with the flesh of a honeydew. Crenshaw melon is oval-shaped with a deep golden rind and no netting.

- Orange varieties include Navel from California and Arizona; Valencia from California, Arizona, Florida and Texas; and mandarins. Mandarins include satsumas, tangerines and miscellaneous hybrids, such as Temple oranges from Florida, a cross between a tangerine and an orange. Murcott is a cross between a sweet orange and a mandarin. Tangelo is a hybrid of a tangerine or mandarin orange and a grapefruit or pomelo.

- Peach varieties are divided into freestone (Elberta, O'Henry and Redtop) and clingstone (Flavorcrest, June Lady, Red Haven and Springcrest). As the names imply, the flesh of the freestone peach separates readily from the pit, whereas the reverse is true of the clingstone. In general, freestones are preferred for eating fresh and for freezing. Both kinds may be canned, but the clingstone maintains the firmer shape.

- Bartlett pears, Forelle and Seckel are summer and early fall pears that are eaten fresh and are also used in canning. Fall and winter pear varieties include Bosc, D'Anjou, Comice and Winter Nellis. These keep well in cold storage.

- Pineapples are picked at the peak of ripeness and flavor; they do not ripen after harvest.

- Plums may be red, green or yellow. Prunes are a variety of freestone plums suitable for drying; they are purplish-black and smaller and more oval than other types of plums.

Storage and Use
- Store citrus fruits — except tangerines — in the refrigerator uncovered. Place tangerines in a plastic bag for refrigerator storage.

- Refrigerate ripe stonefruits uncovered and plan to use within three to five days.

- Store ripe melons in a plastic bag to protect other foods from the pungent melon odor and store in refrigerator for use within a week.

- Let bananas ripen at room temperature and then refrigerate. Cold temperatures darken the skins, but will not affect palatability.

- To ripen firm avocados, let them stand three to five days until softened; then refrigerate.

- To avoid the discoloration of pared apples,

peaches and avocado that occurs when the pared fruits are exposed to air, coat cut fruit with lemon juice or ascorbic acid.

■ To ripen cantaloupe, let stand at room temperature two to four days. Chill a few hours in refrigerator before serving.

■ Most tropical fruits will soften at room temperature, giving slightly to pressure when ripe. Ripe fruit needs to be refrigerated.

PROCESSED FRUITS

Many fruits are available in frozen, canned, dried and dehydrated forms. The number and kinds of processed foods available at the retail market are constantly increasing as new procedures and equipment are developed for processing foods of improved quality. Their convenience and availability all year round have added variety to menus particularly in winter.

Frozen and Canned Fruits

Standards of identity for most canned fruits as well as minimum standards of quality for many of the principal ones have been established by the U.S. Food and Drug Administration. Grade standards which also reflect factors of quality for many frozen and canned fruits have been developed by the U.S. Department of Agriculture. Canners, freezers and distributors often voluntarily use the grade designations on their labels. Grades reflect mainly differences in appearance. The factors most important in evaluating the quality of processed fruits are flavor, color, texture, uniformity of size and shape, ripeness, and absence of defects. The permissive grades established by industry for most processed fruits are A (fancy), B (choice) or C (standard). The terms in parentheses are those in common commercial usage for designating the quality of processed products.

Dried Fruits

Apples, apricots, blueberries, cherries, figs, peaches, prunes and raisins may be sun-dried, mechanically dehydrated, vacuum dried, foam-mat dried or explosively puffed. The moisture content of the dried fruits generally ranges from 15 to 25 percent. Quality levels or grades for most dried fruits are the same as for other fruits. The sizes of dried fruit — small, medium, large, extra large or jumbo — appear on retail packages.

Prunes are size graded according to the number per pound, with size grading varying somewhat with type — French, Italian, Imperials and/or Sugars.

When "sulfur dioxide" appears on the label of dried apples, apricots and peaches, the fruit may have been dipped in sodium bisulfite or treated with sulfur dioxide fumes to prevent darkening of color. The chemical is harmless and disappears in the steam when the fruits are cooked.

Fruit leathers are prepared by dehydrating a puree of selected fruit and sweetener. All dried fruits, including leathers, must be stored in airtight packaging to retain quality and avoid the addition of moisture.

FRUIT JUICES

Juice may be extracted from virtually any fruit

and may be purchased as full strength or concentrate to be reconstituted. In addition to fresh and frozen fruit juices, canned, frozen and powered fruit drinks are available. Fruit drinks are prepared from regular or synthetic fruits juices or from a combination of the two and contain natural or synthetic flavorings, sugar or non-sugar sweetener, color, usually ascorbic acid and preservatives. Nutritionally, fruit juices are a better choice than fruit drinks. The National Juice Products Association has adopted a voluntary policy to label dilute juice beverages for juice content as "contains ____% _____juice."

QUALITY GUIDE FOR FRUITS
Apples
WHAT TO LOOK FOR: Firm, well-colored fruit. Apples must be mature when picked to have good flavor, crisp texture and storing ability.

WHAT TO AVOID: Immature apples that lack color for the particular variety; also fruit with shriveled skin; overripe apples (indicated by a yielding to slight pressure on the skin and soft mealy flesh); and apples affected by freezing (indicated by internal breakdown and bruised areas). Scald on apples (irregularly shaped tan or brown areas) may not seriously affect the eating quality of the apple.

Apricots
WHAT TO LOOK FOR: Apricots that are plump and juicy looking and have a uniform, golden-orange color. Ripe apricots will yield to gentle pressure on the skin.

WHAT TO AVOID: Dull-looking, soft or mushy fruit, and very firm, pale yellow or greenish yellow fruit. These are indications of over-maturity or immaturity, respectively.

Avocados
WHAT TO LOOK FOR: For immediate use, slightly soft avocados which yield to a gentle pressure on the skin. For use in a few days, firm fruits that do not yield to the squeeze test. Leave them at room temperature to ripen. Irregular light brown markings are sometimes found on the outside skin. These markings have no effect on the flesh of the avocado.

WHAT TO AVOID: Avocados with dark sunken spots in irregular patches or cracked or broken surfaces. These are signs of decay.

Bananas
WHAT TO LOOK FOR: Bananas which are firm, bright in appearance and free from bruises or other injury. The stage of ripeness is indicated by the skin color; best eating quality has been reached when the solid yellow color is specked with brown. At this stage, the flesh is mellow and the flavor is fully developed. Bananas with green tips or with practically no yellow color have not developed their full flavor potential.

WHAT TO AVOID: Bruised fruit (which means rapid deterioration and waste); discolored skins (a sign of decay); a dull, grayish, aged appearance (showing that the bananas have been exposed to cold and will not ripen properly). Occasionally, the skin may be entirely brown and yet the flesh will still be in prime condition. Flavor will be fully developed.

Blueberries

WHAT TO LOOK FOR: A dark blue color with a silvery bloom which is a natural, protective waxy coating; blueberries that are plump, firm, uniform, dry and free from stems or leaves.

Cantaloupes (Muskmelons) and Persian Melons

WHAT TO LOOK FOR: Three major signs of full maturity:

1. The stem should be gone, leaving a smooth, symmetrical, shallow basin called a "full-slip." If all or part of the stem base remains or if the stem scar is jagged or torn, the melon is probably not fully matured.
2. The netting, or veining, should be thick, coarse and corky and should stand out in bold relief over some part of the surface.
3. The skin color (ground color) between the netting should have changed from green to a yellowish buff, yellowish gray or pale yellow.

Look for signs of ripeness, for a cantaloupe may be mature, but not ripe. A ripe cantaloupe will have a yellowish cast to the rind, have a pleasant cantaloupe odor when held to the nose, and will yield slightly to light thumb pressure on the blossom end of the melon.

WHAT TO AVOID: Over-ripeness, shown by a pronounced yellow rind color, a softening over the entire rind, and soft, watery and insipid flesh. Small bruises normally will not hurt the fruit, but large bruised areas should be avoided since they generally cause soft, water-soaked areas underneath the rind. Mold growth on the cantaloupe — particularly in the stem scar with wet tissue under the mold — indicates decay.

Casaba

WHAT TO LOOK FOR: Ripe melons with a gold yellow rind color and a slight softening at the blossom end. Casabas have no odor or aroma.

WHAT TO AVOID: Decayed melons, shown by dark, sunken water-soaked spots.

Cherries

WHAT TO LOOK FOR: A very dark color, the most important indication of good flavor and maturity in sweet cherries. Bing, Black Tartarian, Chapman, Republican and Schmidt varieties should range from deep maroon to mahogany red to black, for richest flavor. Lambert cherries should be dark red. Good cherries have bright, glossy, plump-looking surfaces and fresh looking stems.

WHAT TO AVOID: Over-mature cherries lacking in flavor, indicated by shriveling, dried stems, and a generally dull appearance. Decay is fairly common at times on sweet cherries, but because of the normal dark color, decayed areas are often inconspicuous. Soft, leaking fruit, brown discoloration, and mold growth are indications of decay.

Cranberries

WHAT TO LOOK FOR: Plump, firm berries with a lustrous color for the best quality. Duller varieties should at least have some red color. Occasional soft, spongy, or leaky berries should be sorted out before cooking, because they may produce an off-flavor.

Crenshaw

WHAT TO LOOK FOR: A deep golden yellow rind, sometimes with small areas of a lighter shade of yellow; a surface that yields slightly to moderate pressure of the thumb, particularly at the blossom end; a pleasant aroma.

WHAT TO AVOID: Slightly sunken, water-soaked areas on the rind (a sign of decay, which spreads quickly through the melon).

Grapefruit

WHAT TO LOOK FOR: Firm, well-shaped fruits — heavy for their size — are usually the best eating. Thin-skinned fruits have more juice than coarse-skinned ones. If a grapefruit is pointed at the stem end, it is likely to be thick-skinned. Rough, ridged or wrinkled skin can also be an indication of thick skin and lack of juice.

Grapefruit often has skin defects — such as scale, scars, thorn scratches, or discoloration — which usually do not affect the eating quality.

WHAT TO AVOID: Soft, discolored areas on the peel at the stem end; water-soaked areas; loss of bright color; and soft and tender peel that breaks easily with finger pressure. These are all symptoms of decay, which has an objectionable effect on flavor.

Grapes

WHAT TO LOOK FOR: Well-colored, plump grapes that are firmly attached to the stem. White or green grapes are sweetest when the color has a yellowish cast or straw color, with a tinge of amber. Red varieties are better when a good red predominates on all or most of the berries. Bunches are more likely to hold together if the stems are green and pliable. Grapes will not improve in sweetness, quality or color after picking.

WHAT TO AVOID: Soft or wrinkled grapes (showing effects of freezing or drying), grapes with bleached areas around the stem end (indicating injury and poor quality), and grapes leaking brownish fluid (a sign of decay).

Honeyball and Honeydew

WHAT TO LOOK FOR: Maturity, shown by a soft, velvety feel, and for ripeness, shown by a slight softening at the blossom end, a faint pleasant fruit aroma, and a yellowish white to cream rind color.

WHAT TO AVOID: Melons with a dead-white or greenish-white color and hard, smooth feel (which are signs of immaturity), large, water-soaked bruised areas (sign of injury), and cuts or punctures through the rind (which usually lead to decay). Small, superficial, sunken spots do not damage the melon for immediate use but large decayed spots will.

Kiwifruit

WHAT TO LOOK FOR: Kiwifruit is ripe when it yields to gentle pressure. To ripen, place hard fruit in a plastic bag with an apple or banana for one to two days at room temperature.

WHAT TO AVOID: Soft dark areas, indentations, broken skin, uneven color.

Lemons

WHAT TO LOOK FOR: Lemons with a rich yellow color, reasonably smooth-textured skin with a slight gloss, and those which are firm and heavy. A pale or greenish yellow color means very fresh fruit with slightly higher acidity. Coarse or rough skin texture is a sign of thick skin and not much flesh.

WHAT TO AVOID: Lemons with a darker yellow or dull color, or with hardening or shriveling of the skin (sign of age) and those with soft spots, mold on the surface, and punctures of the skin (sign of decay).

Limes

WHAT TO LOOK FOR: Limes with glossy skin and heavy weight for the size.

WHAT TO AVOID: Limes with full, dry skin (a sign of aging and loss of acid flavor), and those showing evidence of decay (soft spots, mold and skin punctures).

Nectarines

WHAT TO LOOK FOR: Rich color and plumpness and a slight softening along the "seam" of the nectarine. Most varieties have an orange-yellow color (ground color) between the red areas, but some varieties have a greenish ground color. Bright-looking fruits which are firm to moderately hard will probably ripen normally within two to three days at room temperature.

WHAT TO AVOID: Hard, dull fruits or slightly shriveled fruits (which may be immature — picked too soon — and of poor eating quality), and soft to overripe fruits or those with cracked or punctured skin or other signs of decay. Russeting or staining of the skin may affect the appearance but not detract from the internal quality of the nectarine.

Oranges

WHAT TO LOOK FOR: Firm and heavy oranges with fresh, bright-looking skin which is reasonably smooth for the variety.

WHAT TO AVOID: Lightweight oranges, which are likely to lack flesh content and juice. Very rough skin texture indicates abnormally thick skin and less flesh. Dull, dry skin and spongy texture indicate aging and deteriorated eating quality. Also avoid decay — shown by cuts or skin punctures, soft spots on the surface, and discolored, weakened areas of skin around the stem end or button.

Peaches

WHAT TO LOOK FOR: Peaches which are fairly firm or becoming a trifle soft. The skin color between the red areas (ground color) should be yellow or at least creamy with a peachy fragrance.

WHAT TO AVOID: Very firm or hard peaches with a distinctly green ground color, which are probable immature and will not ripen properly. Also avoid very soft fruits, which are overripe. Do not buy peaches with large flattened bruises (they will have areas of discolored flesh underneath) or peaches with any sign of decay. Decay starts as a pale tan spot which expands in a circle and gradually turn darker in color.

Pears

WHAT TO LOOK FOR: Firm pears of all varieties. The color depends on variety. For Bartletts, look for a pale yellow to rich yellow color; Bosc — greenish yellow to brownish yellow (the brown cast is caused by skin russeting, a characteristic of the Bosc pear); D'Anjou or Comice — light green to yellowish green; Winter Nellis — medium to light green.

Pears which are hard when purchased will probably ripen if kept at room temperature, but it is wise to select pears that have already begun to soften — to be reasonably sure that they will ripen satisfactorily.

WHAT TO AVOID: Wilted or shriveled pears with dull-appearing skin and slight weakening of the flesh near the stem, which indicates immaturity. These pears will not ripen. Also avoid spots on the sides or blossom ends of the pear, which means that corky tissue may be underneath.

Pineapples

WHAT TO LOOK FOR: The proper color, the fragrant pineapple odor, a very slight separation of the eyes or pips, and the ease with which the "spikes" or leaves can be pulled out from the top. Pineapples are usually dark green in mature hard stage. As the more popular varieties (such as Red Spanish and Smooth Cayenne) ripen, the green color fades and orange and yellow take its place. When full ripe, the pineapples are golden yellow, orange yellow, or reddish brown — depending on the variety, although one seldom-seen pineapple (the Sugar Loaf) remains green even when ripe. Also look for maturity, shown by plump glossy eyes or pips, firmness, a lively color, and fruits which are heavy for their size.

WHAT TO AVOID: Pineapples with sunken or slightly pointed pips, dull yellowish-green color, and dried appearance (all signs of immaturity). Also avoid bruised fruit (shown by discolored or soft spots), which are susceptible to decay. Other signs of decay (which spreads rapidly through the fruit) are: traces of mold, unpleasant odor, and eyes which turn watery and darken in color.

Plums and Prunes

WHAT TO LOOK FOR: Plums and prunes with a good color for the variety, in a fairly firm to slightly soft stage of ripeness.

WHAT TO AVOID: Fruits with skin breaks, punctures or brownish discoloration. Also avoid immature fruits (relatively hard, poorly colored, very tart, sometimes shriveled) and over-mature fruits (excessively soft, possibly leaking or decaying).

Raspberries, Boysenberries, Gooseberries, Loganberries

WHAT TO LOOK FOR: A bright, clean appearance and a uniform good color for the species. The individual small cells making up the berry should be plump and tender but not mushy. Look for berries that are fully ripened and with no attached stem caps.

WHAT TO AVOID: Leaky and moldy berries. Also note wet or stained spots on wood or fiber containers; these are possible signs of poor quality or spoiled berries.

Strawberries

WHAT TO LOOK FOR: Berries with a full red color and a bright luster, firm flesh, and the cap stem still attached. The berries should be dry and clean; usually medium to small strawberries have better eating qualities than do the larger berries.

WHAT TO AVOID: Berries with large uncolored areas or with large seedy areas (poor in flavor and texture), a dull shrunken appearance or softness (sign of decay), or those with mold, which can spread rapidly from one berry to another.

Tangerines

WHAT TO LOOK FOR: Deep yellow or orange color and a bright luster are the best sign of fresh, mature, good-flavored tangerines. Because of the typically loose nature of the tangerine skin, they will frequently not feel firm to the touch.

WHAT TO AVOID: Very pale yellow or greenish fruits, likely to be lacking in flavor (although small green areas on otherwise high-colored fruits are not bad) and tangerines with cut or punctured skins or very soft spots (all signs of decay, which spreads rapidly).

Watermelon

WHAT TO LOOK FOR: In cut melons, firm, juicy flesh with good red color, free of white streaks; seeds which are dark brown or black. In whole melons, a relatively smooth surface, neither shiny nor dull, ends that are rounded and filled out; creamy colored underside.

WHAT TO AVOID: Melons with pale-colored flesh, and white steaks or "white heart," whitish seeds (indicating immaturity). Dry, mealy flesh or watery, stringy flesh are signs of over-maturity or aging after harvest.

Vegetables

FRESH VEGETABLES

Fresh vegetables are available throughout the year due to modern transportation and storage. U.S. markets now sell fresh vegetables grown around the world. Vegetables are classified according to the portion of the plant that is eaten. The following classification is a general list; many more types and varieties are available worldwide.

BULBS: onions (all varieties), garlic, leeks, and shallots

FLOWERS AND FRUITS: Artichoke, broccoli, cauliflower, chayote, cucumber, eggplant, fennel, nopales, okra, pepper, pumpkin, squash, sweet corn, tomato and water chestnuts

LEAVES AND STEMS: Asparagus, brussels sprouts, cabbage, celery, Chinese cabbage, chives, greens, kale, kohlrabi, lettuce, parsley, seaweed, spinach and watercress

LEGUMES: U.S.D.A. describes legumes as the mature, dry seeds of the family Fabaceae or Leguminosae. The list includes: Adzuki, common beans, broadbean (Vicia faba), carob, chickpeas, cowpeas, hyacinth beans (dahl), lentils, lima beans, lupins, mothbeans, mung beans, mungo beans, peas, peanuts, pigeon peas, soybeans, and winged beans.

ROOTS: Beet, carrot, cassava (manioc or tapioca), celeriac, daikon, jicama, kohlrabi, poi (taro), parsnip, radish, rutabaga, salsify, sweet potato and turnip

TUBERS: Jerusalem artichoke, Irish potato, and taro

Crucifers

Bamboo shoots, mushrooms and truffles also are considered to be vegetables. Of special interest nutritionally are the crucifers. Crucifers include Bok choy, broccoli, Brussels sprouts, cabbage, cauliflower, collards, kale, kohlrabi, mustard greens, rutabagas, turnips and their greens.

Grades for Fresh Vegetables

U.S. grading standards for fresh vegetables are voluntary; the principal factors affecting the grade are maturity, decay, shipping quality, appearance and waste caused by various defects. The U.S. No. 1 grade is designed to include a fairly good proportion of the commercial crop. Standards for some commodities provide a fancy grade used by packers of superior vegetables for which a premium is obtained. U.S. No. 1 is the highest grade for most vegetables. Other fresh vegetable grades (No. 2 or Combination) are not likely to appear in retail stores.

CANNED AND FROZEN VEGETABLES

Vegetables may be frozen or canned separately or in combination with other vegetables. The different forms include whole, sliced, diced, mashed, puree, juice, and soup.

Grades for Canned and Frozen Vegetables

The Standards of Quality and Fill as outlined by the FDA are minimal, basic requirements which serve as a pattern for good processing techniques for the commercial food processor. FDA Standards of Identity tell us what a product is.

The U.S. Grade Standards developed by the USDA are essentially market classifications of quality. Processors are not required by law to include the grade on the label. The U.S. grade names are: U.S. Grade A or Fancy, U.S. Grade B or Extra-Standard, and U.S. Grade C or Standard. The four quality characteristics used to determine the grade are: color, uniformity of size, texture, and absence of defects. Additional grading factors which are used include: consistency, clearness of liquid, size and symmetry, drain weight, wholeness and flavor.

Storage of Canned and Frozen Vegetables

Store unopened canned vegetables in a cool, dry place. For best quality, use canned vegetables within a year of purchase. Vegetables lose quality and some nutrients if stored too long, but remain indefinitely safe to eat if the seal is not broken and the can is not bulging.

Frozen vegetables should be stored at 0°F (-18°C) or lower to retain quality and nutritive value for 8 to 12 months. Before buying large quantities of frozen vegetables check the freezer or freezing compartment temperature. If the temperature is above 0°F (-18°C), plan to use frozen vegetables within a few days for best quality.

DRIED AND FREEZE-DRIED VEGETABLES

Dried and freeze-dried vegetables are readily available in markets, but health food and sporting goods sections in large stores may carry a wide selection of dried and freeze-dried foods.

Storage of Dried Vegetables

Optimal storage conditions for dried foods are:
■ storage temperature below 60°F
■ cool, dry, and dark storage area, and
■ airtight and moisture-proof packaging.

For best quality and nutritional value, dried foods should be used within one year of purchase.

Substituting Dried Foods for Fresh

Substitute reconstituted vegetable powders and flakes for finely chopped fresh vegetables in recipes. If you do not reconstitute the powders or flakes before adding to the recipe ingredients, add a small amount of liquid to the recipe. Allow 1/4 cup (60 ml) liquid for each tablespoon of powder and each 1 1/2 tablespoons (23 ml) of flakes.

Substitute 1 tablespoon (15 ml) vegetable powder or 1 1/2 tablespoons vegetable flakes or 2 tablespoons (30 ml) dried pieces for 4 tablespoons (60 ml) chopped fresh vegetables.

QUALITY GUIDE FOR VEGETABLES

Artichokes

WHAT TO LOOK FOR: Plump, globular artichokes that are heavy in relation to size, and compact with thick, green, fresh looking leaf scales. Size is not important in relation to quality.

WHAT TO AVOID: Artichokes with large areas of brown on the scales and with spreading scales (a sign of age, indicating drying and toughening of the edible portions), grayish black discoloration (caused by bruises), mold growth on the scales, and worm injury.

Asparagus

WHAT TO LOOK FOR: Closed, compact tips, smooth, round spears, and a fresh appearance. A rich green color should cover most of the spear. Stalks should be tender almost as far down as the green extends.

WHAT TO AVOID: Tips that are open and spread out, moldy or decayed tips, or ribbed spears (up and down ridges), or spears that are not rounded. These are signs of aging and indicate tough asparagus and poor flavor. Also avoid excessively sandy asparagus because sand grains can lodge beneath the scales and are difficult to wash out.

Bean (Snap Beans)

WHAT TO LOOK FOR: A fresh, bright appearance with good color for the variety. Get young, tender beans with pods in firm crisp condition.

WHAT TO AVOID: Wilted or flabby bean pods, serious blemishes, and decay. Thick, tough, fibrous pods indicate over-maturity.

Beets

WHAT TO LOOK FOR: Beets that are a rich, deep red color, firm, round and smooth over most of the surface and have a slender tap root (the large main root). If beets are bunched, judge their freshness by the condition of the tops. Badly wilted or decayed tops indicate a lack of freshness, but the roots may be satisfactory if they are firm.

WHAT TO AVOID: Elongated beets with round, scaly areas around the top surface; these will be tough, fibrous and strong flavored. Also avoid wilted, flabby beets-which have been exposed to the air too long.

Broccoli

WHAT TO LOOK FOR: A firm, compact cluster of small flower buds, with none opened enough to show the bright yellow flower. Bud clusters should be dark green or sage green or even green with a decidedly purplish cast. Stems should not be too thick or tough.

WHAT TO AVOID: Broccoli with spread bud clusters, enlarged or open buds, yellowish green color or wilted condition - signs of over-maturity and overlong display. Also avoid broccoli with soft, slippery, water soaked spots on the bud cluster. These are signs of decay.

Brussels Sprouts

WHAT TO LOOK FOR: A fresh, bright green color, tight fitting outer leaves, firm body, and freedom from blemishes.

WHAT TO AVOID: Brussels sprouts with yellow or yellowish green leaves or leaves that are loose, soft, or wilted. Small holes or ragged leaves may indicate worm injury.

Cabbage

Cabbage may be red; green with smooth leaves; or green with crinkly leaves — a variety known as Savoy.

WHAT TO LOOK FOR: Firm or hard heads of cabbage that are heavy for their size. Outer leaves should be a good green or red color (depending on type), reasonably fresh, and free from serious blemishes. The outer leaves (called "wrapper" leaves) fit loosely on the head and are usually discarded, but too many loose wrapper leaves on a head cause extra waste. With Savoy cabbage, look for crumpled leaves with developed round heads of dark green color.

Some early crop cabbage may be soft or only fairly firm but is suitable for immediate use if the leaves are fresh and crisp. Cabbage that has been in storage is usually trimmed of all outer leaves and lacks color but is satisfactory if not wilted.

WHAT TO AVOID: New cabbage with wilted or decayed outer leaves or with leaves turning yellow. Worm-eaten outer leaves often indicate that the worm injury penetrates into the head.

Storage cabbage with outer leaves badly discolored, dried or decayed probably is over-aged. Separation of the stems of leaves from the central stem at the base of the head also indicates overage.

Carrots

WHAT TO LOOK FOR: Carrots which are well-formed, smooth, well colored and firm.

WHAT TO AVOID: Roots with large green sunburned areas at the top (which must be trimmed) and roots which are flabby from wilting or show spots of soft decay.

Cauliflower

WHAT TO LOOK FOR: White to creamy compact solid and clean curds (head). A slightly granular texture of the curd will not hurt the eating quality if the surface is compact. Ignore small green leaflets extending through the curd. If jacket leaves are attached, a green color is a sign of freshness.

WHAT TO AVOID: A spreading of the curd — a sign of aging or over-maturity. Also avoid wilting or discolored spots on the curd. A smudgy or speckled appearance of the curd is a sign of insect injury, mold growth or decay and should be avoided.

Celery

WHAT TO LOOK FOR: Freshness and crispness: the stalk should have a solid, rigid feel, and leaflets should be fresh or only slightly wilted. Also look for a glossy surface, light or medium green stalks and green leaflets.

WHAT TO AVOID: Wilted celery with flabby upper branches or leaf stems. Celery with pithy, hollow, or discolored centers in the branches. Celery with internal discoloration will show some gray or brown on the inside surface of the larger branches near the base of the stock. Avoid celery with "blackheart," a brown or black discoloration of the small center branches; insect injury in the center branches or the insides of outer branches; long, thick seedstem in place of the usually small, tender heart branches.

Chard (See Greens.)

Chicory, Endive, Escarole

WHAT TO LOOK FOR: Freshness, crispness and tenderness: look for a good green color of the outer leaves (except for Witloof or Belgian endive, the compact, cigar-shaped creamy white endive grown in complete darkness).

WHAT TO AVOID: Plants with leaves which have brownish or yellowish discoloration or which have insect injury.

Chinese Cabbage

WHAT TO LOOK FOR: Fresh, crisp, green plants that are free from blemishes or decay.

WHAT TO AVOID: Wilted or yellowed plants.

Collards (See Greens.)

Corn

WHAT TO LOOK FOR: Fresh, succulent husks with good green color, silk ends that are free from decay or worm injury, and stem ends (opposite from the silk) that are not too discolored or dried. Select ears that are well covered with plump, not too mature kernels.

WHAT TO AVOID: Ears with undeveloped kernels which lack yellow color (in yellow corn), ears with very large kernels, and ears with dark yellow kernels with depressed areas on the outer surface. Also avoid ears of corn with yellowed, wilted, or dried husks, or discolored and dried-out stem ends.

Cucumbers

WHAT TO LOOK FOR: Cucumbers with good green color which are firm over their entire length. They should be well shaped and well developed, but should not be too large in diameter. Good cucumbers typically have small lumps on their surfaces. They may also have some white or greenish white color and still be of top quality.

WHAT TO AVOID: Overgrown cucumbers which are large in diameter and have a dull color, turning yellowish. Also avoid cucumbers with withered or shriveled ends — signs of toughness and bitter flavor.

Eggplant

WHAT TO LOOK FOR: Firm, heavy, smooth and uniformly dark purple eggplants.

WHAT TO AVOID: Those which are poorly colored, soft, shriveled, cut or which show decay in the form of irregular dark brown spots.

Endive, Escarole (See Chicory.)

Greens

WHAT TO LOOK FOR: Leaves that are fresh, young, tender, free from blemishes and which have a good, healthy green color. Beet tops and ruby chard show reddish color.

WHAT TO AVOID: Leaves with coarse, fibrous stems, yellowish green color, softness (a sign of decay) or a wilted condition. Also avoid greens with evidence of insects - especially aphids - which are sometimes hard to see and equally hard to wash away.

Kale (See Greens.)

Lettuce

WHAT TO LOOK FOR: Iceberg and Romaine lettuce leaves should be crisp. Other lettuce types will have a softer texture, but leaves should not be wilted. Look for a good, bright color, medium to light green in most varieties.

WHAT TO AVOID: Heads of iceberg type which are very hard and which lack green color (signs of over-maturity). Such heads sometimes develop discoloration in the center of the leaves (the "mid-ribs"), and may have a less attractive flavor. Also avoid heads with irregular shapes and hard bumps on top, which indicate the presence of overgrown central stems.

Check the lettuce for tip burn, a tan or brown area (dead tissue) around the margins of the leaves. Slight discoloration of the outer or wrapper leaves usually will not hurt the quality of the lettuce, but serious discoloration or soft decay definitely should be avoided.

Mushrooms

WHAT TO LOOK FOR: Young mushrooms that are small to medium in size. Caps should be either closed around the stem or moderately open with pink or light tan gills. The surface of the cap should be white or creamy or from some producing areas light brown.

WHAT TO AVOID: Overripe mushrooms (shown by wide open caps and dark, discolored gills underneath) and those with pitted or seriously discolored caps.

Okra

WHAT TO LOOK FOR: Tender pods (the tips will bend with very slight pressure) under 4 1/2 inches (11 cm) long. They should have a bright green color and be free from blemishes.

WHAT TO AVOID: Tough, fibrous pods, indicated by tips which are stiff and resist bending, or by a very hard body of the pod, or by pale, faded green color.

Onions (Dry onions)

WHAT TO LOOK FOR: Hard or firm onions which are dry and have small necks. They should be covered with papery outer scales and reasonably free from green sunburn spots and other blemishes.

WHAT TO AVOID: Onions with wet or very soft necks, which usually are immature or affected by decay. Also avoid onions with thick, hollow, woody centers in the neck or with fresh sprouts or green sunburn spots.

Onions (Green), Shallots, Scallions, Leeks

WHAT TO LOOK FOR: Crisp, tender bunches with fresh green tops. Choose those with 2-3 inches (5-7 cm) of white above a slightly bulbed root end.

WHAT TO AVOID: Yellowing, wilted, discolored, or decayed tops (indicating flabby, tough or fibrous condition of the edible portions). Bruised tops will not affect the eating quality of the bulbs if the tops are removed.

Parsnips

WHAT TO LOOK FOR: Parsnips of small or medium width that are well formed, smooth, firm, and free from serious blemishes or decay.

WHAT TO AVOID: Large, coarse roots (which probably have woody, fibrous, or pithy centers), and badly wilted and flabby roots (which will be tough when cooked).

Peas

WHAT TO LOOK FOR: Young, bright-green, angular pods, well filled with well-developed peas that snap readily.

WHAT TO AVOID: Yellow or whitish color indicates overmature and tough product. Mildew, swollen or speckled pods indicate poor quality.

Peppers (Sweet Green and Red)

WHAT TO LOOK FOR: Medium to dark green color (or bright red), glossy sheen, relatively heavy weight, and firm walls or sides.

WHAT TO AVOID: Peppers with very thin walls (shown by light weight and flimsy sides), punctures through the walls, and peppers with soft watery spots on the sides (evidence of decay).

Potatoes

WHAT TO LOOK FOR: In new potatoes — well shaped, firm potatoes that are free from blemishes and sunburn (a green discoloration under the skin). Some amount of skinned surface is normal, but potatoes with large skinned and discolored areas are undesirable. General all-purpose and baking potatoes — reasonably smooth, well shaped firm potatoes free from blemishes, sunburn, and decay. These potatoes should be free from skinned surfaces.

WHAT TO AVOID: Potatoes with large cuts or bruises (they will mean waste in peeling), those with a green color (probably caused by sunburn or exposure to light in store), and potatoes showing any signs of decay. Also avoid sprouted or shriveled potatoes.

Radishes

WHAT TO LOOK FOR: Medium size radishes (3/4 to 1 1/8 inches (2 to 3 cm) in diameter) that are plump, round, firm, and of a good red color.

WHAT TO AVOID: Very large or flabby radishes (likely to have pithy centers). Also avoid radishes with yellow or decayed tops.

Rhubarb

WHAT TO LOOK FOR: Fresh, firm rhubarb stems with a bright, glossy appearance. Stems should have a large amount of pink or red color, although many good quality stems will be predominantly light green. Be sure the stem is tender and not fibrous.

WHAT TO AVOID: Either very slender or extremely thick stems, which are likely to be tough; also avoid wilted or flabby rhubarb.

Rutabagas (See Turnips.)

Spinach (See Greens.)

Squash (Summer)

WHAT TO LOOK FOR: Squash that is tender but firm, well formed and developed, fairly heavy in relation to size and fresh appearing. The skin of a tender squash is glossy instead of dull, and it is neither hard nor tough. Seeds are soft and fully edible.

WHAT TO AVOID: Overmature squash, which will have a dull appearance and a hard, tough surface. Such squash usually have enlarged seeds and dry stringy flesh.

Squash (Fall and Winter)

WHAT TO LOOK FOR: Full maturity, indicated by a hard, tough rind. Also look for squash that is heavy for its size (meaning a thick wall and more edible flesh).

WHAT TO AVOID: Squash with cuts, punctures, sunken or moldy spots on the rind — all indications of decay. A tender rind indicates immaturity which is a sign of poor eating quality in winter squash varieties.

Sweet Potatoes

WHAT TO LOOK FOR: Well shaped firm sweet potatoes with smooth, bright, uniformly colored skins, free from signs of decay. Because they are more perishable than Irish potatoes, extra care should be used in selecting sweet potatoes.

WHAT TO AVOID: Sweet potatoes with worm holes, cuts, grub injury, or any other defects which penetrate the skin; this causes waste and can readily lead to decay. Even when the decayed portion is cut away, the remainder of the potato flesh which looks normal may have a bad taste.

Decay is the worst problem with sweet potatoes and is of three types: wet, soft decay; dry firm decay which begins at the end of the potato, making it discolored and shriveled; and dry rot in the form of sunken, discolored areas on the sides of the potato.

Tomatoes

WHAT TO LOOK FOR: Tomatoes which are well formed, smooth, well-ripened and reasonably free from blemishes. For fully ripe fruit, look for an overall rich red color and a slight softness. Softness is easily detected by gentle handling. For tomatoes slightly less than fully ripe, look for firm texture and color ranging from pink to light red.

WHAT TO AVOID: Overripe and bruised tomatoes (they are both soft and watery) and tomatoes with sunburn (green or yellow areas near the stem scar) and growth cracks (deep cracks around the stem scar). Also avoid decayed tomatoes which will have soft, water-soaked spots. depressed areas, or surface mold.

Turnips (including Rutabagas)

WHAT TO LOOK FOR — TURNIPS: small or medium size, smooth, fairly round, and firm vegetables. If sold in bunches, the tops should be fresh and should have a good green color.

WHAT TO AVOID: Large turnips with too many leaf scars around the top and with flabby, soft or obvious fibrous roots.

WHAT TO LOOK FOR — RUTABAGAS: heavy weight for their size, generally smooth, round or moderately elongated shape. Good quality rutabagas should also be firm to the touch.

WHAT TO AVOID: Rutabagas with hard-texture, pithy, skin punctures, deep cuts, or decay.

Watercress

WHAT TO LOOK FOR: Watercress that is fresh, crisp and bright-green color with rather long stems.

WHAT TO AVOID: Bunches with yellow, wilted, bruised or decayed leaves.

COOKING METHODS
Fresh Vegetables

Vegetables can be cooked by boiling, baking, steaming, stir-frying or steaming under pressure. The length of time required for a given vegetable to cook by any method cannot be stated exactly, because cooking time differs with the variety and maturity of each vegetable, the period and the temperature at which the vegetable was held after it was harvested, and the size of the pieces into which it was cut. Each vegetable should be cooked for the shortest time necessary to give a palatable product. See timetable for cooking fresh vegetables, Table 8.1.

Frozen Vegetables

The length of time required for cooking (boiling) frozen vegetables is usually less than that required for fresh vegetables. This is because the blanching and freezing of vegetables tenderize them to some degree. Frozen vegetables should be brought quickly to a boil, then boiled gently until just tender. Because cooking time varies with different vegetables, package directions are the best guide for proper cooking of frozen vegetables.

Use of Pressure Saucepan

Manufacturer's directions for use of a pressure saucepan are the best guide because they are based on that specific model. Vegetables are usually cooked at 15 pounds (103.4 kPa) pressure. One note of caution: At the end of the cooking time, the pressure saucepan should be placed in cold water or under running cold water to reduce the pressure quickly and stop the cooking.

Use of Microwave

Manufacture's directions for use with a microwave are the best guide since they are based on that specific model. The Timetable for Cooking Vegetables suggests approximately a three-minute resting time following the recommended cooking time. Food continues to cook during this period.

STORAGE AND USE

■ Store the following vegetables in refrigerator crisper or in a plastic bag in refrigerator: asparagus, beets, broccoli, Brussels sprouts, beet greens, cabbage, carrots, cauliflower, celery, chard, collard greens, cucumber, green onions, lettuce, mushrooms, mustard greens, okra, peppers, spinach, summer squash, and turnip greens.

■ Store sweet corn in husks, uncovered in refrigerator.

■ Store ripe tomatoes, uncovered, in the refrigerator. Keep unripe tomatoes at room temperature, but away from direct sunlight until they ripen.

■ Store dry onions in loosely woven or open mesh containers at room temperature or slightly cooler temperatures.

■ Store potatoes in a dark, dry, well ventilated place at temperatures between 45° and 50°F (7° and 10°C). Potatoes stored at room temperature should be used within a week to prevent greening or sprouting and shriveling.

■ Store these vegetables at 60°F (15°C); hard rind squashes, eggplant, rutabagas, and sweet potatoes. Do not refrigerate; temperatures below 50°F (10°C) may cause chilling injury. If these vegetables must be kept at room temperature, plan to use them within a week.

■ Use these vegetables within one or two days, asparagus, beet greens, broccoli,

Brussels sprouts, chard, collard greens, green peas, green onions, kale, lettuce and other salad greens, fresh lima beans, mushrooms, mustard greens, spinach, sweet corn and turnip greens.

■ Use these vegetables within three to five days: cauliflower, celery, cucumbers, green beans (snap), okra, peppers and

summer squash.

■ Use these vegetables within one or two weeks: beets, cabbage, carrots, parsnips and radishes.

If refrigerator crisper is not kept two-thirds full, put vegetables in plastic bags before storing them in the crisper.

Table 8.1

FRESH VEGETABLES COOKING TIMETABLE

VEGETABLE	BOILING*	STEAMING*	MICROWAVE (700 Watts)	BAKING
Artichokes				
French or globe, whole	35 - 45 minutes		High 4 to 5 minutes 1 medium†	
Jerusalem whole	25 - 35 minutes	35 minutes		30 to 60 minutes
Asparagus				
Whole or butts	10 - 20 minutes	12 - 30 minutes	Spears — High 6-9	
Tips	5 - 15 minutes	7 - 14 minutes	min./lb 500g Cuts — High 5-7 min,†	
Beans				
Lima/green	25 - 30 minutes	25 - 35 minutes	Green beans —	
Soy, green	20 - 30 minutes	25 - 35 minutes	High 6-10 min per	
Green, whole			1/2 lb/250 g	
or 1" pieces	15 - 30 minutes	20 - 35 minutes		
French	10 - 20 minutes	15 - 25 minutes	High 5-7 min. per lb/500 g†	
Broccoli				
Heavy stalk, split	10 - 15 minutes	15 - 20 minutes	Spears — High 8 - 12 min. per 1 1/2 lb/500-750 g† Pieces — High 8 to 10 min. per 1 - 1 1/2 lb/500-750 g†	
Brussel sprouts				
Whole	10 - 20 minutes	15 - 20 minutes	High 4 - 8 min. per lb. (4 cups)/500 g (1 l) †	

VEGETABLES	BOILING*	STEAMING*	MICROWAVE (700 Watts)	BAKING
Cabbage				
Green				
quartered	10 - 15 minutes	15 minutes	Green, red or savory wedges — High 7 1/2 - 13 1/2 min. per lb/500 g†	
shredded	3 - 10 minutes	8 - 12 minutes	7 1/2-13 1/2 min. per lb./500 g	
Red				
shredded	8 - 12 minutes	10 - 15 minutes	7 - 13 min.per lb./ 500 g†	
Carrots				
Young				
whole	15 - 20 minutes	20 - 30 minutes	High 6 - 8 min. per	35 - 40 minutes
sliced	10 - 20 minutes	15 - 25 minutes	12 oz./340 g†	30 - 40 minutes
Mature			Cut (2") or 10-12	60 minutes
whole	20 - 30 minutes	40 - 50 minutes	med. High 6-8 minutes	
sliced	15 - 25 minutes	25 - 30 minutes	Slices (1/4") — High 4-7 min. High 7-8 min. per lb./500 g†	
Cauliflower				
Whole	15 - 25 minutes	25 - 30 minutes	High 5 1/2 - 7 1/2 min. per lb./500 g†	
Flowerets	8 - 15 minutes	10 - 20 minutes	High 4 - 7 min. per lb./500 g†	
Celery				
Diced	15 - 18 minutes	25 - 30 minutes	Slices (1/4") High 5 - 8 min. per lb./500 g†	
Chard				
Swiss	10 - 20 minutes	15 - 25 minutes	High 5 1/2 - 6 1/2 min. per lb./500 g†	
Collards	10 - 20 minutes		High 5 1/2 - 6 1/2 min. per lb./500 g†	

(continued on the next page)

* For altitude cookery, increase cooking time 4 - 11% at 5,000 feet (1524 m); 20 - 25% at 7,200 feet (2194 m); and 55 - 66% at 10,000 feet (3048 m) and more water added.

† Rest covered 3 minutes

Vegetables ■ 141

FRESH VEGETABLES COOKING TIMETABLE (continued)

VEGETABLE	BOILING*	STEAMING*	MICROWAVE (700 Watts)	BAKING
Corn				
Kernel	10 - 12 minutes	10 - 12 minutes	High 6 - 7 min. per lb./500 g†	
On cob	6 - 12 minutes	10 - 15 minutes	Husked — High 2 - 5 min. for one ear; 4 1/2 - 10 min. for two ears. †	
Eggplant				
Sliced	10 - 20 minutes	15 - 20 minutes	High 7 - 10 min. per lb./500 g†	
Kale	10 - 15 minutes		High 6 - 7 min. per lb./500 g†	
Kohlrabi				
Sliced	20 - 25 minutes	30 minutes	High — 10 - 15 min. per 4 - 5 med. (2 lbs/1 kg)†	
Okra				
Sliced	10 - 15 minutes	20 minutes	High 7 - 10 min. per lb./500 g†	
Onions				
Small				
whole	15 - 30 minutes	25 - 35 minutes	High 7 - 10 minutes (4 medium†	
Large				
whole	20 - 40 minutes	35 - 40 minutes		50 - 60 minutes
Parsnips				
Whole	20 - 40 minutes	30 - 45 minutes	High 7 - 8 min. per lb./500 g†	45 - 60 minutes
Quartered	8 - 15 minutes	30 - 40 minutes		
Peas				
Green	12 - 16 minutes	10 - 20 minutes	High 5 - 7 min. per lb. (2 cups)/500 g (500 ml) Pea Pod — High 2 - 4 min. 1/4 lb./125 g.†	

VEGETABLE	BOILING*	STEAMING*	MICROWAVE (700 Watts)	BAKING
Potatoes				
White medium, whole	25 - 40 minutes	30 - 45 minutes	Baked — High 3 - 5 min. one med; 5 - 7 1/2 min, two med.†	45 - 60 minutes
quartered	20 - 25 minutes	20 - 30 minutes	Boiled whole — High 5 - 8 min. per eight med. Slices — (1/4") 5 - 7 min per 4 med.†	
Rutabaga				
Diced	20 - 30 minutes	35 - 40 minutes	High 14 - 18 min. per 1 1/2 lbs. (3-4 cups)/750 g (0.7-1 l)†	
Spinach	3 - 10 minutes	5 - 12 minutes	High 7 - 8 1/2 min. per lb./500 g†	
Squash				
Hubbard 2" pieces	15 - 20 minutes	25 - 40 minutes	Winter — High 6 - 7 min. per lb./500 g†	40 - 60 minutes
Summer sliced	8 - 15 minutes	15 - 20 minutes	Summer — (1/4" slices) High 2 1/2 - 6 1/2 min. per 2 cups/500 ml†	30 minutes
Sweet Potatoes, Yams				
Whole	35 - 55 minutes	30 - 35 minutes	High 3 - 5 min. per potato; 5 - 9 min. for two potatoes†	30 - 45 minutes
Quartered	15 - 25 minutes	25 - 30 minutes		
Tomatoes	7 - 15 minutes		High 4 - 6 min. per lb./500 g†	15 - 30 minutes
Turnips				
Whole	20 - 30 minutes		Slices (1/4") High 9 - 11 min., 4 med. Cubes (1/2") High 12 - 14 min. per 4 med.†	
Sliced	15 - 20 minutes	20 to 25 minutes		

* *For altitude cookery, increase cooking time 4 - 11% at 5,000 feet (1524 m); 20 - 25% at 7,200 feet (2194 m); and 55 - 66% at 10,000 feet (3048 m) and more water added.*

† *Rest covered 3 minutes*

Table 8.2
GUIDE TO HERB-VEGETABLE COOKERY

VEGETABLE	APPROPRIATE SPICE OR HERB
Asparagus	Cayenne or red pepper, celery flakes, cinnamon, mustard seed, nutmeg, poppy seeds, sesame seed or tarragon
Lima beans	Marjoram, oregano, rosemary, sage, savory, tarragon or thyme
Green beans	Basil, dill, marjoram, mint, mustard seed, nutmeg, oregano, poultry seasoning, rosemary, savory, tarragon or thyme
Beets	Allspice, bay leaves, caraway seed, cloves, cinnamon, dill, ginger, mustard seed, savory or thyme
Broccoli	Caraway seed, cayenne or red pepper, celery flakes, dill, herb seasoning, lemon or orange bits, mustard seed, nutmeg, tarragon or thyme
Brussels sprouts	Basil, caraway seed, dill, mustard seed, rosemary, sage or thyme
Cabbage	Caraway seed, celery seed, dill, mint, mustard seed, nutmeg, rosemary, savory or tarragon
Carrots	Allspice, bay leaves, basil leaves, caraway seed, chili powder, cinnamon, dill, fennel, ginger, lemon or orange bits, mace, marjoram, mint, nutmeg, oregano, parsley flakes, poppy seed, pumpkin pie spice, rosemary or thyme
Cauliflower	Basil leaves, caraway seed, celery salt, dill, mace, mustard seeds, parsley flakes, rosemary or tarragon
Corn	Cayenne or red pepper, celery flakes, chili powder or mustard seeds
Cucumbers	Basil, dill, mint or tarragon
Eggplant	Allspice, cayenne or red pepper, chili powder, basil leaves, herb seasoning, marjoram, oregano, parsley flakes, poultry seasoning or sage
Mushrooms	Herb seasoning, marjoram or sesame seed
Okra	Celery seed

VEGETABLE	APPROPRIATE SPICE OR HERB
Onions	Caraway seed, cayenne or red pepper, chili powder, cloves, mustard seed, nutmeg, oregano, parsley flakes, poultry seasoning, sage or thyme
Peas	Basil leaves, dill, marjoram, mint, oregano, poppy seed, rosemary, sage or savory
Potatoes	Basil leaves, bay leaves, caraway seed, celery seed, chives, dill, herb seasoning, mustard seed, oregano, parsley flakes, poppy seed, rosemary or thyme
Rutabagas	Pumpkin pie spice
Spinach	Allspice, basil leaves, lemon or orange bits, mace, marjoram, nutmeg or oregano
Squash	Allspice, basil leaves, cardamon, cinnamon, cloves, fennel, ginger, lemon or orange bits, marjoram, mustard seed, nutmeg, oregano, pumpkin pie spice, rosemary or thyme
Sweet potatoes	Allspice, cardamon, cinnamon, cloves, ginger, lemon or orange bits, or nutmeg
Tomatoes	Basil, bay leaves, celery seed, cloves, herb seasoning, oregano, parsley flakes, rosemary, sage, sesame seed, tarragon or thyme
Turnips	Oregano, poppy seed or rosemary
Green salads	Basil, chives, dill or tarragon

NOTE: Curry powder adds piquancy to creamed vegetables. Pepper and parsley may be used with any of the vegetables.

Based on "Spices and Herbs, Vegetables in Family Meals," *Home and Garden Bulletin No. 105*, U.S. Department of Agriculture, 1965, and "Cooking Magic with Herbs and Spices Schilling," McCormick and Co., Inc.

Grain Products

Cereal grains are the seeds of cultivated grasses, including barley, corn, oats, rice, and wheat. The kernels of the various grains are similar in structure, but differ in size and shape. The three main structural parts of the kernel are bran which is the outer protective covering of the kernel; endosperm which comprises about 85 percent of the kernel and contains the food supply of the plant; and germ which contains elements necessary for new plant life.

BARLEY PRODUCTS

In the United States, this grain is sold mainly as pearl barley which is the whole grain with hull and bran removed. It is used principally as a soup ingredient. Pearl barley may be used in casseroles, pilafs, or salads. The grain may also be made into a flour by a process similar to that for making wheat flour. Barley flour and milling fractions such as bran, middlings, and shorts are used in baked products and breakfast cereals. Barley products are high in soluble fiber.

CORN PRODUCTS

Cornmeal is made by grinding white or yellow corn kernels to a fineness specified by federal standards. Cornmeals contain small amounts of fat and crude fiber and not more than 15 percent moisture. Degermed cornmeal is made by grinding the kernel after the germ is removed.

Bolted white or yellow cornmeal is ground finer than the above type but otherwise is similar.

Enriched cornmeal contains added vitamins and minerals. It is enriched with thiamin, riboflavin, niacin, and iron. It may also contain calcium and Vitamin D.

Corn flour may be a by-product in the preparation of cornmeal or may be prepared especially by milling and sifting yellow or white corn.

Corn grits, grits, or hominy grits are made from white or yellow corn from which the bran and germ have been removed. Grits are more coarsely ground than cornmeal.

Hominy is corn with the hull and germ removed, left whole, or broken into particles. Pearl hominy is whole grain hominy with the hulls removed by machinery. Lye hominy is whole grain hominy that has been soaked in lye water to remove the hulls. Granulated hominy is a ground form of hominy. Hominy grits are broken grains.

Cornstarch is the refined starch obtained from the endosperm of corn.

Waxy cornstarch is prepared from waxy corn. It is composed almost completely of amylopectin with little or no amylose. This starch acts as a stabilizer for frozen sauces and pie fillings.

Flavored cornstarch mixes are blends of cornstarch, sugar, and flavorings for making puddings and pie fillings.

Instant cornstarch puddings usually contain dehydrated gelatinized cornstarch, sugar or sugar substitute, and flavoring.

Corn cereals are usually ready-to-eat flakes or puffs, made from corn grits that have been cooked and dried or toasted. Corn cereals may be flavored, sugar-coated, and enriched with thiamin, riboflavin, niacin, and iron, or fortified with vitamins and minerals.

OAT PRODUCTS

Oatmeal, or rolled oats, also called oats, is made by rolling the groats (oats with hulls removed) to form flakes. Regular oats and quick-cooking oats differ only in thinness of flakes. For quick-cooking oats, the finished groats (edible portion of the kernel) are cut into tiny particles which are then rolled into thin, small flakes. Steel-cut oats, those that are not flaked, are the most resistant of the oat products to overcooking. Although oatmeal is primarily considered a breakfast cereal, many recipes call for its use in cooking and baking.

Oat bran is essentially the envelope of the groat, composed of the outermost pericarp. Oat bran is high in soluble fiber and can be used in many types of recipes.

RICE PRODUCTS

Rice grains are classified as long grain, medium grain, and short grain, according to varieties. Medium and short grain rice have a higher proportion of amylopectin than long grain rice and therefore the grains cling together after cooking. Brown rice is the grain from which only the hull has been removed. White rice has the bran layers removed and is the starchy endosperm of the grain.

Aromatic rice has a natural aroma when cooked. Special varieties of rice are aromatic; nothing is added to the grains. Basmati rice and jasmine rice are imported aromatic rices. Aromatic rice is also grown in the U.S.

Enriched rice contains thiamin, riboflavin, niacin, and iron. Over 90 percent of milled rice in the U.S. is enriched. Enriched rice should not be rinsed before cooking.

Imported rice includes arborio rice from Italy which is used to make risotto, a creamy rice dish. U.S. medium or short grain rice may be substituted for arborio rice.

Precooked rice is packaged long grain rice (brown or white) that has been cooked, rinsed, and dried by a patented process. This rice needs to be rehydrated during preparation.

Parboiled rice has been steeped in warm or hot water, drained, steamed under pressure, and dried before it is hulled and milled. This steaming process causes vitamins and minerals present in the outer coats to migrate to the interior of the kernel. Parboiling gelatinizes some of the starch, which results in translucent golden grains.

Rice bran consists of bran and germ. It is a smooth brown powder with a faintly sweet taste; it is rich in nutrients and fiber.

Rice polish consists of inner bran layers and some endosperm. It is a smooth yellow powder with a sweet taste.

Rice flour is made from white or brown rice ground into flour. It is gluten-free and can be used by those who are allergic to wheat flour.

Waxy rice flour is made from waxy rice. It is composed almost completely of amylopectin with little or no amylose. It acts as a stabilizer in sauces and gravies and is especially useful in preventing separation in these products when they are frozen.

CLASSES OF WHEAT

There are six classes of wheat grown in the United States. They are durum wheat for pasta; hard red spring, hard red winter and hard white for yeast breads and hard rolls; soft red winter for flat breads, cakes, pastries, and crackers; soft white wheat for flat breads, cakes, pastries, crackers, and noodles.

WHEAT PRODUCTS

Bulgur wheat is whole wheat that has been cooked, dried, partly debranned, and cracked into coarse, angular fragments. Rehydration requires simmering for 15 to 25 minutes. It may be used as an alternate for rice in many recipes, and resembles whole wheat in nutritive properties.

Cracked wheat is similar to bulgur in nutrition and texture, but it has not been precooked. It is the whole kernel broken into smaller pieces which serves as a hot cereal or an addition to baked goods. Cracked wheat should be pre-soaked or cooked before addition to baked products.

Farina is the coarsely ground endosperm of

wheats other than durum. It is the prime ingredient in many hot breakfast cereals and is occasionally used for pasta. Enriched farina contains thiamin, riboflavin, niacin, and iron. Calcium and Vitamin D may also be added.

Semolina is the coarsely ground endosperm of durum wheat. The primary use of semolina is for pasta; however, it is also used for couscous, a Moroccan dish.

Wheat bran is the outer layer of the kernel. It is high in insoluble fiber and can be added to baked goods, casseroles, cereals, and meat dishes.

Wheat germ is the germ of the kernel and is often added to baked goods, casseroles, and beverages to enhance the nutritional value and give a nutty, crunchy texture. Because of the oil content, it should be tightly covered and stored in the refrigerator or freezer.

Wheat kernels (berries) are the whole-grain kernel and can be sprouted and added to salads and baked goods. The cooked berries can be used as a meat extender, breakfast cereal, or a substitute for beans in chili, salads, and baked dishes.

FLOURS

The term flour when used in recipes is understood to mean refined all-purpose wheat flour unless otherwise designated as, for example, bread flour, cake flour, self-rising flour, oat flour, or rice flour. The majority of states require white flour to be enriched. Therefore, the major mills in the United States enrich all their flour so it can be shipped interstate. The Federal standards for enriched corn, rice, macaroni, and wheat flour are presented in Table 9.1. The following describes in more detail the various types of wheat flour available in most markets.

All-purpose flour is the finely-ground endosperm of the wheat kernel separated from the bran and germ during milling. It is made from hard wheats (other than durum) or a combination of hard and soft wheats. It is best for quick breads and may be used for yeast breads, cakes, pastry, and cookies.

Bread flour is the ground endosperm from hard wheats and is best for yeast breads because of its high gluten content (higher than all-purpose flour).

Cake flour is milled from the endosperm of soft wheats and is especially suited for cakes, cookies, and crackers. Because it is so fine and uniform, it feels soft and satiny. It is low in gluten. It is usually bleached for improved crumb quality.

Semolina is finely ground endosperm of durum wheat which is used primarily for pasta.

Enriched flour is white flour which contains added vitamins and minerals. Thiamin, riboflavin, niacin, and iron are added; the addition of calcium is optional.

Table 9.1
FEDERAL STANDARDS FOR ENRICHED
CORN, RICE, MACARONI AND WHEAT FLOUR

NUTRIENT	FARINA	CORN MEAL	RICE	MACARONI	WHEAT
Required per pound (454 g) of flour:					
Thiamin	2.0 - 2.5 mg	2.0 - 3.0 mg	2.0 - 4.0 mg	4.0 - 5.0 mg	2.9 mg
Riboflavin	1.2 - 1.5 mg	1.2 - 1.8 mg		1.7 - 2.2 mg	1.8 mg
Niacin	16 - 20 mg	16 - 24 mg	16 - 32 mg	27 - 34 mg	24 mg
Iron	13 mg	13 - 26 mg	13 - 26 mg	13 - 16.5 mg	13 - 16.5 mg
Optional per pound (454 g) of flour:					
Calcium	500 mg	500 - 750 mg		500 - 625 mg	960 mg
Vitamin D	250 IU	250 - 1000 IU		250 - 1000 IU	
Riboflavin			1.2 - 2.4 mg		

Gluten flour is a mixture of wheat flour and gluten with a protein content of about 45 percent.

Instant, instantized, instant-blending or quick mixing flour is a granular all-purpose flour which blends more readily with liquids than regular flour. It is made by exposing all-purpose flour to hot water or steam to combine the individual particles into agglomerates. It is excellent for gravies and as a thickener, but can also be used in baked goods with some adaptations.

Pastry flour is milled from the endosperm of soft wheats and is used in pastries.

Self-rising flour is an all-purpose flour with 1-1/2 teaspoons (7.5 ml) of baking powder and 1/2 teaspoon (2.5 ml) of salt added per cup (250 ml) of flour. It can be substituted for an all-purpose flour by reducing the baking powder and salt in the recipe accordingly. Self-rising flour is used primarily in the southeastern U.S. for biscuits, cornbread, waffles, and shortbread.

Vital wheat gluten is used by bakers to enhance the gluten quality in flour or bread products containing fiber. It contains about 75 percent protein and is made by gently washing a flour-water dough which separates the gluten portion from the starch. The protein fraction is then dried to form a powder. Very little vital wheat gluten is needed to enhance a recipe. Use 1 teaspoon (5 ml) of gluten for every 6 cups (1.4 l) of flour and add an additional 1-1/2 teaspoons (7 ml) water.

White-wheat flour is made from hard white wheat and is becoming popular in the U.S. When the whole kernel is ground, it produces a flour with the fiber and nutritional content of the darker whole-wheat flour, but with a lighter, golden color and less bitter flavor. It has excellent baking qualities but is not readily available nationally in grocery stores.

Whole-wheat flour, also called graham flour, is coarse in texture and is ground from the entire wheat kernel. Bran inhibits the gluten development and absorbs water, giving a heavier, denser loaf of bread. Many recipes call for a mixture of whole-wheat and white flour. Whole-wheat flour contains more dietary fiber than white flour, but the other nutrients are very similar to white flour.

PASTA

Pasta includes macaroni, noodles, and spaghetti in one of 150 shapes. Durum wheat is used to make semolina, which is enriched with thiamin, riboflavin, niacin, and iron; pasta dough is made from semolina and water. Noodles are made from a more finely ground semolina and have eggs added. Pasta dough is kneaded and then forced through dies to create the many different forms of pasta available.

The pasta is dried by automatic dryers which remove moisture under carefully controlled conditions. Fresh pasta is available in the refrigerated section of the grocery store. Pasta should be cooked until "al dente" (tender but firm). It is best to follow package directions, but keep in mind the following: use at least one quart (1 l) of water for every four ounces (115 g) of dry pasta; add pasta to boiling water; stir the pasta when you add it, when the water returns to a boil, and occasionally during cooking; drain in a colander; and undercook slightly if the pasta will be used as part of a dish that requires further cooking.

OTHER FLOURS, CEREALS, GRAINS, AND SEEDS

Amaranth is a tall willowy plant similar in height to corn. It has a large shaggy head containing thousands of tiny seeds. The seed can be milled into a whole grain flour, or puffed like rice or corn.

Buckwheat is neither a wheat nor a cereal grain, but the seed from any of the *Fagopyrum* family of herbs. Kasha is a word commonly used to describe cooked buckwheat groats, a Russian dish. Buckwheat is ground and used for its unique flavor to replace part of the wheat flour in buckwheat pancake mixes. It has more starch and less protein than wheat.

Millet has a stronger flavor than most cereals. It can be eaten as the whole grain. Millet can be husked, soaked, boiled, and ground into a meal. It is added in bread making.

Potato flour is prepared from cooked potatoes that have been dried and ground.

Quinoa (pronounced keenwah) is a small, disk-shaped seed that can come in many colors. It is not a cereal grain; it is the fruit of an annual herb. It has been grown in the mountain regions of Peru and Bolivia for 3,000 years. The whole grain is cooked like rice, and quinoa can also be ground into flour and used for baked goods.

Rye flour is the finely ground product obtained by sifting rye meal. It is available in three grades: white, medium, and dark. Rye and wheat flours are the only flours containing gluten-forming proteins that are so important in baked products. Rye flour produces gluten of low elasticity.

Sorghum is a tropical grass similar to Indian corn and has an unusual flavor that can be improved by steaming or dry heat processing. Small amounts of sorghum are sometimes added to crackers and snack foods. Sorghum is also used to make a syrup.

Soy flour is highly flavored. It must be combined with wheat flour when used in baked products, because it lacks gluten-forming proteins. The amount of liquid in a recipe must be increased when soy flour is substituted for part of the wheat flour. Full-fat soy flour is make by grinding soybeans that have only the hull removed. Low-fat soy flour is made from the press cake after all or nearly all of the oil is taken out of the soybeans. The soybeans may be heat treated or conditioned with steam prior to oil extraction.

Soy grits are made from coarsely ground soy press cakes and are a low-fat product.

Spelt (*triticum spelta*) is a predecessor of wheat (*triticum sativum*) and has a very strong hull that is difficult to remove when milling. It is available primarily as flour.

Teff is the smallest grain in the world; 150 grains weigh the same as one grain of wheat. It is available as the whole grain and flour. Teff flour can be used with other flours in baked goods and as a thickener in gravy, soups, and stews.

Triticale is a hybrid cereal derived from crossing wheat and rye. It can be cooked as a whole grain, ground into flour for use in baking, or processed into cereal flakes.

Wild rice is the long brownish grain of a reedlike water plant. It is hulled, but not milled.

BREAKFAST CEREALS

Whole-grain cereals retain the natural proportion of bran, germ, and endosperm, and the specific nutrients that are normally contained in the whole unprocessed grain.

Enriched cereals contain replaced amounts of thiamin, riboflavin, niacin, and iron. The levels of nutrient enrichment are established by the FDA.

Fortified cereals contain added amounts of selected nutrients that may or may not have been present in the grain before processing.

Restored cereals contain added amounts of selected nutrients to supply the same approximate levels of these nutrients in the finished grain products as were present in the whole grain before processing.

Varieties of hot and ready-to-eat cereals include extruded, flaked, granulated, puffed, rolled, and shredded. Hot cereals include regular, quick-cooking, and instant varieties. Instant hot cereals are prepared from precooked dried grains. Disodium phosphate is added, or the kernels are modified with a small amount of an enzyme preparation to permit quick entry of water into the starch granules. Some ready-to-eat cereals are presweetened.

STORAGE AND MEASUREMENT OF GRAINS AND CEREAL PRODUCTS

■ Store flours, grains, and cereals in tightly covered containers to keep out dust, moisture, and insects; store in a dry place at room temperature. Whole grains should be stored in the refrigerator or freezer due to their oil content.

■ Store dried pasta or egg noodles tightly covered or well wrapped. These products may be stored for one year. Follow package directions for storage of commercially prepared fresh pasta. Fresh pasta must be refrigerated and should be eaten within two days or frozen for later use.

■ Cereals may be stored satisfactorily for two to three months; corn meal and hominy grits for four to six months; bulgur and brown or wild rice for six months; and other rices for one year.

■ To measure sifted or unsifted all-purpose flour, spoon rounded tablespoons of the flour lightly into a fractional measuring cup until the flour overflows the cup. Level with the straight edge of a spatula or knife.

■ To measure whole-grain flours, instant flour, and meals, stir lightly with a fork or spoon but do not sift before measuring. Follow measuring directions for all-purpose flour.

The dietary fiber content of grains and cereal products are shown in Table 9.2. Cereal sources of various fiber components are as follows:

Cellulose
whole wheat flour
bran
Gums
oat products
barley products
Hemicellulose
bran
cereals
whole grains
Lignin
whole wheat flour

Table 9.2
DIETARY FIBER CONTENT OF GRAINS AND CEREAL PRODUCTS
(in commonly served portions)

FIBER CATEGORIES	<1 g	1 - 1.9 g	2 - 2.9 g	3 - 3.9 g
Foods				
Cereals (1 oz., 28 g)	There are cereals in every fiber category. Check labels			
Pasta (1 cup, 250 ml)		macaroni spaghetti		whole wheat spaghetti
Rice (1/2 cup, 125 ml)	white	brown		

Sweetening agents, Fats and oils, Leavening agents

SWEETENING AGENTS

Sugars

The term sugar, when unqualified as to source, refers to refined sucrose derived from sugar beets or sugarcane. These two sugars are the same and are 99.9 percent pure sucrose.

White Sugar

Granulated sugar is the standard product for general use, variously branded "granulated," "fine granulated," or "ultra-fine granulated." The variation indicates preference in terminology of the manufacturer rather than any definite particle size. It is available in numerous sizes and types of packages, from one-pound cartons to 100-pound bags.

Ultra-fine granulated sugar is a specially screened, uniformly fine-grained sugar designed for special use in cakes and in mixed drinks and other uses where quick creaming or rapid dissolving is desirable. It is available in one-pound cartons.

Powdered or confectioner's sugar is granu-

lated sugar crushed and screened to a desired fineness. These are available in several degrees of fineness designated by name or number of x's following the name. Although 10x is finer than 4x, no standard terminology applies to all brands. It is used in frostings and icings and for dusting on baked products. It usually contains three percent cornstarch to prevent caking.

Special Forms of Sugar

Cut tablets are made from sugar which is molded into slabs that are afterward cut or clipped. Cut tablets of various sizes and shapes are packed in one- and two-pound cartons.

Pressed tablets are made by compressing moist, white sugar into molds to form the tablets which are afterward oven-dried to produce hard, smooth tablets. Tablets of various sizes and shapes come in one- and two-pound cartons.

Cubes, like pressed tablets, are formed in

molds. Sizes range from 200 to 80 pieces to a pound. Cubes are packed in one- and two-pound cartons.

Brown Sugar

Brown sugar is a product which contains varying quantities of molasses, non-sugars (ash) naturally present in molasses, and moisture. It may be produced from the syrup remaining after the removal of commercially extractable white sugar or by the addition of refined syrups to specially graded, uniformly minute white sugar crystals. Four grades are available for food manufacturing but only two for consumer purchase. These are variously designated as "golden brown" or "light brown" and "dark" or "old-fashioned brown," indicating the color characteristic. Intensity of molasses flavor increases with color. The granulated (Brownulated®) form of brown sugar contains enough molasses to provide a flavor of an intensity between the light and dark brown sugars; its use in baking requires adjustments in amounts of ingredients. Brown sugar imparts flavor and color to candies, condiments, baked goods, and the like. It is packed in 14 oz. and one-pound cartons and two-pound plastic bags.

Other Sugars

Raw sugar is the product crystallized at the stage in cane-sugar manufacture at which sugar goes from the mill to the refiner. Raw sugar may contain molds, fibers, waxes, and other contaminants.

Turbinado sugar is a partially refined sugar similar in appearance to raw sugar, which is sold for consumption without further refining.

Blended sugar is a combination of sugar and dextrose which may be used in place of an equal quantity of sugar, although its properties are somewhat different.

Corn sugar is dextrose (glucose) obtained by treating cornstarch with acid.

Fructose (levulose) is one of two sugars that result when sucrose reacts chemically with water. It may be produced industrially by the use of an enzyme (isomerase) to change the structure of glucose. It is highly soluble and is approximately one and one-half times as sweet as sucrose in sugar solutions.

Maple sugar is the solid product resulting from the evaporation of maple sap or maple syrup. It consists mostly of sucrose with some invert sugar and ash.

Syrups
FROM SUGARCANE

Cane syrup is the concentrated sap of sugar cane. It is made by evaporation of the juice of sugarcane or by solution of sugar cane concrete (concentrate). The recommended maximum ash content of the unsulfured product is 4.5 percent; sulfured, six percent.

Molasses is the mother liquid from which raw cane sugar has crystallized. The following types are usually found:

Table molasses, which is light in color, contains a higher percentage of sugar and a smaller percentage of ash than are present in cooking molasses.

Cooking (blackstrap) molasses is dark in color. Barbados molasses, which is specially treated cooking molasses, resembles cane syrup more than molasses in composition.

Refiners' syrup is the residual product obtained in the process of refining raw cane sugar which has been subjected to clarification and decolorization. It is a solution, or solution and suspension, of sucrose and partially inverted sucrose, containing not more than 28 percent moisture. It is used extensively for flavoring corn syrup.

FROM SORGHUM CANE

Sorghum syrup is obtained by concentration of the juice of the sugar sorghum. It contains not more than 30 percent water nor more than 6.25 percent ash calculated on a dry basis.

FROM CORN

Corn syrup (unmixed) is obtained by partial hydrolysis of cornstarch by use of acid or enzymatic catalysts or a combination of these. The resulting liquid is neutralized, clarified, and concentrated to syrup consistency. The principal ingredients are dextrose, maltose, and dextrins. Two types are commonly marketed.

Light corn syrup is corn syrup that has been clarified and decolorized. Retail products may have HFCS and/or flavoring added.

Dark corn syrup is a mixture of corn syrup

and refiners' syrup. It is used as a table syrup and also for the same purposes as light corn syrup in combinations that give a desirable darker color and distinctive flavor. Color and flavors may be added to retail products.

A third form available to food processors is high **fructose corn syrup (HFCS).** An enzymatic process is used to produce syrup with 42 percent, 55 percent or 90 percent fructose.

FROM MAPLE TREES

Maple syrup is made by evaporation of maple sap or by solution of maple sugar. It contains not more than 35 percent water and weighs not less than 11 pounds to the gallon.

FROM BEES

Honey is the nectar of plants, gathered, modified, stored, and concentrated by honey bees. The water content of honey is limited to about 20 percent. Its principal ingredients are levulose (fructose) and dextrose (glucose). The term honey in cookery refers to honey extracted from the comb. The different flavors of honey are classified according to the plant from which the nectar is derived.

BY SPECIAL PROCESSES

Blended syrups are mixtures of different, but somewhat similar, types of syrups which are sold for table purposes. The composition of blended syrups is stated on the label.

Spray-dried syrups consist essentially of the solids of syrup which have been spray-dried.

Storage and Use

- To store honey and syrups, keep the unopened containers at room temperature. Once the containers have been opened, refrigerate honey and syrups to protect against mold. If crystals form, place the container in hot water.

- Store white granulated sugar, covered, in a dry place. If the sugar becomes lumpy, sift before measuring.

- Store brown sugar in a plastic bag in airtight container. If sugar hardens, place a piece of foil or plastic wrap directly on the sugar and set a wad of dampened paper towel on the foil. Cover container tightly. The sugar will absorb the moisture and become soft. Remove paper when it has dried out.

- To soften brown sugar quickly, warm in a 250°F oven (120°C) and measure as soon as the sugar becomes soft. Sugar may also be heated in an open microwavable container in the microwave unit with a second container of 1/2 cup (125 ml) water for one - three minutes (depending on quantity and unit). It will harden again upon cooling.

- When measuring brown sugar, pack it firmly enough into the measuring cup for the sugar to retain the shape of the cup when turned out.

- Store powdered sugar in an airtight container to keep out moisture. If sugar becomes lumpy, sift before measuring.

No-Calorie and Low-Calorie Sweeteners

No-Calorie and Low-Calorie Sweeteners are sugar substitutes which provide sweetness but cause little change in viscosity or density of solutions and lack other functional properties of sugar. Because of the intensity of sweetness, very small amounts need to be used and calorie contributions, even of those which are metabolized, are considered to be insignificant. For best flavor, several are frequently combined and dextrin, lactose, or other bulking material included in the product. Generally a one-serving package equals the sweetness of two teaspoons sugar.

Currently, sweeteners which have been approved by the Food and Drug Administration or for which petitions for approval have been submitted are shown in Table 10.1.

Related Products

Polydextrose is a condensation polymer of dextrose, containing minor amounts of bound sorbitol and citric acid. It has one calorie per gram. As a bulking agent, it gives texture and body to foods when used to partially replace sugar or fat in some foods. Since it has no sweetness, sweeteners may also be needed.

Polyols (polyhydric alcohols). Sugar alcohols, such as sorbitol, mannitol, and xylitol have limited use in foods. Although less sweet than sugar, they contribute to texture and are non-cariogenic.

Tables 10.2 and 10.3 on pages 160 and 161 present information on Solubility of Sugar and Temperatures and Tests for Syrup and Candies, respectively.

FATS AND OILS

Fats and oils are substances of plant and animal origin which belong to a class of chemical compounds called lipids. The terms commonly used are "fats" that are lipids solid at room temperature, while "oils" are lipids that are liquid at room temperature. Most of the lipids found in foods are triglycerides, which are esters of glycerol and three fatty acids. Other lipids found in small amounts include mono- and diglycerides (esters of glycerol and one or two fatty acids), phospholipids such as lecithin, and sterols such as cholesterol. The last is synthesized only by animals.

Fatty acids are responsible for the varied characteristics of different triglycerides. Fatty acids are organic acids generally with an even number of carbon atoms. Triglycerides with short-chain fatty acids are usually liquid or soft at room temperature; the triglycerides become harder as chain lengths increase. Fatty acids may be saturated (having no double bonds), monounsaturated (having one double bond), or polyunsaturated (having two or more

Table 10.1
HIGH INTENSITY SWEETENERS

PRODUCT	SWEETENERS INDEX (Sugar = 1)	FDA STATUS	STABILITY	COMPOSITION
Acesulfame-K	200	Approved	Stable	Derivative of (potassium) acetoacetic acid
Alitame	2000	Under review	Stable	Dipeptide of D-alanine and L-aspartic acid
Aspartame	180	Approved — must be labeled that it contains phenylalanine	Unstable when heated or when stored at pH extremes	Methylester of dipeptide of phenylalanine and aspartic acid
Cyclamate	30	Banned in US in 1970	Stable	Sulfonated cyclohexylamine
Saccharin	300	Approved	Stable	Benzoic sulphimide
Sucralose	600	Under review	Stable	Chlorinated derivative of sucrose

Table 10.2
SOLUBILITY OF SUGARS

SUGAR	TEMPERATURE °F	°C	PERCENTAGE OF SUGAR IN SATURATED SOLUTION %	AMOUNT DISSOLVED BY 100 GRAMS OF WATER g	DISSOLVED BY 1 CUP WATER (236.6 ml) (calculated on the assumption that 1 cup sugar weighs 200 g) c
Common Sugars					
Fructose	68	20	78.9	375.0	
Glucose	68	20	49.7	83.1	
Lactose	77	25	17.8	21.7	
Maltose	70	21	44.1	78.9	
Sucrose	32	0	64.2	179.2	2.1
	68	20	67.1	203.9	2.4
	104	40	70.4	238.1	2.8
	140	60	74.2	287.3	3.4
	176	80	78.4	362.1	4.3
	194	90	80.6	415.7	4.9
	212	100	83.0	487.2	5.8

double bonds). Saturated fatty acids are harder (more likely to be solid at room temperature) than unsaturated fatty acids, which tend to be liquid at room temperature.

Many commercially-available fats are made from oils by hydrogenation. Hydrogenation is the process of adding hydrogen to unsaturated fatty acids under carefully controlled conditions to reduce the number of double bonds and increase saturation. Regardless of source and fatty acid composition, all fats and oils provide 9 kilocalories per gram.

Animal Fat Shortenings

These products are made from fat extracted from animal tissue by dry or wet rendering. The fats are then deodorized, and/or partially hydrogenated, and plasticized.

Lard — This is a plastic fat extracted from hogs. It is used in refried beans, pies, and pastries.

Tallow — This is fat extracted from sheep or cattle. It is more saturated than lard and has a more distinctive, meaty flavor. The flavor has made this a popular frying fat for french fries. Tallow currently makes up about 17 percent of the fat and oils used in shortening manufacture.

Table 10.3
TEMPERATURES AND TESTS FOR SYRUP AND CANDIES

PRODUCT	FINAL TEMPERATURE OF SYRUP AT SEA LEVEL*		TEST OF DONENESS	DESCRIPTION OF TEST
	°F	°C		
Jelly	220	104	———	Syrup runs off a cool metal spoon in drops that merge to form a sheet.
Syrup	230 to 234	110 to 112	Thread	Syrup spins a 2" (5 cm) thread when dropped from fork or spoon.
Fondant Fudge Panocha	234 to 240	112 to 115	Soft ball	Syrup, when dropped into very cold water, forms a soft ball which flattens on removal from water.
Caramels	244 to 248	118 to 120	Firm ball	Syrup, when dropped into very cold water, forms a firm ball which does not flatten on removal from water.
Divinity Marshmallows Popcorn Balls	250 to 266	121 to 130	Hard ball	Syrup, when dropped into very cold water, forms a ball which is hard enough to hold its shape, yet plastic.
Butterscotch Taffies	270 to 290	132 to 143	Soft Crack	Syrup, when dropped into very cold water, separates into threads which are hard but not brittle.
Brittle Glacé	300 to 310	149 to 154	Hard Crack	Syrup, when dropped into very cold water, separates into threads which are hard and brittle.
Barley sugar	320	160	Clear liquid	The sugar liquefies.
Caramel	338	170	Brown liquid	The liquid becomes brown.

* For each increase of 500 feet in elevation, cook the syrup to a temperature 1°F lower than temperature called for at sea level. If readings are taken in Celsius, for each 900 feet of elevation cook the syrup to a temperature 1°C lower than called for at sea level.

Vegetable Oils

The edible oils used in the American home are of vegetable origin. Vegetable oils are pressed or squeezed from the seeds or fruits of the plant under heavy pressure (a method known as expelling), or the oils are dissolved out with an organic solvent which is later evaporated off (a method called solvent extraction). The raw oils are refined, bleached, and deodorized before being packaged. Oils to be used as salad oils are winterized by exposure to low temperatures for a period of time. These oils are then filtered to remove high-melting portions of the oil so that the remainder will stay clear at refrigerator temperatures.

Soybean, corn, peanut, safflower and sunflower oils are widely used. All are bland in flavor and useful in a variety of food products. Safflower and sunflower oils, however, are poor frying oils due to their high unsaturation. Of increasing popularity is canola oil, which is extracted from a variety of rape seed and was approved for food use in 1985. This oil is 94 percent unsaturated and performs well in food products and for frying. Cottonseed oil makes up a very small percentage of the market, with its main use in restaurant frying operations.

Olive Oil — This oil is pressed from fully ripe black olives. "Extra virgin" and "virgin" olive oil are obtained from the first pressings; refined olive oil is derived from additional pressings of the fruit and is then filtered through layers of felt to remove impurities. Refined olive oil is not bleached or deodorized. Olive oil is popular because of its distinctive flavor and very high composition of monounsaturated fatty acids.

Tropical Oils — Palm oil, palm kernel oil and coconut oil are sometimes referred to as tropical oils. These oils are more saturated than other vegetable oils and are popular with food manufacturers because of their shelf stability. Each oil makes up less than 3 percent of the fat in the U.S. food supply.

Sesame Oil — Sesame oil ranges from a distinctively flavored straw- to amber-colored oil (found in Oriental food stores) to a more highly refined yellow product having a mild flavor (found in grocery stores). The oil is usually relatively expensive and is used primarily as a condiment for flavoring rather than for cooking. Sesame oil consists primarily of polyunsaturated fatty acids.

Marine Oils — These are oils extracted from herring, menhaden, whale and sardines. Only menhaden oil is currently approved for use in the US. These oils are the subject of current research since they are high in omega-3 fatty acids, unsaturated fatty acids linked with a decreased risk of heart disease.

Hydrogenated All-Vegetable Shortenings

Essentially these are solidified vegetable oils. Soybean oil is used primarily, but varying amounts of other oils such as corn oil, peanut oil and cottonseed oil are sometimes used.

The vegetable oils are refined to remove free fatty acids, and then bleached with absorbent materials to remove coloring materials. The purified oils are then hydrogenated and deodorized to produce a bland-flavored fat.

Mono- and diglycerides are added to enhance their emulsifying capability.

Spreads

Butter — see pages 71-72 (In Dairy Section).

Margarine — Margarines are made from refined vegetable oils or a combination of animal fats and vegetable oils emulsified with cultured milk, sweet milk, nonfat dry milk solids, water, or a mixture of these. The emulsion is then cooled and kneaded by machine to produce the desired consistency. Today almost all margarines are enriched with carotenes to enhance color. Salt and butter flavoring may be added, too. The law requires that margarine contain 80 percent fat unless the product is intended as a diet substitute, in which case the package must be labeled imitation or diet. Ingredient labels must also state the type of fat or fats used.

Regular margarine varies in hardness due to the type of oil or fat used and the amount of hydrogenation. Spreads and liquid margarines generally are higher in polyunsaturated fatty acids than regular stick margarine. Both regular and soft margarines provide 100 kcal/Tbsp (15 ml) and contain no cholesterol if produced from vegetable oils. Whipped margarines have added air and provide about 60 kcal/Tbsp (15 ml). Diet margarines contain 40-45 percent fat and added water; they provide 50-80 percent fewer calories than regular margarine.

Blends — Blends are mixtures of margarine and butter. The products offer a butter-like taste with one-third to one-sixth less cholesterol than butter.

Fat Substitutions

Oils may be substituted for solid shortening in batters and doughs by reducing the amount of oil 1 1/2 tablespoon (22.5 ml) per cup (236.6 ml). However, a product made with oil will be different from that made with shortening. Pastries will be crumbly and mealy in texture because the oil is spread homogeneously throughout the flour mixture. Cakes prepared by the creaming or traditional method are lower in volume and more coarse when oil is used as a replacement for shortening. Less air is incorporated during the creaming stage of the shortening and sugars, reducing the number of air cells that expand and divide during the baking process. To use oil in a cake, the mixing can be modified to a muffin method whereby the oil is added with other liquids; an egg white foam folded into the batter at the end of mixing helps to increase the volume.

Fat Substitutes

Modified foods that may be labeled light, reduced calorie, or reduced fat are available in the market. The foods may be of a fat reduced formula or contain a fat substitute that is either not metabolized or has an energy value of 4 kilocalories (17 kJ) or less per gram compared to the 9 kilocalories (38 kJ) per gram for fats.

Protein-based fat substitutes such as Simplesse® are made from egg white and milk protein that have been heated and formed into tiny spheres, by a process called microparticulation, which give the creamy mouthfeel of fat to frozen products, cream cheese, cheese spreads, or yogurt.

Carbohydrate-based fat substitutes are

combinations of gums and other carbohydrates such as polydextrose that act as a bulking agent. N-Oil® is made from tapioca dextrin and maltodextrins made from hydrolyzed cornstarch. These products contribute to viscosity and impart the mouthfeel of fat. Both protein and carbohydrate substitutes have water blended in ratios that result in a final product that may range from two to four kilocalories (eight to 17 kJ) per gram.

Synthetic based fat substitutes include triglyceride modification (sucrose polyester), polycarboxylic acid esters (trialkoxy-tricarballylate or TATCA by Best Foods), sterically hindered esters and polyglycerines. Triglyceride modifications are composed of modified molecules of sugars linked with long chain fatty acids. The synthetic substitutes have the look and feel of fat but the large molecules are not metabolized and, therefore, have no caloric value. Currently, such a product, Olestra®, is waiting approval from the Food and Drug Administration for use in foods.

Storage and Use

- Store lards and home-rendered fats such as poultry fat in the refrigerator.

- Refrigerate vegetable shortenings intended for storage of several months or more. These fats, however, will keep well at room temperature for shorter periods of time.

- Keep oils capped tightly and store at room temperature. Some oils may become thick and cloudy when stored in the refrigerator due to partial solidification. Store in dark containers or in a dark storage area.

Frying with Fats and Oils

Fats and oils are used as a cooking medium for pan frying or deep fat frying. Oils may be preferred since they generally are more stable and have a higher smoke point than solid shortenings. Some shortenings contain mono- and diglycerides that are desirable for use in cakes, but contribute a lower smoke point. The smoke point is the lowest temperature at which a continuous stream of thin, visible smoke is observed , along with a strong odor and eye irritation. The smoke is symptomatic of a rapid breakdown of the fat resulting in off flavor to the food cooked in the fat. The smoke point of the oil/fat must be above the temperature used in food preparation. The smoke point is lowered greatly by the presence of free fatty acids.

The formation of free fatty acids and other products from fat deterioration are accelerated with exposure to light, food particles in the fat, water from the food cooked in the fat, and a wide container with a large surface area. To maintain high quality of fat or oil to be reused for deep fat frying, the oil should be strained and stored in a closed container in cool darkness. Approximately 1/5 of the fat should be replaced with new fat or oil for each use.

Smoke Points of Fats and Oils

Lard	361°- 401°F (183°- 205°C)
Vegetable Oil	441°- 450°F (227°- 232°C)
Vegetable shortenings with mono- and diglycerides	356°- 370°F (180°- 188°C)
Vegetable and animal shortenings with mono-and diglycerides	351°- 363°F (177°- 184°C)
Vegetable and animal shortenings without mono- and diglycerides	448°F (231°C)

Fat absorption is reduced by maintaining a recommended cooking temperature of the oil that allows the food to cook quickly but not brown so rapidly that the interior is undercooked. Other factors that increase fat absorption are increased amounts of fat and sugar in the batter of the product and a lower protein content of the flour used.

Ways to Measure Fats and Oils

Butter or margarine purchased in bar form need not be measured with measuring equipment. Simply keep in mind that a 1/4 pound bar equals 1/2 cup (125 ml) or 8 tablespoons (120 ml). Two bars equal 1 cup (250 ml).

For other fats not in bar form use standard measuring cups or spoons. Press fat firmly into the utensil until it is full. Level with the straight edge of a spatula or knife.

Water displacement method may be used if water that clings to the fat will not affect the product. Pour cold water into a liquid measuring cup up to the measure that will equal 1 cup (250 ml) when the desired amount of fat is added. For example, if 1/4 cup (60 ml) is needed, pour 3/4 cup (175 ml) water into the measurer. Add enough fat to the water to make the water level rise to the mark for 1 cup (250 ml), being sure that the fat is entirely covered with water. Drain off the water.

For oils or melted fats, use a standard glass measuring cup or spoons and pour the oil or melted fat to the desired mark.

LEAVENING AGENTS

A leavening agent is a gas incorporated or formed in a batter or dough to make it rise, increase in volume or bulk, and become light and porous during preparation and subsequent heating. The amount of leavening gas in a mixture and the rate at which it is formed are of importance in establishing texture and other characteristics of leavened products. There are three principal leavening gases:

AIR

Air contributes to some of the volume of leavened products. Air is beaten or folded into mixtures or introduced into ingredients by beating, creaming and sifting. It leavens by expansion during heating.

WATER VAPOR

Water vapor or steam is formed in any batter or dough as it is heated. It is the principal leavening agent in products having a high proportion of liquid to flour, such as popovers and cream puffs.

CARBON DIOXIDE

Carbon dioxide is a leavening agent produced in a batter or dough by chemical or biological reactions. Currently it is produced in breads and cakes from baking soda (sodium bicarbonate) in combination with acid ingredient(s), baking powder, yeast or other microorganisms metabolizing sugar.

From Sodium Bicarbonate and Acids

Baking soda plus an acid ingredient form carbon dioxide gas, salts and water. Common sources of acids are sour or acidified milk, buttermilk, citrus fruit juice, vinegar, applesauce, molasses, and brown sugar. The acidity of sour milk varies with its age and degree of sourness; the acidity of molasses also varies. The acidity of corn syrup, honey and chocolate is too low for them to be used as the only source of acid. When sour milk or molasses is used, the baking soda should be mixed with the dry ingredients, since the reaction between baking soda and acid is immediate in a liquid medium. For proportions of baking soda and acid to use in place of baking powder see "Substitution of Ingredients,"page 39.

From Baking Powders

Baking powders are mixtures of dry acid or acid salts and an alkali (carbonate of soda) separated by an inert filler such as cornstarch or powdered calcium carbonate added to standardize and help stabilize the mixtures. According to federal standards, baking powders must liberate at least 12 percent of available carbon dioxide. Baking powders are classified according to type of acid components. Those commonly found in the supermarket for home use are SAS and low-sodium.

■ Tartrate powders, in which the acid ingredients are potassium acid tartrate (cream of tartar) and tartaric acid. These are quick acting or single acting baking powders that form gas bubbles as soon as the batter is mixed.

■ Phosphate powders, in which the acid ingredient is either calcium acid phosphate or sodium acid pyrophosphate or a combination of these. Phosphate powders may be double acting.

■ Sodium free powders or low sodium powder, may be double acting in which potas-sium bicarbonate replaces the sodium bicarbonate. Use 1.5 teaspoonful (7 ml) for each teaspoonful of baking powder in the recipe.

■ SAS-phosphate powders, in which the acid ingredients are sodium aluminum sulfate and calcium acid phosphate. This type is often referred to as combination or double-acting powder and may be so considered from the point of view that the acid phosphate reacts with the baking soda while the mixture is cold, whereas the sodium aluminum sulfate produces carbon dioxide when the batter is heated. This type is usually available in supermarkets and used in home baking.

Tartrate powders release essentially all of their carbon dioxide while the mixture is cold and SAS-phosphate powders release most of their carbon dioxide when heated; phosphate powders are intermediate. Different amounts of carbon dioxide are lost during mixing, depending on the type of baking powder used.

From Sugar

Carbon dioxide is formed by the action of yeast or certain bacteria with sugar. These reactions require a fermentation or proofing period prior to baking in order to produce the leavening gas.

Yeast — a microscopic, unicellular plant — under suitable conditions of temperature, nutrients and moisture produces carbon dioxide from simple sugars formed from starch and/or granulated sugar. Yeast is marketed in three forms, which are interchangeable:

Compressed yeast is a moist mixture of yeast and starch. The yeast is in an active state. Presence of approximately 70 percent moisture makes the product perishable; therefore, it should be refrigerated.

Active Dry Yeast is similar to compressed yeast except the yeast-and-filler mixture has been dried and is then packaged in granular form. It should be rehydrated before mixing with the flour in making a dough.

Quick rising Yeast (rapid rising or instant) is a more active strain of yeast packaged in a dried form. It does not need to be rehydrated before mixing and is, therefore, more suitable for use in a home bread machine. For a one pound loaf, 2.25 teaspoons may be better than a whole package. Up to 50 percent less rising time is needed with this yeast than with active dry yeast.

Bacteria of certain species, under suitable conditions of temperature and moisture, grow rapidly and produce gases from sugar. Salt-rising and sour dough breads are made from dough leavened in this manner. These doughs will have a distinctive taste.

Acidic (sour) doughs contain *Saccharomyces exigus* and *Saccharomyces inusitatus*. The high acidity of the dough results in the distinctive flavor of sour dough. San Francisco sour dough bread uses in conjunction *Lactobacillus sanfrancisco* which produces lactic acid. Other breads made from sour dough include rye breads and pumpernickel.

Storage and Use

■ Store baking powder, baking soda and cream of tartar tightly covered in a dry place.

■ Check the label for the expiration date, and plan to use it before that date.

■ Before measuring dry leavening agents, stir the product to break up any lumps. For best results, use standard measuring spoons. Be sure the spoon is dry when the product is measured.

Miscellaneous Foods

DEFINITIONS

Bouillon

Bouillon may be a clarified liquid prepared by simmering meat or poultry.

Bouillon cube or powder is a dehydrated cube or powder containing hydrolyzed vegetable protein, salt, fat, dextrin, sugar, meat extract, flavorings and coloring.

Bread Crumbs

Dry bread crumbs are those that can be rolled fine. They are used for stuffings, for buttered crumbs, and for coating foods for frying. Packaged bread crumbs are of this type.

Soft bread crumbs are those prepared by crumbling two- to four-day-old bread. These are used for bread puddings, fondues, timbales, stuffings, and buttered crumbs.

Croutons are dried bread cubes sold commercially. They may have a variety of herb and spice mix coatings.

Catsup

Catsup, catchup, or ketchup is prepared from concentrated tomato pulp and liquid, seasoned with onions and/or garlic, salt, vinegar, spices, and/or flavorings, and sweetened with sugar, dextrose, or corn syrup.

Chili Sauce

Chili sauce is similar to catsup but contains pieces of the whole peeled tomato with seeds and more sugar and onion than does catsup.

Chocolate

Chocolate is the product resulting from the grinding of cocoa nibs (cocoa, or cacao, beans that have been roasted and shelled).

Sweet Chocolate (sweet chocolate coating) is chocolate mixed with sugar and may also contain added cocoa butter and flavorings. It is used for dipping confections.

Semisweet chocolate pieces or squares are formed from slightly sweetened chocolate.

Unsweetened chocolate is the original baking or cooking chocolate with no sweeteners or flavorings added.

White chocolate is milk chocolate that contains mild flavored cocoa butter (the fat of the cocoa bean), but no additional cocoa solids. White chocolate keeps for a shorter time than the more familiar chocolates.

Cocoa

Cocoa is powdered chocolate from which a portion of the cocoa butter has been removed.

Breakfast cocoa is a high-fat cocoa which must contain at least 22 percent cocoa fat.

Cocoa has a medium fat content (from 10 to 21 percent cocoa fat).

Dutch process cocoa can be either "breakfast cocoa" or "cocoa" which is processed with one or more alkaline materials, as permitted under government regulations.

Instant cocoa is a mixture of cocoa, sugar, and an emulsifier. It can be prepared as a beverage by adding hot liquid.

Coconut

Flaked or grated coconut is coconut meat cut into uniform shreds or flakes.

Coffee

Coffee is prepared by roasting green coffee beans, and then blending, and usually grinding. Flavor of the brewed beverage depends on the degree of roasting. In some parts of the country—notably Louisiana—coffee blended with chicory is favored.

Instant coffee is prepared by freeze-drying or by various extraction, evaporation, and drying processes.

Decaffeinated coffee is prepared either by steaming and soaking green coffee with a chlorinated organic solvent or by a water soaking process.

Fruit Pectin

Fruit pectin is part of the water-soluble fiber found in fruit. In the right proportion with sugar and acid, pectin forms a gel. Commercially, pectin is refined from citrus or apple pectin and marketed as liquid or powdered pectin.

Gelatin

The term gelatin usually means the granulated, unflavored, unacidulated product. Gelatin is obtained by hydrolysis of collagen in bones and good-grade skin stock. In processing, gelatin may be alkaline- or acid-extracted.

Fruit-flavored gelatin is a mixture of plain gelatin, sugar or sugar substitute, fruit acids, flavors, and coloring. It is sold in packages standardized to gel 1 pint or 1 quart of liquid (500 - 1000 ml). For industrial use, this product is packaged in one-pound (454 g) or larger containers.

Imitation Dairy Products

Some imitation dairy products resemble ice cream or ice milk, depending on the fat content. The products differ from the dairy products in that a fat such as hydrogenated vegetable oil replaces the butter fat used in ice cream or ice milk. Only a few states permit sale of these products.

Imitation milk and the cream substitutes known as nondairy creamers or whipped toppings are combinations of nondairy ingredients made to resemble milk or cream. The ingredients include a vegetable fat, protein such as sodium caseinate or soya solids, corn syrup solids, flavoring agents, stabilizers, emulsifiers, and water. Nondairy substitutes for cream are also marketed in powdered form.

Filled milk is a combination of skim milk and vegetable fat or nonfat dry milk, water, and vegetable fat. Nutrient standards have not been established for filled milk.

Infant Foods

A wide variety of strained and junior or chopped foods is available. These include small containers, usually glass, of cooked cereals, strained fruits, strained vegetables, egg yolk, homogenized meat, and combinations or mixtures of these foods. In addition, frozen dinners (usually of meat, vegetable, and pasta) are available for infants, toddlers and juniors.

Mayonnaise and Salad Dressings

Mayonnaise is a permanent emulsion of oil droplets in water, stabilized with egg yolk. It is prepared from vegetable oil, vinegar or lime or lemon juice, eggs or egg yolks, and spices. Commercial mayonnaise must contain a minimum of 65 percent vegetable oil.

Salad dressings have substantially the same ingredients as those in mayonnaise, but a portion of the egg is replaced with a cooked starch paste, and the amount of oil is less than in mayonnaise. Salad dressing is 30 percent vegetable oil.

Some French dressings are temporary emulsions. Other commercial French dressings are emulsified with small amounts of vegetable gums or pectins. These dressings also contain tomato paste or purée and a minimum of 35 percent vegetable oil.

Low-calorie or fat-free dressings may have a fruit or vegetable base, and contain water, sugar, vinegar, modified starches, spices, vegetable gums, and emulsifiers, with very little or no oil. They may also be sweetened artificially .

Mustard

A pungent condiment consisting of black and/or yellow mustard seeds pulverized and made into a paste with water and/or vinegar. The paste may then be mixed with spices, sugar, and/or salt. Ground mustard seeds are available as a dry powdered spice.

Nuts

Nuts are dry fruits which generally consist of a single kernel inside a woody shell. True nuts include filberts, hazelnuts, almonds, pecans, and Brazil nuts. Peanuts are the pods of a vine of the pea family and are classified as a legume.

Nuts are available either in the shell or shelled. Shelled nuts may be chopped, ground, blanched, halved, slivered, plain, toasted, and/or salted.

Peanut butter is a spread prepared from finely ground nuts which may be blanched or unblanched. Commercially prepared peanut butter may be hydrogenated and contain salt and/or a sweetener.

Olives and Olive Oil

The edible fruit of the olive tree is available in cans or jars as ripe olives, green fermented, or salt-cured olives, as well as an oil.

Both green and ripe olives are treated to remove the characteristic bitterness of the nut. Ripe olives are packed in salt with or without spices and are available pitted, unpitted, whole, sliced, or chopped.

Green olives are fermented, and packed in brine, either whole, pitted, or pitted and stuffed with pimiento, almonds, capers, onions, or celery.

Dried or salt-cured olives are also known as Greek or Italian olives.

The U.S. grades for ripe or green olives are: Grade A (Fancy), Grade B (Choice), Grade C (Standard), and Substandard.

Green olives are available in the following sizes. Ripe olives have a similar size range:

No. 1 (small)	128 to 140 per lb
No. 2 (medium)	106 to 127 per lb
No. 3 (large)	91 to 105 per lb
No. 4 (extra large)	76 to 90 per lb
No. 5 (mammoth)	65 to 75 per lb
No. 6 (giant)	53 to 64 per lb
No. 7 (jumbo)	46 to 52 per lb
No. 8 (colossal)	33 to 45 per lb
No. 9 (super colossal)	32 maximum

Pickles

Pickles are cucumbers, other vegetables, or fruits, prepared by fermentation or in vinegar, usually with salt, sugar, and spices added. There are three general groups: (1) fermented (salt and dill) pickles; (2) unfermented (fresh pasteurized); and (3) sweet, sour, and mixed pickles and relishes of various mixtures.

Pudding

Instant pudding comes in a variety of flavors. It generally contains a modified starch, milk solids, surfactants and a variety of flavorings and colorings.

Salt

Salt is sodium chloride unless otherwise identified as, for example, potassium chloride. Salt (sodium chloride) is used to season and preserve foods. Sometimes spices and/or herbs or other seasonings are added as in onion, garlic, or celery salt. Salt may also be iodized.

Salt is made "free flowing" by the addition of a substance (sodium silico aluminate) that prevents absorption of moisture from the air.

Pickling salt differs from common salt in that pickling salt does not contain additives that would cloud the pickle liquid. Pickling salt may be granulated or flaked. One cup (250 ml) of the granulated salt is equal to 1 1/2 cups (375 ml) of flake salt.

Rock salt is a granular salt used in salt mills and in ice cream making.

Salt substitutes contain calcium, potassium, or ammonium in place of sodium.

Soups

Soups may be clear or thick and may be served hot or cold. Bisque is a rich cream soup sometimes containing shellfish. Bouillabaisse is a fish soup or stew. Bouillon or broth is a thin soup prepared by simmering meat, fish, or vegetables in water to extract their flavor. Consomme is a clarified, double strength brown broth. Chowder is a heavy thick soup prepared from meat, poultry, fish, and/or vegetables. Fruit soups are served as a dessert. Gazpacho is a clear soup of fresh vegetables and herbs, including tomatoes. Vichyssoise is a cream stock of puréed potatoes, leeks and chicken stock served cold.

Spices and Herbs

Most spices are grown in tropical climates and herbs in temperate climates. Spices and herbs are used to season food and include various plant parts that have aromatic odors and pungent flavors. They include:

Aril (a lacy layer of the nutmeg seed)—mace
Bark — cassia, cinnamon
Berry — allspice, juniper, peppercorn
Bud — capers, cloves
Flower Stigma — saffron
Fruit — cayenne pepper, paprika
Kernels or seeds — anise, caraway, cardamom, celery, coriander, cumin, dill, fennel, fenugreek, mustard, nutmeg, poppy, sesame
Leaves and stems — basil, bay, chervil, celery, chives, dill weed, marjoram, mint, parsley, oregano, rosemary, sage, savory, tarragon, thyme
Root — ginger, horseradish, turmeric

Tapioca

Tapioca is made from flour obtained from the cassava root and is marketed in two forms:

Pearl tapioca consists of small pellets that thicken and become translucent in cooking. Pearl tapioca is made by mixing the tapioca flour with water and cooking it on heated metal surfaces just enough to form a shell on the pellets.

Quick-cooking tapioca consists of very fine pellets. It is made by grinding a cooked dough prepared from tapioca flour or by crushing pearl or native flake tapioca.

Flavored tapioca mixes are blends of quick-cooking tapioca, cornstarch, sugar, and flavorings.

Tea

Tea is prepared from the leaves of an evergreen tree or shrub (*Thea sinensis*). The treatment of the leaves after they are picked produces three types of teas. Black tea is prepared by allowing dried and rolled tea leaves to ferment before they are fired. Green tea is steamed, rolled, dried, and fired without fermentation. Oolong tea has partially fermented leaves. For special teas, including herbal, the leaves are mixed with jasmine, gardenia, mint, orange, or other spices.

Comfrey, as a tea, is a health hazard when taken internally because of toxic pyrrolizidine alkaloids shown to be carcinogenic in rats.

Chamomile and *yarrow* have long been used as teas for digestive disorders. Those allergic to ragweed, asters, or chrysanthemums should drink these with caution.

Sassafras has been used as a tea; it contains safrole, a volatile oil, and a carcinogenic agent in rats.

Textured Vegetable Proteins

Textured vegetable protein products are made from edible protein sources. Extruded products are colored and flavored to resemble a food such as ground beef and are most often used as extenders. Spun soy products are also colored and flavored and shaped to resemble products such as ham, chicken cubes, beef or bacon pieces. Also available are frozen, canned, and dehydrated spun soy products.

Vinegars

The acidity of vinegars ranges between four and six percent (40 to 60 grain).

Vinegar or cider vinegar is the product made by fermenting apple juice.

Malt vinegar is the product made by the alcoholic and subsequent fermentations of an infusion of barley malt or cereals whose starch has been converted by malt.

Wine vinegar is the product made by the alcoholic and subsequent acetous fermentations of the juice of grapes.

Spirit, distilled, or grain vinegar is made by the acetous fermentation of dilute distilled alcohol.

STORAGE AND USE

■ Store nuts tightly covered in a cool, dry, dark place or in the freezer. Exposure to air, light, warmth, and moisture can cause rancidity.

■ Store spices in a tightly closed container in a cool, dry place. Refrigeration or freezing extends their self-life.

■ Keep mayonnaise and salad dressings made with eggs in the refrigerator once the jar has been opened.

■ Keep gelatin in unopened package until ready for use, and store in a dry place.

■ To substitute fresh herbs for dried, use 2 teaspoons (10 ml) minced fresh herbs for each 1/4 teaspoon (1 ml) of the dried product.

■ Melt chocolate for cooking purposes in small container over hot water unless recipe states otherwise. Chocolate scorches easily when exposed to direct heat.

■ Follow storage directions when provided on package labels.

Food Buying Guides

BUYING GUIDE FOR FATS AND OILS

FOOD ITEM AND FORM	MARKET UNIT		APPROXIMATE VOLUME PER MARKET PRICE		APPROXIMATE WEIGHT PER CUP	
Butter (See Dairy Products)						
Oils: corn, cottonseed, olive, peanut, and safflower	1 qt.	946 ml	4 c	946 ml	218 g	7.7 oz
Margarine	1 lb	454 g	2 c	473 ml	227 g	8.0 oz
Whipped	1 lb	454 g	3 c	710 ml	150 g	5.3 oz
Soft tub	8 oz	227 g	1 c	237 ml	227 g	8.0 oz
Imitation (40% fat)	1 lb	454 g	2 c	473 ml	232 g	8.2 oz
Hydrogenated fat	1 lb	454 g	2 1/2 c	551 ml	204 g	7.2 oz
Lard	1 lb	454 g	2 1/3 c	551 ml	204 g	7.2 oz
Beef Tallow	1 lb	454 g	3 3/4 c	887 ml	204 g	7.2 oz
Mutton tallow					204 g	7.2 oz

BUYING GUIDE FOR POULTRY

FOOD ITEM AND FORM	MARKET UNIT		APPROXIMATE NUMBER OF SERVINGS PER MARKET UNIT*	APPROXIMATE WEIGHT PER CUP	
Chicken					
Ready-to-cook					
Broiler-fryer	1 lb	454 g	2		
Roaster	1 lb	454 g	2		
Rock Cornish hen	1 lb	454 g	1		
Capon	1 lb	454 g	2		
Stewing					
Cooked, boned	1 lb	454 g	2		
diced			1 1/2	139 g	4.9 oz
Canned, boned	5 oz	140 g	1 1/2 to 2		
Duck					
Ready-to-cook	1 lb	454 g	1		
Goose					
Ready-to-cook	1 lb	454 g	1 1/2 to 2		
Turkey					
Ready-to-cook					
bone in	1 lb	454 g	2		
boneless roast	1 lb	454 g	3		
ground	1 lb	454 g	4		
cooked, boned, diced	5 oz	140 g	1 to 2	139 g	4.9 oz
canned, boned	5 oz	140 g	1 to 2		

* Amounts are based on three ounces of cooked poultry meat without bone per serving

BUYING GUIDE FOR EGGS

FOOD ITEM AND FORM	MARKET UNIT		APPROXIMATE VOLUME OR NUMBER PER MARKET UNIT		APPROXIMATE WEIGHT PER CUP	
Eggs, Whole						
Fresh	1 doz		12 eggs		244 g	8.6 oz
Jumbo, 63 g	1 doz		3 c	710 ml	244 g	8.6 oz
Extra large, 56 g	1 doz		2 3/4 c	651 ml	244 g	8.6 oz
Large, 50 g	1 doz		2 1/4 c	532 ml	244 g	8.6 oz
Medium, 44 g	1 doz		2 c	473 ml	244 g	8.6 oz
Small, 38 g	1 doz		1 7/8 c	444 ml	244 g	8.6 oz
Frozen	1 lb	454 g	1 7/8 c	444 ml	244 g	8.6 oz
Dried, sifted	1 lb	454 g	5 1/3 c	1.3 l	82 g	2.9 oz
Whites						
Fresh	1 doz		12 whites		244 g	8.6 oz
Jumbo, 42 g	1 doz		2 c	473 ml	244 g	8.6 oz
Extra large, 37.4 g	1 doz		1 7/8 c	444 ml	244 g	8.6 oz
Large, 33.4 g	1 doz		1 2/3 c	393 ml	244 g	8.6 oz
Medium, 30.4 g	1 doz		1 1/2 c	355 ml	244 g	8.6 oz
Small, 25.4 g	1 doz		1 1/4 c	296 ml	244 g	8.6 oz
Frozen	1 lb	454 g	1 7/8 c	444 ml	244 g	8.6 oz
Dried	1 lb	454 g	4 1/4 c	1.0 l	108 g	3.8 oz
Yolks						
Fresh	1 doz		12 yolks		244 g	8.6 oz
Jumbo, 21 g	1 doz		1 c	237 ml	244 g	8.6 oz
Extra large, 18.6 g	1 doz		7/8 c	207 ml	244 g	8.6 oz
Large, 16.6 g	1 doz		5/6 c	197 ml	244 g	8.6 oz
Medium, 14.6 g	1 doz		2/3 c	156 ml	244 g	8.6 oz
Small, 12.6 g	1 doz		5/8 c	148 ml	244 g	8.6 oz
Frozen	1 lb	454 g	1 7/8 c	444 ml	244 g	8.6 oz
Dried	1 lb	454 g	6 3/4 c	1.6 l	65 g	2.3 oz
Substitutes	16 oz	454 g	2 c	473 ml	227 g	8 oz

BUYING GUIDE FOR FISH AND SHELLFISH

FOOD ITEM AND FORM	MARKET UNIT		APPROXIMATE SERVINGS PER MARKET UNIT*	APPROXIMATE WEIGHT PER CUP	
Fish, Fresh or Frozen					
Whole	1 lb	454 g	1 1/2		
Chunks	1 lb	454 g	3		
Dressed	1 lb	454 g	2 1/3		
Fillets	1 lb	454 g	3 1/3		
Steaks	1 lb	454 g	3		
Cakes, frozen	1 lb	454 g	5 1/3		
frozen portions					
unbreaded	1 lb	454 g	4		
breaded, fried					
or raw	1 lb	454 g	5 1/3		
Sticks, frozen	1 lb	454 g	5 1/3		
Fish, canned					
Gefilte fish	1 lb	454 g	3	162 g	5.7 oz
Mackerel	15 oz	424 g	4 1/4	181 g	6.4 oz
Sardines	12 oz	340 g	3 3/4	159 g	5.6 oz
Salmon	1 lb	454 g	4 1/4	167 g	5.9 oz
Tuna	7 oz	198 g	2	170 g	6.0 oz
Fish, cured					
Lox	1 lb	454 g	5 1/3		
Salt fish	1 lb	454 g	5 1/3		
Smoked fish	1 lb	454 g	3 1/2		
Shellfish					
Clams					
in shell (hard)	1 doz		2		
in shell (soft)	1 doz		1		
shucked	1 lb	454 g	2 1/2		
frozen,					
breaded, raw	1 lb	454 g	4 1/2		
canned, minced	7.5 oz	213 g	2 1/2	159 g	5.6 oz
Crabs					
in shell (Blue)	1 lb	454 g	3/4		
in shell					
(Dungeness)	1 lb	454 g	1 1/4		
crab meat	1 lb	454 g	5	162 g	5.7 oz
crab cakes,					
frozen	1 lb	454 g	5		
crab legs and					
sections,					
frozen	1 lb	454 g	2 1/2		
deviled, frozen	1 lb	454 g	5 1/3		
crab meat,					
canned	6.5 oz	184 g	1 3/4		

FOOD ITEM AND FORM	MARKET UNIT		APPROXIMATE SERVINGS PER MARKET UNIT*	APPROXIMATE WEIGHT PER CUP	
Lobsters					
in shell	1 lb	454 g	1 1/4		
meat	1 lb	454 g	4 3/4	153	5.4 oz
spiny tails,					
frozen	1 lb	454 g	2 2/3		
Oysters					
in shell	1 doz		2		
shucked	1 lb	454 g	2	235 g	8.3 oz
breaded, frozen	1 lb	454 g	4 2/3		
canned	5 oz	142 g	1 2/3	156 g	5.5 oz
Scallops					
shucked	1 lb	454 g	3 1/3		
breaded, frozen	1 lb	454 g	4		
Shrimp					
in shell	1 lb	454 g	2 2/3		
raw, peeled	1 lb	454 g	3 1/3		
cooked, peeled	1 lb	454 g	5 1/3		
breaded, frozen	1 lb	454 g	4 1/2		
canned	13.25 oz	376 g	4 1/3	130 g	4.6 oz

* One serving equals three ounces (85 g) of cooked boneless fish or shellfish

BUYING GUIDE FOR MEATS

MEAT FORM	MARKET UNIT		VOLUME/ NUMBER SERVINGS PER MARKET UNIT *
Fresh or Frozen			
Boneless or Ground Meat	1 lb	454 g	4 servings
Meat with minimum amount of bone (steaks, roasts, chops, etc.)	1 lb	454 g	2 to 3 servings
Meat with large amount of bone (shoulder cuts, short ribs, neck, etc.)	1 lb	454 g	1 to 2 servings
Cured and/or Smoked			
Ham, boneless	1 lb	454 g	4 to 5 servings
Bacon	1 lb	454 g	24 slices
Frankfurters	1 lb	454 g	8 to 10 frankfurters

*Three ounces (85 g) of cooked trimmed meat is the usual amount for one serving.

BUYING GUIDE FOR DAIRY PRODUCTS

FOOD ITEM AND FORM	MARKET UNIT		APPROXIMATE VOLUME PER MARKET UNIT		APPROXIMATE WEIGHT PER CUP	
Butter	1 lb	454 g	2 c	473 ml	224 g	7.9 oz
Whipped	1 lb	454 g	3 c	710 ml	152 g	5.2 oz
Cheese						
Cheddar (natural or processed)	1 lb	454 g				
grated or chopped			4 c	946 ml	113 g	4.0 oz
Cheddar or Swiss sliced	1 lb	454 g	8 slices			
Cottage	12 oz	340 g	1 1/2 c	355 ml	236 g	8.3 oz
Cream	8 oz	227 g	1 c	237 ml	230 g	8.1 oz
Spread	5 oz	142 g	1/2 c	118 ml		
Parmesan, grated	3 oz	85 g	1 c	237 ml	92 g	3.3 oz
Cream						
Light (table)	1/2 pt	237 ml	1 c	237 ml	240 g	8.5 oz
Heavy (whipping)			1 c	237 ml	236 g	8.3 oz
whipped	1/2 pt	237 ml	2 c	473 ml		
Sour	1/2 pt	237 ml	1 c	237 ml	241 g	8.5 oz
Half and Half (cream + milk)						
sweet	1 pt	473 ml	2 c	473 ml	242 g	8.5 oz
sour	1/2 pt	237 ml	1 c	237 ml	242 g	8.5 oz
Milk						
Whole or skim	1 qt	946 ml	4 c	946 ml	242 g	8.5 oz
Buttermilk	1 qt	946 ml	4 c	946 ml	242 g	8.5 oz
Sweedened condensed	15 oz	425 g	1 1/3 c	315 ml	306 g	10.8 oz
Evaporated whole or skim	14.5 oz	411 g	1 2/3 c	393 ml	252 g	8.9 oz
reconstituted			3 1/3 c	788 ml		
Dry, nonfat	1 lb	454 g	3 2/3 c	866 ml	131 g	4.6 oz
instant	9 5/8 lb	4.4 kg	4 c	946 ml	75 g	2.6 oz
reconstituted			14 c	3.3 l	242 g	8.5 oz
Milk desserts						
Ice cream	1 qt	946 ml	4 c	946 ml	142 g	5.0 oz
brick, sliced	1 qt	946 ml	8 slices			
Ice milk	1 qt	946 ml	4 c	946 ml	187 g	6.6 oz
Sherbet	1 qt	946 ml	4 c	946 ml	193 g	6.8 oz
Yogurt	1/2 pt	237 ml	1 c	237 ml	246 g	8.7 oz

BUYING GUIDE FOR CEREALS AND FLOURS

FOOD ITEM AND FORM	MARKET UNIT		APPROXIMATE VOLUME OR PIECES PER MARKET UNIT		APPROXIMATE WEIGHT PER CUP	
Cereals/Grains						
Amaranth	1 lb	454 g	2 1/2 c	592 ml	179 g	6.3 oz
Bulgur	1 lb	454 g	2 3/4 c	651 ml	162 g	5.7 oz
cooked			8 c	1.9 l	230 g	8.1 oz
Cornmeal						
white	1 lb	454 g	3 1/2 c	828 ml	130 g	4.6 oz
yellow	1 lb	454 g	3 c	710 ml	153 g	5.4 oz
cooked			16 2/3 c	3.9 l	238 g	8.4 oz
Farina	1 lb	454 g	3 c	710 ml		
cooked			16 2/3 c	3.9 l	238 g	8.4 oz
Hominy, whole	1 lb	454 g	2 1/2 c	592 ml	181 g	6.4 oz
cooked			16 2/3 c	3.9 l		
Grits	1 lb	454 g	3 c	710 ml	153 g	5.4 oz
cooked			10 c	2.4 l	235 g	8.3 oz
Oats, rolled	1 lb	454 g	6 1/4 c	1.5 l	71 g	2.5 oz
cooked			8 c	1.9 l	241 g	8.5 oz
Quinoa, whole	14 oz	397 g	2 1/2 c	592 ml	159 g	5.6 oz
Ready-to-eat						
flaked					31 g	1.1 oz
granulated					88 g	3.1 oz
puffed					23 g	0.8 oz
shredded					37 g	1.3 oz
Rice, brown	1 lb	454 g	2 1/2 c	592 ml	184 g	6.5 oz
Rice, white						
polished						
long grain	1 lb	454 g	2 1/2 c	592 ml	181 g	6.4 oz
medium grain	1 lb	454 g	2 1/3 c	551 ml	193 g	6.8 oz
short grain	1 lb	454 g	2 1/4 c	532 ml	201 g	7.1 oz
Rice, all types						
cooked	1 lb	454 g	8 c	1.9 l	170 g	6.0 oz
precooked	8 oz	227 g			184 g	6.5 oz
prepared			2 c	473 ml	164 g	5.8 oz
parboiled	14 oz	397 g	2 c	473 ml	198 g	7.0 oz
Soy grits, stirred						
low-fat	1 lb	454 g	3 c	710 ml	150 g	5.3 oz
Teff	12 oz	340 g	1 2/3 c	393 ml	198 g	7.0 oz
Wheat germ	12 oz	340 g	3 c	710 ml	113 g	4.0 oz

(continued on the next page)

BUYING GUIDE FOR CEREALS AND FLOURS (continued)

FOOD ITEM AND FORM	MARKET UNIT		APPROXIMATE VOLUME OR PIECES PER MARKET UNIT		APPROXIMATE WEIGHT PER CUP	
Flours						
Amaranth	1 lb	454 g	4 1/2 c	1.1 l	102 g	3.6 oz
Corn	2 lb	908 g	8 c	1.9 l	116 g	4.1 oz
Gluten	2 lb	908 g	6 1/2 c	1.5 l		
sifted					142 g	5.0 oz
Quinoa	24 oz	680 g	5 1/2 c	1.3 l	122 g	4.3 oz
Rice	2 lb	908 g				
sifted			7 c	1.6 l	125 g	4.4 oz
stirred, spooned			5 3/4 c	1.3 l	159 g	5.6 oz
Rye	2 lb	908 g				
light, sifted			10 c	2.4 l	88 g	3.1 oz
dark, sifted			7 c	1.6 l	128 g	4.5 oz
Soy	2 lb	908 g				
full-fat, sifted			15 c	3.5 l	60 g	2.1 oz
low fat			11 c	2.6 l	82 g	2.9 oz
Spelt	1 lb	454 g	4 1/4 c	1.0 l	113 g	4.0 oz
Teff	12 oz	340 g	2 1/3 c	551 ml	147 g	5.2 oz
Wheat						
all-purpose						
sifted	2 lb	908 g	8 c	1.9 l	116 g	4.1 oz
unsifted,						
spooned			7 c	1.6 l	125 g	4.4 oz
instant			7 1/4 c	1.7 l	130 g	4.6 oz
bread, sifted	2 lb	908 g	8 c	1.9 l	113 g	4.0 oz
cake, sifted	2 lb	908 g	9 1/4 c	2.2 l	96 g	3.4 oz
spooned			8 1/4 c	2.0 l	110 g	3.9 oz
pastry, sifted	2 lb	908 g	9 c	2.1 l	99 g	3.5 oz
self-rising, sifted	2 lb	908 g	8 c	1.9 l	105 g	3.7 oz
whole wheat						
stirred	2 lb	908 g	6 2/3 c	1.6 l	133 g	4.7 oz
Pastas						
Macaroni						
1" pieces	1 lb	454 g	3 3/4 c	887 ml	123 g	4.3 oz
cooked			9 c	2.1 l	140 g	4.9 oz
Shell	1 lb	454 g	4 - 5 c	0.9 - 1.2 l	115 g	4.1 oz
cooked			9 c	2.1 l		
Noodles						
1" pieces	1 lb	454 g	6 - 8 c	1.4 - 1.9 l	73 g	2.6 oz
cooked			8 c	1.9 l		

FOOD ITEM AND FORM	MARKET UNIT		APPROXIMATE VOLUME OR PIECES PER MARKET UNIT		APPROXIMATE WEIGHT PER CUP	
Pastas (con't.)						
Spaghetti						
2" pieces	1 lb	454 g	4 - 5 c	0.9 - 1.2 l	94 g	3.3 oz
cooked			9 c	2.1 l	159 g	5.6 oz
Starch						
Corn						
stirred	1 lb	454 g	3 1/2 c	828 ml	128 g	4.5 oz
Potato						
stirred	1 lb	454 g	3 1/4 c	769 ml	142 g	5.0 oz

BUYING GUIDE FOR FRUITS

FOOD ITEM AND FORM	MARKET UNIT		APPROXIMATE VOLUME OR PIECES PER MARKET UNIT		APPROXIMATE WEIGHT PER CUP*	
Apples						
Fresh						
whole	1 lb	454 g	3 medium			
pared and sliced			2 3/4 c	651 ml	122 g	4.3 oz
sauce						
sweetened						
(not canned)			1 3/4 c	414 ml	252 g	8.9 oz
Frozen						
sliced,						
sweetened	20 oz	567 g	2 1/2 c	592 ml	205 g	7.2 oz
Canned						
sliced	20 oz	567 g	2 1/2 c	592 ml	231 g	7.5 oz
juice	46 fl oz	1.4 l	4 3/4 c	1.1 l	249 g	8.8 oz
sauce	1 lb	454 g	1 3/4 c	414 ml	259 g	9.1 oz
Dried	1 lb	454 g	4 1/3 c	1.0 l	104 g	3.7 oz
cooked			8 c	1.9 l	244 g	8.6 oz

(continued on the next page)

BUYING GUIDE FOR FRUITS (continued)

FOOD ITEM AND FORM	MARKET UNIT		APPROXIMATE VOLUME OR PIECES PER MARKET UNIT		APPROXIMATE WEIGHT PER CUP*	
Apricots						
Fresh						
whole	1 lb	454 g	8 to 12		115 g	4.1 oz
sliced or halved			2 1/2 c	592 ml	156 g	5.5 oz
Canned						
whole (medium)	1 lb	454 g	8 to 12		225 g	7.9 oz
halved (medium)	1 lb	454 g	12 to 20 halves		217 g	7.7 oz
Dried	11 oz	312 g	2 1/4 c	532 ml	150 g	5.3 oz
cooked, fruit and liquid			4 1/3 c	1.0 l	285 g	10.0 oz
Avocado						
Fresh	1 lb	454 g				
sliced, diced, wedges			2 1/2 c	592 ml	142 g	5.0 oz
Bananas						
Fresh						
whole	1 lb	454 g	3 to 4			
sliced			2 c	473 ml	142 g	5.0 oz
mashed			1 1/3 c	315 ml	232 g	8.2 oz
Dried	1 lb	454 g	4 1/2 c	1.1 l	100 g	3.5 oz
Blueberries						
Fresh	1 lb	454 g	2 c	473 ml	146 g	5.2 oz
Frozen	10 oz	284 g	1 1/2 c	355 ml	161 g	5.7 oz
Canned	14 oz	397 g	1 1/2 c	355 ml	170 g	6.0 oz
Cherries						
Fresh, red, pitted	1 lb	454 g	2 1/3 c	551 ml	154 g	5.4 oz
Frozen, red, tart, pitted	20 oz	567 g	2 c	473 ml	242 g	8.5 oz
Canned, red, tart, pitted	1 lb	454 g	1 1/2 c	355 ml	177 g	6.2 oz
Sweet, unpitted	1 lb	454 g	1 3/4 c	414 ml	177 g	6.2 oz
Cranberries						
Fresh						
uncooked	1 lb	454 g	4 c	946 ml	151 g	5.3 oz
sauce			4 c	946 ml	215 g	7.6 oz
Canned						
sauce	1 lb	454 g	1 2/3 c	393 ml	278 g	9.8 oz
juice	1 qt	946 ml	4 c	946 ml	250 g	8.8 oz
Currants						
Dried	1 lb	454 g	3 1/4 c	769 ml	140 g	4.9 oz

FOOD ITEM AND FORM	MARKET UNIT		APPROXIMATE VOLUME OR PIECES PER MARKET UNIT		APPROXIMATE WEIGHT PER CUP*	
Dates						
Dried, whole	1 lb	454 g	60 dates			
Pitted, cut	1 lb	454 g	2 1/2 c	592 ml	178 g	6.3 oz
Figs						
Fresh	1 lb	454 g	12 medium			
Canned	1 lb	454 g	12 to 15 figs		230 g	8.1 oz
Dried						
whole	1 lb	454 g	44 figs			
cut fine			2 2/3 c	551 ml	168 g	5.9 oz
Fruit Juice						
Frozen	6 fl oz	177 ml	3/4 c	177 ml		
Canned	46 fl oz	1.4 l	5 3/4 c	1.4 l	247 g	8.7 oz
Fruits						
Frozen, mixed	12 oz	340 g	1 1/3 c	315 ml		
Canned, cocktail						
or salad	17 oz	482 g	2 c	473 ml	229 g	8.1 oz
Grapefruit						
Fresh	1 lb	454 g	1 medium			
sections			1 c	237 ml	194 g	6.8 oz
Frozen sections	13.5 oz	383 g	1 1/2 c	355 ml	219 g	7.7 oz
Canned sections	16 oz	454 g	2 c	473 ml	241 g	8.5 oz
Grapes						
Fresh						
seeded	1 lb	454 g	2 c	473 ml	184 g	6.5 oz
seedless	1 lb	454 g	2 1/2 c	592 ml	169 g	6.0 oz
Kiwi						
Fresh	1 lb	454 g	3 medium			
Lemons						
Fresh	3 lb	1.4 kg	1 dozen			
Juice			2 c	473 ml	247 g	8.7 oz
Frozen juice	6 fl oz	177 ml	3/4 c	177 ml	283 g	10.0 oz
Canned juice	8 fl oz	237 ml	1 c	237 ml	245 g	8.6 oz
Melons						
Frozen balls	12 oz	340 g	1 1/2 c	355 ml	231 g	8.2 oz
Oranges						
Fresh	6 lb	2.7 kg	1 dozen			
diced or						
sectioned			12 c	2.8 l	214 g	7.5 oz
juice			4 c	946	247 g	8.7 oz

(continued on the next page)

BUYING GUIDE FOR FRUITS (continued)

FOOD ITEM AND FORM	MARKET UNIT		APPROXIMATE VOLUME OR PIECES PER MARKET UNIT		APPROXIMATE WEIGHT PER CUP*	
Oranges (con't.)						
Frozen juice						
reconstituted	6 fl oz	177 ml	3 c	710 ml	268 g	9.5 oz
Canned juice	46 fl oz	1.4 l	5 3/4 c	1.4 l	247 g	8.7 oz
Canned mandarin						
fruit and juice	11 oz	312 g	1 1/4 c	296 ml	250 g	8.8 oz
Peaches						
Fresh	1 lb	454 g	4 medium			
sliced			2 c	473 ml	177 g	6.2 oz
Frozen slices and						
juice	10 oz	284 g	1 1/8 c	266 ml	251 g	8.8 oz
Canned						
halves	1 lb	454 g	6 to 10 halves		224 g	7.9 oz
slices	1 lb	454 g	2 c	473 ml	218 g	7.7 oz
Dried	1 lb	454 g	3 c	710 ml	160 g	5.6 oz
cooked	1 lb	454 g	6 c	1.4 l	244 g	8.6 oz
Pears						
Fresh	1 lb	454 g	4 medium			
sliced			2 1/8 c	503 ml	213 g	7.5 oz
Canned halves	1 lb	454 g	6 to 10 halves		227 g	8.0 oz
Pineapple						
Fresh	2 lb	907 g	1 medium			
cubed			3 c	710 ml	146 g	5.2 oz
Frozen chunks	13.5 oz	383 g	1 1/2 c	355 ml	204 g	7.2 oz
Canned						
chunks, tidbits	29 oz	822 g	3 3/4 c	887 ml	198 g	7.0 oz
crushed	29 oz	822 g	3 3/4 c	887 ml	260 g	9.2 oz
sliced	20 oz	567 g	10 slices		208 g	7.3 oz
juice	46 fl oz	1.4 l	5 3/4 c	1.4 l		
Plums						
Fresh	1 lb	454 g	8 to 20 plums			
halved			2 c	473 ml	185 g	6.5 oz
Canned, whole	1 lb	454 g	10 to 14 plums		223 g	7.9 oz
Prunes						
Canned	1 lb	454 g	10 to 14 prunes		196 g	6.9 oz
Dried						
whole	1 lb	454 g	2 1/2 c	592 ml	176 g	6.2 oz
cooked			4 - 4 1/2 c		229 g	8.1 oz
				946-1065 ml		

FOOD ITEM AND FORM	MARKET UNIT		APPROXIMATE VOLUME OR PIECES PER MARKET UNIT		APPROXIMATE WEIGHT PER CUP*	
Prunes (con't.)						
Dried						
pitted	1 lb	454 g	2 1/4 c	532 ml	162 g	5.7 oz
cooked			4 - 4 1/2 c		210 g	7.4 oz
				946 - 1065 ml		
Raisins						
Seeded						
whole	1 lb	454 g	3 1/4 c	769 ml	142 g	5.0 oz
chopped			2 1/2 c	592 ml	182 g	6.4 oz
Seedless						
whole	1 lb	454 g	2 3/4 c	651 ml	146 g	5.2 oz
cooked			2 3/4 c	651 ml	183 g	6.5 oz
chopped			2 c	473 ml	189 g	6.7 oz
Rhubarb						
Fresh	1 lb	454 g	4 to 8 pieces			
cut					122 g	4.3 oz
cooked			2 c	473 ml	242 g	8.5 oz
Frozen, sliced	12 oz	340 g	1 1/2 c	355 ml	168 g	5.9 oz
Strawberries						
Fresh						
whole	1.5 lb	680 g	4 c	946 ml	144 g	5.1 oz
sliced			4 c	946 ml	148 g	5.2 oz
Frozen						
whole	1 lb	454 g	1 1/3 c	315 ml	204 g	7.2 oz
sliced or halved	10 oz	284 g	1 c	237 ml	235 g	8.3 oz

* Weight per cup is that of food alone without liquid, unless otherwise noted.

BUYING GUIDE FOR VEGETABLES

FOOD ITEM AND FORM	MARKET UNIT		APPROXIMATE VOLUME OR PIECES PER MARKET UNIT		APPROXIMATE WEIGHT PER CUP (food alone, without liquid)	
Asparagus, spears						
Fresh	1 lb	454 g	16 to 20			
cooked			2 c	473 ml	181 g	6.4 oz
canned	15 oz	425 g	12 to 18		195 g	6.9 oz
Frozen spears, cuts, and tips	10 oz	284 g	2 c	473 ml	181 g	6.4 oz
Artichokes/Heart						
Bottoms			5 buttons/			
canned	14 oz	397 g	1 c	237 ml	212 g	7.5 oz
Bamboo Shoots						
Canned	16 oz	454 g	1 c	237 ml	12 g	4.3 oz
Bean Sprouts						
Alfalfa, Mung	8 oz	227 g	3 c	710 ml	75 g	2.0 oz
Beans — Green						
Fresh	1 lb	454 g	3 c	710 ml	114 g	4.0 oz
cooked			2 1/2 c	592 ml	125 g	4.4 oz
Frozen	9 oz	255 g	1 1/2 c	355 ml	161 g	5.7 oz
Canned	16 oz	454 g	1 3/4 c	414 ml	135 g	4.8 oz
Beans — Kidney, Pinto, Red, Pink, Black						
dried	1 lb	454 g	2 1/4 c	532 ml	187 g	6.5 oz
canned	15-16 oz	425-454 g	2 c	473 ml	187 g	6.5 oz
dried, cooked	1 lb	454 g	5-6 c	1.2-1.4 l	185 g	6.5 oz
Beans — Lima						
shelled						
Fresh	1 lb	454 g	2 c	473 ml	155 g	5.5 oz
cooked			1 2/3 - 2 c	393-473 ml	166 g	5.9 oz
Frozen	10 oz	284 g	1 3/4 c	414 ml	173 g	6.1 oz
Canned	16 oz	454 g	2 c	473 ml	170 g	6.0 oz
Dried	1 lb	454 g	2 1/2 c	592 ml	180 g	6.3 oz
cooked			5 1/2 c	1.3 l	186 g	6.6 oz
Beans — Navy and Small White						
Dried	1 lb	454 g	2 1/3 c	551 ml	190 g	6.7 oz
cooked	1 lb	454 g	5 1/2 c	1.3 l	191 g	6.7 oz
Beans — Soybeans						
Dried	1 lb	454 g	2 c	473 ml	210 g	7.4 oz

FOOD ITEM AND FORM	MARKET UNIT		APPROXIMATE VOLUME OR PIECES PER MARKET UNIT		APPROXIMATE WEIGHT PER CUP (food alone, without liquid)	
Beets, without tops						
Fresh	1 lb	454 g	2 c	473 ml	145 g	5.1 oz
cooked			2 c	473 ml	180 g	6.3 oz
Canned	16 oz	454 g	2 c	473 ml	167 g	5.9 oz
Beet Greens	16 oz	454 g	2 c	473 ml	227 g	8 oz
Broccoli						
Fresh						
cooked	1 lb	454 g	2 c	473 ml	164 g	5.8 oz
Spears, chopped						
frozen	10 oz	284 g	1 1/2 c	355 ml	188 g	6.6 oz
Brussels sprouts						
Fresh	1 lb	454 g	4 c	946 ml	102 g	3.6 oz
cooked			2 1/2 c	592 ml	180 g	6.4 oz
Frozen	10 oz	284 g	18-24 sprouts			
	16 oz	454 g				
	20 oz	567 g				
Cabbage						
Fresh	1 lb	454 g				
shredded			3 1/2 - 4 1/2 c		80 g	2.8 oz
			0.8 - 1.1 l			
cooked			2 c	473 ml	146 g	5.2 oz
Cabbage, Chinese	1 lb	454 g	2 c	473 ml	146 g	5.2 oz
Carrots, without tops						
Fresh	1 lb	454 g	3 c	710 ml	130 g	4.6 oz
shredded			2 1/2 c	592 ml	112 g	4.0 oz
diced					137 g	4.8 oz
cooked			2 - 2 1/2 c		160 g	5.6 oz
			473 - 592 ml			
Frozen	1 lb	454 g				
cooked			2 1/2 c	592 ml	165 g	5.8 oz
Canned	16 oz	454 g	2 c	473 ml	159 g	5.6 oz
Cauliflower						
Fresh	1 lb	454 g	1 1/2 c	355 ml	104 g	3.7 oz
cooked			1 1/2 c	355 ml	125 g	4.4 oz
Frozen	10 oz	284 g	2 c	473 ml	152 g	5.4 oz
cooked			1 1/2 c	355 ml	179 g	6.3 oz
Celery						
Fresh	1 lb	454 g	2 bunches		121 g	4.3 oz
Stalk	1 stalk		1 c	237 ml	150 g	5.3 oz

(continued on the next page)

BUYING GUIDE FOR VEGETABLES (continued)

FOOD ITEM AND FORM	MARKET UNIT		APPROXIMATE VOLUME OR PIECES PER MARKET UNIT		APPROXIMATE WEIGHT PER CUP (food alone, without liquid)	
Celery (con't.)						
Cooked			2 - 2 1/2 c		153 g	5.4 oz
			473 - 592 ml			
Corn						
Fresh ears	1 dozen					
cooked			5 - 6 c	1.2-1.4 l	165 g	5.8 oz
Frozen	10 oz	284 g	1 3/4 c	414 ml	135 g	4.8 oz
cut kernels	1 ear		1/2 c	118 ml	82 g	2.9 oz
cooked			1 1/2 - 2 c		182 g	6.4 oz
			355 - 473 ml			
Canned						
cream style	16 oz	454 g	2 c	473 ml	249 g	8.8 oz
whole kernel	16 oz	454 g	2 c	473 ml	170 g	6.0 oz
Eggplant, fresh	1 lb	454 g				
diced			2 1/2 c	592 ml	99 g	3.5 oz
cooked			2 1/2 c	592 ml	213 g	7.5 oz
Greens, fresh	1 lb	454 g			77 g	2.7 oz
cooked			3 c	710 ml	190 g	6.7 oz
frozen	10 oz	284 g	1 1/2 - 2 c		187 g	6.6 oz
			355 - 473 ml			
	16 oz	454 g				
Juice						
Tomato	46 oz	1.4 kg	5 3/4 c	1.4 l	265 g	9.3 oz
Mixed vegetable	46 oz	1.4 kg	5 3/4 c	1.4 l	265 g	9.3 oz
Kolhrabi	1 lb	454 g				
Fresh, raw			1 1/2 c slices	355 ml	140 g	4.9 oz
Lentils, dried	1 lb	454 g	2 1/4 c	532 ml	191 g	6.7 oz
cooked			5 c	1.2 l	202 g	7.1 oz
Lettuce						
Head	1 lb	454 g	6 1/4 c	1.5 l		
Leaf	1 lb	454 g	6 1/4 c	1.5 l		
Romaine	1 lb	454 g	6 c	1.4 l		
Endive	1 lb	454 g	4 1/4 c	1.0 l		
Mixed vegetables						
Frozen	10 oz	284 g	2 c	473 ml	182 g	6.4 oz
	16 oz	454 g				
	32 oz	907 g				
Canned	16 oz	454 g	2 c	473 ml	179 g	6.3 oz

FOOD ITEM AND FORM	MARKET UNIT		APPROXIMATE VOLUME OR PIECES PER MARKET UNIT		APPROXIMATE WEIGHT PER CUP (food alone, without liquid)	
Mushrooms						
Fresh, sliced	1 lb	454 g	2 - 3 c	473-710 ml	68 g	2.4 oz
Canned	4 oz	113 g	2/3 c	156 ml	161 g	5.7 oz
Okra						
Fresh, cooked	1 lb	454 g	2 1/4 c	532 ml	177 g	6.2 oz
Frozen	10 oz	284 g	1 1/4 c	296 ml	209 g	7.4 oz
Canned	14 1/2 oz	411 g	1 3/4 c	414 ml	171 g	6.0 oz
Onions						
Fresh	1 lb	454 g	3 large			
chopped			2 - 2 1/2 c	473 - 592 ml	135 g	4.8 oz
Cooked					197 g	6.9 oz
Frozen, chopped	12 oz	340 g	3 c	710 ml		
Canned	16 - 17 oz	454 - 482 g	2 c	473 ml		
Dried					64 g	2.3 oz
Parsnips						
Fresh	1 lb	454 g	4 medium			
cooked			2 c	473 ml	211 g	7.4 oz
Peas, green						
Fresh, in pod	1 lb	454 g				
shelled			1 c	237 ml	138 g	4.9 oz
cooked			1 c	237 ml	163 g	5.7 oz
Frozen	10 oz	284 g	2 c	473 ml	156 g	5.5 oz
cooked			2 c	473 ml	167 g	5.9 oz
Canned	17 oz	482 g	2 c	473 ml	168 g	5.9 oz
Dried, split	1 lb	454 g	2 1/4 c	532 ml	200 g	7.1 oz
cooked			5 c	1.2 l	194 g	6.8 oz
Peas, black-eyed						
Fresh	1 lb	454 g			144 g	5.1 oz
cooked			2 1/3 c	551 ml	162 g	5.7 oz
Frozen, cooked	16 oz	454 g	1 1/2 c	355 ml	171 g	6.0 oz
Canned	15 oz	425 g	2 c	473 ml	205 g	7.2 oz
Dried, split	1 lb	454 g			200 g	7.1 oz
cooked					248 g	8.7 oz
Peppers — Sweet, Bell, Green, Red, Yellow						
Fresh	1 lb	454 g	3 medium			

(continued on the next page)

BUYING GUIDE FOR VEGETABLES (continued)

FOOD ITEM AND FORM	MARKET UNIT		APPROXIMATE VOLUME OR PIECES PER MARKET UNIT		APPROXIMATE WEIGHT PER CUP (food alone, without liquid)	
Peppers (con't.)						
strips			3 1/2 c	828 ml	114 g	4.0 oz
diced			3 c	710 ml	126 g	4.4 oz
Cooked strips			2 1/2 - 3 c		138 g	4.8 oz
				592-710 ml		
Poi	1 lb	454 g	1 c	237 ml	240 g	8.4 oz
Potatoes, white						
Fresh	1 lb	454 g	3 medium		164 g	5.8 oz
cooked, diced						
or sliced			2 1/4 c	532 ml	163 g	5.7 oz
mashed			1 3/4 c	414 ml	207 g	7.3 oz
Frozen, french						
fried or puffs	20 oz	567 g	4 1/2 c	1.1 l	113 g	4.0 oz
	32 oz	907 g	8 c	1.9 l	113 g	4.0 oz
Canned, whole	15-16 oz	425-454 g	8-12 c	1.9-2.8 l	179 g	6.3 oz
Dried flakes	6-7 oz	170-198 g	4 1/2 c	1.1 l	36 g	1.3 oz
reconstituted			10 3/4 c	2.5 l	212 g	7.5 oz
Dried granules	1 lb	454 g	2 1/4 c	532 ml	201 g	7.1 oz
reconstituted			10 1/2 c	2.5 l	212 g	7.5 oz
Hash browns						
frozen	10 oz	284 g	4 c	946 ml	114 g	4.0 oz
	32 oz	907 g	8 c	1.9 l	114 g	4.0 oz
Pumpkin						
Fresh						
cooked, mashed	1 lb	454 g	1 c	237 ml	247 g	8.7 oz
Canned	16 oz	454 g	2 c	473 ml	244 g	8.6 oz
	29 oz	822 g	3 c	710 ml	244 g	8.6 oz
Radishes, sliced	6 oz	170 g	1 1/4 c	296 ml		
Rutabaga						
Fresh						
cubed	1 lb	454 g	2 1/2 c	592 ml	139 g	4.9 oz
cooked			2 c	473 ml	163 g	5.7 oz
Saukerkraut						
Canned	16 oz	454 g	3 c	710 ml	188 g	6.6 oz
	29 oz	822 g	5 1/2 c	1.3 l	188 g	6.6 oz
Spinach						
Fresh	1 lb	454 g	3 c	710 ml	54 g	1.9 oz
cooked			1 c	237 ml	200 g	7.1 oz
Frozen	10 oz	284 g	1 1/2 c	355 ml	190 g	6.7 oz
Canned	15 oz	425 g	2 c	473 ml	221 g	7.8 oz

FOOD ITEM AND FORM	MARKET UNIT		APPROXIMATE VOLUME OR PIECES PER MARKET UNIT		APPROXIMATE WEIGHT PER CUP (food alone, without liquid)	
Squash, winter						
Fresh	1 lb	454 g				
cooked, mashed			1 c	237 ml	244 g	8.6 oz
Frozen	12 oz	340 g	1 1/2 c	355 ml	242 g	8.5 oz
Canned, drained						
Solids	16 oz	454 g	1 3/4 -2c	414-473 ml		
Squash, summer						
Fresh	1 lb	454 g			136 g	4.8 oz
cooked, mashed			1 2/3 c	393 ml	238 g	8.4 oz
Frozen	10 oz	284 g	1 1/2 c	355 ml	211 g	7.4 oz
Canned	1 lb	454 g				
Sweet potatoes/ Yams						
Fresh	1 lb	454 g	3 medium			
cooked, sliced					232 g	8.2 oz
Frozen	12 oz	340 g	3-4		200 g	7.1 oz
Canned	16 oz	454 g	1 3/4 c-2 c	414-473 ml	220 g	7.8 oz
	29 oz	822 g	3 1/2 c	828 ml	220 g	7.8 oz
Dried, flakes	1 lb	454 g			115 g	4.1 oz
reconstituted					255 g	9.0 oz
Tomatoes						
Fresh	1 lb	454 g	3-4 small		162 g	5.7 oz
cooked			1 1/2 c	355 ml		
Canned, whole	16 oz	454 g	2 c	473 ml	238 g	8.4 oz
	28 oz	794 g	3 1/2 c	828 ml	238 g	8.4 oz
Sauce	8 oz	227 g	1 c	237 ml	258 g	9.1 oz
	16 oz	454 g	2 c	473 ml	258 g	9.1 oz
Turnips						
Fresh	1 lb	454 g	3 medium		134 g	4.7 oz
cooked			2 c	473 ml	196 g	6.9 oz

BUYING GUIDE FOR SPICES AND HERBS

FOOD ITEM AND FORM	MARKET UNIT		APPROXIMATE VOLUME PER MARKET UNIT		APPROXIMATE WEIGHT PER CUP	
Allspice	1.1 oz	31 g	1.5 T	22 ml	96 g	3.4 oz
Anise	0.7 oz	20 g	3 T	45 ml	108 g	3.8 oz
Basil					71 g	2.5 oz
Bay Laurel	0.1 oz	3 g			28 g	1.0 oz
Caraway					108 g	3.8 oz
Cardamom					94 g	3.3 oz
Cayenne Pepper ground	2 oz	57 g	1/2 c	118 ml	85 g	3.0 oz
Celery Seed	1.6 oz	45 g	7 T	105 ml	105 g	3.7 oz
Chervil					28 g	1.0 oz
Chili Powder	1.5 oz	42 g	5 T	75 ml	119 g	4.2 oz
Cinnamon, ground	1.6 oz	45 g	6 T	90 ml	108 g	3.8 oz
Clove, ground	1.4·oz	40 g	5 T	75 ml	105 g	3.7 oz
Coriander Seed, ground	1.7 oz	48 g	9 T	135 ml	79 g	2.8 oz
Cumin Seed	1.4 oz	40 g	6 T	90 ml	96 g	3.4 oz
Dill Seed	1.6 oz	45 g	7 T	105 ml	105 g	3.7 oz
Fennel	1.8 oz	51 g	9 T	135 ml	94 g	3.3 oz
Ginger					85 g	3.0 oz
Mace, ground					85 g	3.0 oz
Marjoram, ground	0.9 oz	26 g			28 g	1.0 oz
Mustard Seed	2.4 oz	68 g	6 T	90 ml	179 g	6.3 oz
Nutmeg, ground	1.3 oz	37 g	6 T	90 ml	110 g	3.9 oz
Oregano, ground	1 oz	28 g	6 T	90 ml	71 g	2.5 oz
Paprika	1.4 oz	40 g	5 T	75 ml	110 g	3.9 oz
Parsley	0.2 oz	6 g	5 T	75 ml	20 g	0.7 oz
Pepper, black	4 oz	113 g	1 c	237 ml	102 g	3.6 oz
Poppy Seed	1 oz	28 g	3 T	45 ml	142 g	5.0 oz
Rosemary	0.2 oz	6 g	2 T	30 ml	54 g	1.9 oz
Saffron	0.05 oz	1 g	2 T	30 ml	34 g	1.2 oz
Sage, ground	0.4 oz	11 g	6 T	90 ml	31 g	1.1 oz
Savory, ground					71 g	2.5 oz
Sesame Seed	2.1 oz	60 g	7 T	105 ml	128 g	4.5 oz
Tarragon					76 g	2.7 oz
Thyme, ground	0.9 oz	26 g	6 T	90 ml	68 g	2.4 oz
Tumeric, ground	0.7 oz	20 g	3 T	45 ml	108 g	3.8 oz

BUYING GUIDE FOR SWEETENING AGENTS

FOOD ITEM AND FORM	MARKET UNIT		APPROXIMATE VOLUME PER MARKET UNIT		APPROXIMATE WEIGHT PER CUP	
Sugar						
Brown, packed						
light	1 lb	454 g	2 1/4 c	532 ml	201 g	7.1 oz
dark	1 lb	454 g	2 1/4 c	532 ml	201 g	7.1 oz
granulated	1 lb	454 g	3 c	710 ml	153 g	5.4 oz
Cane or beet						
granulated	5 lb	2.3 kg	11 1/4 c	2.7 l	201 g	7.1 oz
ultrafine	2 lb	907 g	4 2/3 c	1.1 l	196 g	6.9 oz
confectioner's						
unsifted	1 lb	454 g	3-4 c	710-946 ml	122 g	4.3 oz
sifted			4 1/2 c	1.1 l	96 g	3.4 oz
Corn Syrup						
Light & dark	16 fl oz	473 ml	2 c	473 ml	329 g	11.6 oz
Honey	1 lb	454 g	1 1/3 c	315 ml	332 g	11.7 oz
Maple Syrup	12 fl oz	355 ml	1 1/2 c	355 ml	312 g	11.0 oz
Molasses						
Cane	12 fl oz	355 ml	1 1/2 c	355 ml	309 g	10.9 oz
Sorghum	1 lb	454 g	1 1/3 c	315 ml	329 g	11.6 oz
Sugar						
Fructose	5.3 oz	150 g	50 packets		194 g	6.8 oz
	10.0 oz	284 g	2 c	473 ml		
High Intensity Sweeteners						
Saccharin*	3.5 oz	99 g	1 g packets		142 g	5.0 oz
	2.8 oz	80 g	1 g packets		29 g	1.0 oz
Aspartame	7 oz	198 g	1 g packets		159 g	5.6 oz
	2 oz	56.7 g	2 3/8 c	557 ml		
Acesulfame						
Potassium	1.75 oz	50 g	1 g packets		144 g	5.1 oz

* Brands of saccharin sweeteners vary in weight per cup.

BUYING GUIDE FOR LEAVENING AGENTS

FOOD ITEM AND FORM	MARKET UNIT		APPROXIMATE VOLUME PER MARKET UNIT		APPROXIMATE WEIGHT IN GRAMS	
					Per tsp	per Tbsp
Baking powder						
SAS-Phosphate	14 oz	397 g	2 1/2 c	592 ml	3.8 g	11.4 g
Low sodium or						
sodium-free	8 oz	227 g	1 1/3 c	315 ml	3.5 g	10.5 g
Baking soda	1 lb	454 g	2 1/3 c	551 ml	4.0 g	12.2 g
Cream of tartar	1.75 oz	50 g	5 1/4 Tsp	79 ml	3.1 g	9.4 g
Yeast						
Active dry &						
quick	0.25 oz	7 g	1 Tbsp	15 ml	2.3 g	7.0 g
Compressed	0.60 oz	17 g	4 tsp	20 ml	4.2 g	12.8 g

BUYING GUIDE FOR MISCELLANEOUS FOODS[1]

FOOD ITEM AND FORM	MARKET UNIT[1]		APPROXIMATE VOLUME PER MARKET UNIT		APPROXIMATE WEIGHT PER CUP	
Bouillon						
cube	3.25 oz	92 g	25 cubes			
powder	6.25 oz	177 g			177 g	6.25 oz
Bread						
Sliced	1 lb	454 g	12-16 slices			
crumbs						
soft			10 c	2.4 l	45 g	1.6 oz
dry	10 oz	283 g	2 3/4 c	651 ml	102 g	3.6 oz
Croutons, cubed	6 oz	170 g			51 g	1.8 oz
Catsup, tomato	14 oz	397 g	1 1/2 c	355 ml	272 g	9.6 oz
Chocolate						
Bitter/semisweet	8 oz	227 g	1 c	237 ml	224 g	7.9 oz
chips	12 oz	340 g	2 c	473 ml	196 g	6.9 oz
Prepared drink			30 c	7.1 l		

[1] The market unit may reflect only one arbitrarily selected market unit. The market place now permits considerable variety.

BUYING GUIDE FOR MISCELLANEOUS FOODS [1] (continued)

FOOD ITEM AND FORM	MARKET UNIT[1]		APPROXIMATE VOLUME PER MARKET UNIT		APPROXIMATE WEIGHT PER CUP	
Cocoa	8 oz	227 g	2 c	473 ml	113 g	4.0 oz
Prepared drink			50 c	11.8 l		
Instant	8 oz	227 g	1 2/3 c	393 ml	139 g	4.9 oz
prepared drink			28 c	6.6 l		
Coconut						
long thread	1 lb	454 g	5 2/3 c	1.3 l	79 g	2.8 oz
canned, moist	1 lb	454 g	5 c	1.2 l	85 g	3.0 oz
Coffee	1 lb	454 g	5 c	1.2 l	85 g	3.0 oz
Brewed			40-50 c	9.5-11.8 l		
Instant	2 oz	57 g	1 1/4-1 1/2 c	296-355 ml	40 g	1.4 oz
brewed			60 c	14 l		
Freeze-dried	4 oz	113 g	2 c	473 ml	54 g	1.9 oz
beverage	10 oz	284 g	40 tsp	200 ml		
Crackers						
Graham	1 lb	454 g	66			
crumbs			4 1/3 c	1.0 l	85 g	3.0 oz
Soda	1 lb	454 g	82			
crumbs			7 c	1.6 l		
fine	10 oz	284 g	4 c	946 ml	71 g	2.5 oz
Saltines	1 lb	454 g	130-140			
Gelatin						
Granulated						
unflavored	1 oz	28 g	1/4 c	59 ml	150 g	5.3 oz
flavored	3 oz	85 g	7 Tbsp	105 ml	179 g	6.3 oz
prepared			2 c	473 ml	269 g	9.5 oz
Infant foods						
Strained and						
junior (chopped)	3.25-3.5 oz 92-99 g		6 Tbsp	90 ml		
	4.25-4.75 oz 120-135 g		9 Tbsp	135 ml		
	7.5-8 oz 213-284 g		15 Tbsp	225 ml		
Juice	4 fl oz	118 ml	1/2 c	118 ml		

[1] The market unit may reflect only one arbitrarily selected market unit. The market place now permits considerable variety.

BUYING GUIDE FOR MISCELLANEOUS FOODS[1] (continued)

FOOD ITEM AND FORM	MARKET UNIT[1]		APPROXIMATE VOLUME PER MARKET UNIT		APPROXIMATE WEIGHT PER CUP	
Mayonnaise	1 pt	473 ml			244 g	8.6 oz
Nuts, shelled						
Almonds						
blanched	1 lb	454 g	3 c	710 ml	153 g	5.4 oz
Filberts						
whole	1 lb	454 g	3 1/2 c	828 ml	133 g	4.7 oz
Peanuts	1 lb	454 g	3 c	710 ml	144 g	5.1 oz
Pecans						
halved	1 lb	454 g	4 c	946 ml	108 g	3.8 oz
chopped	1 lb	454 g	3 1/2-4 c 828-946 ml		119 g	4.2 oz
Pistachio	1 lb	454 g	3 1/4-4 c 769-946 ml		125 g	4.4 oz
Walnuts						
Persian, English						
halved	1 lb	454 g	3 1/2 c	828 ml	99 g	3.5 oz
chopped	1 lb	454 g	3 1/2 c	828 ml	119 g	4.2 oz
Paste, Almond	8 oz	227 g				
Peanut butter	18 oz	510 g	2 c	473 ml	252 g	8.9 oz
Pudding						
instant mix	6 oz	170 g	13 Tbsp	195 ml	210 g	7.4 oz
Salad dressing						
French	1 pt	473 ml	2 c	473 ml	249 g	8.8 oz
Salt						
free-running	1 lb	454 g	1 1/2 c	355 ml	289 g	10.2 oz
Soups						
Frozen						
condensed	10-10.5 oz 284-298 g		1-1 1/2 c 237-355 ml			
Ready-to-serve	15 oz	425 g	1 1/2-2 c 355-473 ml			
Canned						
condensed	10.5-11.5 oz 298-326 g		1 1/4 c	296 ml		

[1] The market unit may reflect only one arbitrarily selected market unit. The market place now permits considerable variety.

BUYING GUIDE FOR MISCELLANEOUS FOODS[1] (continued)

FOOD ITEM AND FORM	MARKET UNIT[1]		APPROXIMATE VOLUME PER MARKET UNIT		APPROXIMATE WEIGHT PER CUP	
Soups (con't.)						
prepared			2 1/2 c	591 ml		
ready-to-serve	8 oz	227 g	1 c	237 ml	227 g	8.0 oz
Dried	2.75 oz	78 g				
reconstituted			3 c	710 ml	232 g	8.2 oz
Tapioca						
Quick cooking	8 oz	227 g	1 1/2 c	355 ml	153 g	5.4 oz
Tea, leaves	1 lb	454 g	6 1/3 c	1.5 l	71 g	2.5 oz
Brewed			300 c	71 l		
Instant	1.5 oz	42 g	1 1/4 c	296 ml	71 g	2.5 oz
brewed			64 c	15 l		
Herbal	2 oz	57 g	24 bags			
Water					237 g	8.4 oz
Whipped toppings						
dry mix	1.3 oz	37 g	6 Tbsp	90 ml	108 g	3.8 oz

[1] The market unit may reflect only one arbitrarily selected market unit. The market place now permits considerable variety.

VOLUME AND WEIGHT OF COMMERCIAL SIZE CONTAINERS

CAN SIZE	NET WEIGHT		PRODUCTS PACKAGED	APPROXIMATE MEASURE	
6 oz 8 oz	6 oz 8 oz	170 g 227 g	Frozen juices concentrates, individual serving juices, vegetables and fruits, tomato paste and sauce	0.75 c 1 c	177 ml 237 ml
No. 1 Picnic	10 1/2 oz	298 g	Condensed soups, some fruits, vegetables, meat and fish products	1.25 c	296 ml
No. 2 Vacuum	12 oz 14 1/2 oz 15 oz	340 g 411 g 425 g	Vegetables Evaporated milk Sweetened condensed milk	1.50 c	355 ml
No. 300	15 1/2 oz	439 g	Pork and beans, spaghetti, macaroni, chili, date and nut bread, cranberry sauce and blueberries	1.75 c	414 ml
No. 303	15 oz	425 g	Vegetables, fruits	2 c	473 ml
No. 2	20 oz (1 lb 4 oz)	567 g	Juices, vegetables, fruits	2.5 c	592 ml
No. 2 1/2	29 oz (1 lb 13 oz)	822 g	Fruits, vegetables	3.5 c	828 ml
No. 3	46 oz (1 qt 14 fl oz)	1.4 l	Juices whole chicken	5.75 c	1.4 l
No. 10	6 lb 9 oz	3 kg	Institutional or restaurant size for many canned products	3 qt	2.8 l

Food Preservation

DRYING

Some state Cooperative Extension services offer bulletins with instructions for drying foods and for constructing dehydrators. There are a few accurate commercial books available on how to dry foods. Consider the following facts before drying is begun:

■ Most fruits, some vegetables, meats, poultry, fish, herbs, nuts, and seeds dry well, but they must be fresh and of high quality to produce a quality product.

■ Pretreatment of foods prior to dehydrating is essential. Methods of pre-treating include: ascorbic acid treatment, salt (sodium chloride) solution, blanching, and cracking skins. Blanching can be either in water or steam. Steam blanching is preferred over boiling water for some vegetables since more water soluble nutrients are retained. Steam blanching requires 50 percent more time than water blanching. Blanching will inactivate enzymes and retard vitamin C loss. Sulfur treatment is not recommended because some individuals are sensitive to it. However, it is useful in preventing discoloration in some fruits, such as apricots. Pretreatment is required for most fruits and vegetables.

■ Drying racks may be homemade or commercial, but they should not include such harmful metals as galvanized or cadmium-coated products or copper.

■ Drying temperatures must be high enough to prevent foodborne illness, but not so high as to cause deterioration of the product. Generally, temperatures between 120°F and 140°F (50°C°- 60°C) are used. For best results, use 140°F (60°C).

■ Testing for dryness should be done when the food is at room temperature, as hot food will respond differently.

■ Conditioning the food in a large glass jar for one week after drying will ensure evenness and thoroughness in drying.

■ Dried foods are drastically reduced in

volume, often one-quarter of the original volume. As a result, they are often consumed in large amounts since they seem small and light-weight, without attention given to their high caloric content and nutrient density.

■ Dried foods store well in glass jars in a cool, dry, dark place for maximum shelf life. Containers should be of appropriate size for the amount of food to keep air space to a minimum. Plastic bags sometimes do not protect from insect damage.

■ When rehydrating dried foods, any thin liquid that combines well with the food can be used. Examples of liquids are: water, milk, fruit juices, bouillon or ginger ale. For best results with fruit, pour just enough boiling liquid over them to cover. For vegetables, cover and soak in a cold liquid until nearly restored to their original texture. Cover meat with boiling water or broth. Let sit for 30 to 60 minutes, followed by 15 to 20 minutes of simmering before using.

■ Regardless of the equipment or techniques used in drying food, vitamin C loss will be great.

■ Microwave ovens are not recommended for drying. The food tends to burn or dry excessively in one spot while being moist in others, and the oven may be damaged.

Food for Drying
Most fruits dry well. Those which do not dry well include: avocados and olives because of high fat content; berries (other than straw-

berries), guavas, and pomegranates because of high seed content; citrus fruits because of juice content and soft pulp; crabapples, quince, and muskmelon because of objectionable flavors when dried. Berries need to be sieved to remove seeds prior to drying to make fruit leather.

■ Select firm, ripe fruits. Bruised fruits can often be used in fruit leather after bruises are cut out, but are not suitable for halves or slices.

■ Drying times may vary due to humidity, load, type of food and efficiency of the dehydrator. The usual range is 3-5 hours for small fruits, 4-7 hours for other fruits except pineapple (8-12 hours).

■ Many vegetables are difficult to dry or to rehydrate satisfactorily. Carrots, corn, mushrooms, onions, parsnips, peas and peppers dry well. These are inexpensive and available fresh year-round, but drying home-grown vegetables is practical and convenient.

■ Select absolutely fresh, mature vegetables of high quality. They should be washed well just before drying.

■ Drying times will vary from 1-2 hours for herbs, 2-4 hours for other vegetables. The thinner the piece, the shorter the drying time.

■ Meat, poultry, or fish should be lean because fat becomes rancid during storage. Meat must be very fresh. Eggs should not be dried in a home dehydrator as quality will be poor.

- Collect herbs for drying as follows: Leaves should be collected just before the plant flowers; flowers should be collected just after the blossoms have opened; seeds should be collected when mature and no longer green.

- Select freshly picked herbs, gathered just after the dew is off. Herbs dry well at room temperature if household dust is not a problem.

- Nuts and seeds are foods naturally preserved by drying. They are usually used in dried form for making desserts and salads or eaten as snacks.

CANNING

Organisms that cause food spoilage — molds, yeast, and bacteria — are always present in the air, water, and soil. Enzymes that may cause undesirable changes in flavor, color, and texture are present in raw fruits and vegetables. When food is canned, it must be processed at a high enough temperature and for a period that is long enough to destroy any spoilage organisms. This heating process also stops the action of enzymes. The method of canning is determined by the pH or acidity of the food.

Pressure Canning

This processing method, utilizing a pressure canner (not a pressure saucepan or steamer), is used for low-acid foods. At sea level, all vegetables (except pickled vegetables), all meat, poultry, and seafood are processed at 10 pounds of pressure with a weighted gauge and 11 pounds with a dial gauge (70 kPa, 240°F or 116°C). Above 1,000 feet in elevation the pressure must be increased to offset the decreasing atmospheric pressure. The higher the elevation, the less atmospheric pressure, hence the lower the boiling point of water. Lower boiling temperatures are less effective in killing bacteria. Increased pressure raises the boiling temperature. *Clostridium botulinum* spores can survive boiling water canner temperatures, but are killed by the high temperature reached in a pressure canner when processing follows the recommended time and pressure. The pressure canner dial gauge should be tested for accuracy each canning season. County extension offices can tell you where to have your gauge tested. Dial gauges should be replaced if they read inaccurately.

There are two methods of packing vegetables into jars. Check for specific vegetables in Table 13.1.

Raw Pack — Pack cold, raw vegetables tightly into canning jars or cans and cover with boiling water, wipe the jar rim, and seal with the lid. Place jars in the pressure canner.

Hot Pack — Prepare vegetables by boiling in water a short time (varies with specific vegetable). Loosely fill canning jars with hot vegetable and then add liquid, leaving 1-inch headspace. Wipe the jar rim and adjust lid.

Processing — Follow the manufacturer's directions for the canner you are using.

Table 13.1
TIMETABLE FOR HOME CANNING VEGETABLES IN PRESSURE CANNER [1,2]

VEGETABLE	PACKING METHOD	PINT JAR	QUART JAR
Asparagus, 1" (2.5 cm) pieces	raw or hot	30 min	40 min
Beans, green, 1" (2.5 cm) pieces	raw or hot	20 min	25 min
Beans, lima, fresh	raw or hot	40 min	50 min
Beets, small or sliced	hot	30 min	35 min
Carrots, sliced or diced	raw or hot	25 min	30 min
Corn, cream style	hot	85 min	not recommended
Corn, whole kernel	raw or hot	55 min	85 min
Mushrooms, small, whole or large, halved or quartered	hot	45 min	not recommended
Okra, cut or whole	hot	25 min	40 min
Peas, green	raw or hot	40 min	40 min
Peppers	hot	35 min	not recommended
Potatoes, small whole	hot	35 min	40 min
Pumpkin, 1" (2.5 cm) cubes	hot	55 min	90 min
Pumpkin, strained	not recommended		
Spinach	hot	70 min	90 min
Squash, winter, 1" (2.5 cm) cubes	hot	55 min	90 min
Squash, winter, strained	not recommended		
Sweet potatoes, cooked	hot	65 min	90 min
Tomato juice	hot	15 min	15 min
Tomatoes, whole or halved	raw or hot	25 min	25 min

[1] at 10 pounds in a weighted gauge canner; 11 pounds in a dial gauge canner (70 kPa, 240°F or 116°C).

[2] pressure must be adjusted for altitude by increasing the pressure 1 pound (6.9 kPa) for each 2000 feet (609 m) above sea level for the dial gauge canner and to 15 pounds (103.4 kPa) for all altitudes above 1,000 feet (304 m) for the weighted-gauge pressure canner.

Here are a few pointers on the use of most pressure canners:

- Preheat two to three inches of water to 180° F (82°C) in the bottom of the canner.

- Set filled jars on rack in pressure canner so that steam can flow around each jar.

- Fasten lid securely so that no steam can escape except through vent (petcock or weighted-gauge opening).

- Watch until steam pours steadily from vent as directed. Close petcock or place weighted gauge on vent.

- Let pressure rise to appropriate pounds required for processing. (See Table 13.1). The moment this pressure is reached, start counting processing time. Keep pressure constant by regulating heat under the canner. Do not lower pressure by opening petcock. Keep drafts from blowing on canner.

■ When processing time is up, remove canner from heat immediately. Let canner stand at room temperature until pressure is zero. Never try to rush the cooling. When pressure registers zero, wait two minutes, then slowly open petcock. Unfasten lid and tilt the far side up so steam escapes away from you. Remove jars from canner.

When canning meat, poultry and seafood, purchase fresh, high quality products and process within 24 hours. When processing homegrown meat or poultry, processing should occur within 24-48 hours after slaughter. The hot pack method of pressure canning is recommended.

■ Place large, cut-to-measure pieces of boned, defatted meat in a large shallow pan. Add just enough water to keep meat from sticking. Cover and cook slowly on top of the range or in a 350°F (180°C) oven until the meat is medium done or it reaches an internal temperature of 155°F.(68°C.), turning it occasionally so it precooks evenly.

■ Pack hot meat loosely in jar, leaving one inch (2.5 cm) headspace. Add 1 teaspoon (5 ml) salt per quart (1 l) if desired. Add boiling meat juice (extended with boiling water if necessary), leaving one inch (2.5 cm) of headspace. Wipe jar rims thoroughly; adjust lids according to manufacturer's instructions.

■ Pressure-process at 90 minutes at 10 pounds pressure with a weighted gauge; 11 pounds with a dial gauge (70 kPa, 240°F or 116°C). Be sure to adjust for altitude.

Boiling Water Canner Method

This processing method is used for all acid foods: fruits, tomatoes with added acid, jams, jellies, and pickled vegetables. The canner must be at least four inches (10 cm) higher than the tops of the jars. It needs a lid and wire rack. A pressure canner may be used, with the petcock left wide open to prevent pressure buildup. See Table 13.2 for correct processing time. As is also true for pressure canning, never use a jar unless it is a canning jar.

Pack food either raw or hot:

Raw Pack — Put raw fruits into container and cover with boiling hot syrup, juice, or water. Press tomatoes down in the containers so they are covered with their own juice. See directions listed under hot pack for acidifying tomatoes.

Hot Pack — Heat fruits in syrup, water, or steam, or in extracted juice before packing. Juicy fruits and tomatoes may be preheated without added liquid and packed in the juice of cooked fruit. To acidify tomatoes add two tablespoons (30 ml) of bottled lemon juice or 1/2 teaspoon (3 ml) of citric acid per quart (l) of tomatoes.

Sugar syrup concentrations used in canning fruits are as follows:

SUGAR TYPE	SUGAR %	WATER		SUGAR		YIELD	
				c	ml	c	l
Very light	10	6 1/2	1.6	3/4	175	6 3/4	1.6
Light	20	5 3/4	1.4	1 1/2	375	6 1/2	1.5
Medium	30	5 1/4	1.3	2 1/4	550	6	1.4
Heavy	40	5	1.2	3 1/4	800	6 1/2	1.5
Very heavy	50	4 1/4	1.0	4 1/4	1050	6 1/2	1.5

■ Fill jars, leaving 1/2 inch (1.2 cm) headspace. Put on cap, screw band firmly. Put filled and capped glass jars into half-filled water bath canner of preheated water, 140°F (60°C) for raw pack and 180°F (82°C) fot hot-packed foods.

■ Add boiling water, if needed, to bring water an inch or two (2.5 - 5 cm) over tops of jars. Do not pour boiling water directly on glass jars. Put lid on canner.

■ When water in canner comes to a rolling boil, start to count processing time. See Table 13.2. Boil gently and steadily for time recommended for the food being canned. Add boiling water during processing, if needed, to keep jars covered. Immediately remove jars from the canner when processing time is complete.

■ Cool overnight before testing for seal and removing screws bands. Wash jars, dry, label, and store without bands.

See Table 13.3 for estimation of yield and jars needed for canning fruits and vegetables.

Pickles and Relishes

For all pickle and relish products, processing in the boiling water canner is recom-mended. See Table 13.2 for recommended times. **DO NOT USE OPEN KETTLE CANNING.**

■ Use vinegar with five to six percent acidity. Canning and pickling salt should be used for all brines.

■ Processing times for relishes depend on the combination of vegetables. Obtain a USDA recipe to insure safety.

■ For brined or fermented pickles, use a USDA recipe and a fermenting time of two to four weeks.

■ For fresh pack pickles, cure them in brine for several hours or overnight.

■ For relishes prepared from fruits and vegetables, chop, season, and then cook. Hot pack.

■ For fruit pickles, prepare them from whole fruits and simmer in a spicy, sweet-sour syrup. Hot pack.

CAUTION: Developing your own recipes and using combinations of foods are not rec-ommended in home canning. If you choose to do this, freeze the product. Only recipes based

Table 13.2
BOILING WATER CANNER PROCESSING

FOOD ITEM	STYLE OF PACK	JAR SIZE	TIME IN MINUTES			
			0-1000' (0-304 m)	1001-3000' (303-913 m)	3001-6000' (914-1826 m)	Above 6000' (1826 m +)
Apple slices	hot	pt	20	25	30	35
		qt	20	25	30	35
Applesauce	hot	pt	15	20	20	25
		qt	20	25	30	35
Apricots, peaches, nectarines	hot	pt	20	25	30	35
		qt	25	30	35	40
	raw	pt	25	30	35	40
		qt	30	35	40	45
Berries	hot	pt	15	20	20	25
		qt	15	20	20	25
	raw	pt	15	20	20	25
		qt	20	25	30	35
Cherries	hot	pt	15	20	20	25
		qt	20	25	30	35
	raw	pt	25	30	35	40
		qt	25	30	35	40
Fruit puree except figs and tomatoes	hot	pt	15	20	20	25
		qt	15	20	20	25
Grapefruit, orange sections	raw	pt	10	15	15	20
		qt	10	15	15	20
Pears	hot	pt	20	25	30	35
		qt	25	30	35	40
Plums	hot/raw	pt	20	25	30	35
		qt	25	30	35	40
Rhubarb	hot	pt	15	20	20	25
		qt	15	20	20	25
Tomato						
juice	hot	pt	35	40	45	50
		qt	45	50	55	60
whole/halved water pack	hot/raw	pt	40	45	50	55
		qt	45	50	55	60
whole/halved juice pack	hot/raw	pt	85	90	95	100
		qt	85	90	95	100
no added liquid	raw	pt	85	90	95	100
		qt	85	90	95	100

(continued on the next page)

BOILING WATER CANNER PROCESSING (continued)

FOOD ITEM	STYLE OF PACK	JAR SIZE	TIME IN MINUTES			
			0-1000' (0-304 m)	1001-3000' (305-913 m)	3001-6000' (914-1826 m)	Above 6000' (1826 m +)
OTHER FOOD ITEMS						
Jams and jellies	hot	1/2 pt/pt	5	10	10	15
Spreads	hot	1/2 pt/pt	15	20	20	25
			20	30	30	35
Dill pickles	raw	pt	10	15	15	20
		qt	15	20	20	25
Bread & butter pickles	hot	pt	10	15	15	20
		qt	10	15	15	20
14-day sweet pickles	raw	pt	5	10	10	15
		qt	10	15	15	20
Sauerkraut	hot	pt	10	15	15	20
		qt	15	20	20	25
	raw	pt	20	25	30	35
		qt	25	30	35	40

on recommendations of the USDA should be used. Changing ingredients can result in different density and acidity resulting in an under processed and unsafe food.

JELLIES AND JAMS

Jelly, jam, conserve, marmalade, and preserves are all fruit products that add zest to meals. These methods provide a way to use inferior fruit, the largest or smallest fruits and berries and those that are irregularly shaped, that are not suitable for canning or freezing. Basically, these products are similar; all of them are preserved by means of sugar and usually gelled to some extent. Pectin, sugar, and acid levels of fruit vary, making it impossible to develop formulas that will always give the same results. In products made with pectin, use 1/4 to 1/2 cup (50 to 125 ml) more fruit or juice to make a softer product. Use 1/4 to 1/2 cup (50 to 125 ml) less fruit or juice to make a firmer product. In products made without added pectin, a shorter cooking time gives a softer product. Lengthen the cooking time for a firmer product.

Jelly is made from fruit juice; the product is clear and firm enough to hold its shape when turned out of the container.

Jam is made from crushed or ground fruit. It tends to hold its shape but generally is less firm than jelly.

Freezer jam is made with added pectin and is not processed. The taste and color are more like fresh fruit.

Conserves are jams made from a mixture of fruits, usually including citrus fruits; often raisins and nuts are added.

Marmalade is a tender jelly with small pieces of fruit distributed evenly throughout. A marmalade commonly contains citrus fruit.

Preserves are whole fruits or large pieces of fruit in a thick syrup, often slightly gelled.

Fruit butter is a smooth, less sweet preserve made from fruit pulp run through a sieve and cooked slowly.

Some fruits have enough natural pectin to make high-quality products. These fruits are: citrus, apples, grapes, blackberries, boysenberries, cranberries and plums. Other fruits require added pectin for making jellies that are firm enough to hold their shape. These fruits are: peaches, pears, apricots, elderberries, strawberries and raspberries. All fruits have less pectin when they are fully ripe than when they are underripe.

Commercial fruit pectins made from apples or citrus fruits are on the market in both liquid and powdered form. Either form is satisfactory when used in a recipe developed especially for that form. Commercial pectins can lose their gelling capabilities if stored too long or cooked too long when preparing the product. Unused pectin should be stored in a cool dry place.

The advantages of using pectin are that fully ripe fruit can be used, cooking time is short, and the yield is greater.

The acid content varies in different fruits and is higher in underripe fruits. With fruits low in acid, lemon juice or citric acid is commonly added to make gelled products. Commercial fruit pectins contain some acid. Lemon juice is usually added to increase acid content of fruit. If desired, 1/8 teaspoon (0.6 ml) of citric acid can be substituted for each tablespoon (15 ml) of lemon juice.

When using cane or beet sugar, the ratio of sugar to fruit is 3/4:1 for most fruits. It is best to add sugar before cooking. Sugar helps in gel formation, serves as a preserving agent, and contributes to the flavor. It also has a firming effect on fruit, a property that is useful in the making of preserves. To use corn syrup or honey in jelly making, use a tested recipe to ensure success.

Gelling tests for making jelly without pectin are:

Spoon or sheet test: dip a cool metal spoon in boiling jelly, then carry it out of the steam and pour from the spoon. Jelly is done when syrup forms two drops that flow together and sheet off the edge of the spoon.

Freezer test: remove jelly from heat. Pour a small amount of boiling jelly on a cold plate and place in freezer. When it is cooled, see if it is gelled.

To make jelly with pectin using the short boil method, mix powdered pectin with unheated fruit juice, bring mixture to a boil, add sugar and boil for one minute at a full boil. If using liquid pectin, add it to the boiling juice and sugar mixture and boil for one minute at a full rolling boil. Follow directions for the specific product.

Filling and sealing containers when jelly is done:

For jelly, fill to 1/4 inch (0.6 cm) from top and seal. Process according to Table 13.2.

Table 13.3
ESTIMATION OF YIELD AND JARS NEEDED
FOR CANNING FRUITS AND VEGETABLES[1]

RAW PRODUCE	MEASURES	APPROXIMATE NUMBER QUART (950 ML) JARS NEEDED	APPROXIMATE POUNDS NEEDED FOR 1 QUART JAR
FRUITS			
Apples	1 bu. (48 lb)	16 - 20	2 1/2 to 3
Applesauce	1 bu. (48 lb)	15 - 18	2 1/2 to 3 1/2
Apricots	1 lug (22 lb)	7 - 11	2 to 2 1/2
Berries	24 quart crate	12 - 18	1 1/2 to 3
Cherries	1 bu. (56 lb)	22 - 33 (unpitted)	2 to 2 1/2
	1 lug (22 lb)	9 - 11 (unpitted)	2 to 2 1/2
Peaches	1 bu. (48 lb)	18 - 24	2 to 3
	1 lug (22 lb)	8 - 12	2 to 3
Pears	1 bu. (50 lb)	20 - 25	2 to 3
	1 box (35 lb)	14 - 17	2 to 3
Plums	1 bu. (56 lb)	24 - 30	1 1/2 to 2 1/2
	1 lug (24 lb)	12	1 1/2 to 2 1/2
Tomatoes	1 bu. (53 lb)	15 - 20	2 1/2 to 3 1/2
	1 lug (30 lb)	10	2 1/2 to 3 1/2
Tomatoes for juice	1 bu. (53 lb)	12 - 16	3 to 3 1/2
VEGETABLES			
Beans, lima			
(in pods)	1 bu. (32 lb)	6 - 10	3 to 5
Beans, green or wax	1 bu. (30 lb)	12 - 20	1 1/2 to 2 1/2
Beets (without tops)	1 bu. (52 lb)	15 - 24	2 to 3 1/2
Carrots			
(without tops)	1 bu. (50 lb)	16 - 25	2 to 3
Corn, sweet		6 - 10	3 to 6
(in husks)	1 bu. (35 lb)	(whole kernel)	
Okra	1 bu. (26 lb)	16 - 18	1 1/2
Peas (in pods)	1 bu. (30 lb)	5 - 10	3 to 6
Spinach and other			
greens	1 bu. (18 lb)	3 - 8	2 to 6
Squash, summer	1 bu. (40 lb)	10 - 20	2 to 4
Sweet potatoes	1 bu. (50 lb)	18 - 25	2 to 3

NOTE: The actual number of jars needed in canning depends on the size and condition of the produce and the manner of preparing and packing into jars. The standard weight of a bushel, lug or box is not the same in all states.

[1]*Ball Blue Book*, Edition 32, Ball Corporation, Muncie, Indiana, 1992.

For sweet spreads, let stand 5 minutes, stirring occasionally to keep fruit from floating. Place in jars and seal. Then process in boiling water canner according to Table 13.2.

Reduced-sugar fruit spreads are made with several different gelling or thickening agents, each of which gives somewhat different characteristics to the product. Reduced or no sugar may be used. Sweet fruits, apple juice, and/or a liquid low or non-caloric sweetener may be added for flavor. Preservation is dependent on boiling water canner processing, refrigerator storage, or frozen storage. Directions given for the commercial thickening ingredient being used should be followed. If unflavored gelatin powder is used as the gelling agent, the products must be refrigerated and used within 4 weeks.

FREEZING

Freezing preserves many foods with little change in flavor, color, texture, and nutritional value. Freezing, one of the simplest methods of home food preservation, does not sterilize the product; it simply retards the growth of harmful bacteria and molds. Therefore, good sanitation procedures are necessary for freezing. The wrapping or container for the food that is being frozen is very important. Boxes, jars, and bags especially made for freezing are available. A freezer container or wrap should:

- be impermeable to oxygen

- be odorless

- possess high wet strength

- be greaseproof

- be nonadherent to the frozen product

- be puncture resistant

- be easy to mark

- not crack at low temperature.

Plastic freezer containers or other sealed rigid containers are preferred for liquid packs. Canning jars designed for freezing used with home canning lids are excellent for freezing liquids. Jars are easily resealed after removing a portion of their contents. Allow enough headspace for expansion of liquid during freezing to prevent breakage. Be sure to follow manufacturer's directions.

Flexible bags or wrappings of moisture-vapor resistant polyethylene, cellophane, nylon, or plastic are suitable for dry-pack vegetables, fruits, meats, poultry, and fish. Bags may also be used for liquid packs, but breakage and leakage should be expected.

Laminated freezer papers made of various combinations of paper, foil or plastic are suitable for dry-pack meats, fish, and poultry. Metal foils are easily torn or punctured.

Basic Steps in Freezing

- Use only quality fresh products.

- Work under very sanitary conditions.

- Organize everything that is needed to save time and energy.

- Use appropriate packing materials.

- Follow directions for the product you are freezing:

    blanch or scald vegetables; blanch 1 minute longer at 5000 feet (1524 m) and above; cool quickly

    use ascorbic acid for light colored fruits to prevent discoloration

    use appropriate pack for fruits

    keep meats cold while preparing for freezing.

- Package, removing all air.

- Label with date and name of product.

- Promptly place in freezer in single layers.

- Maintain 0°F (-18°C) in freezer.

- Keep an inventory.

- Use all products within recommended storage period for best quality.

How To Pack Fruits

Fruits should be slightly riper than for canning. Fruits can be packed in syrup or dry sugar. The intended use of the fruit will determine the type of pack used. Forty percent syrup is recommended for most fruits. See Table 13.4 for quantities needed.

- Syrup pack: dissolve sugar in water until solution is clear. Use just enough cool syrup to cover the fruit in the container. Allow 1/2 inch (1.2 cm) headspace.

Type of Syrup %	Sugar c	l	Water c	l	Amount of Syrup c	l
30	2	0.5	4	1	5	1.2
40	3	0.8	4	1	5 1/2	1.4
50	4 3/4	1.2	4	1	6 1/2	1.6
60	7	1.8	4	1	7 3/4	1.9

- Sugar pack: works well for soft fruits such as strawberries. Add sugar to clean, prepared fruits. Let stand 10 to 15 minutes. Stir to coat each piece. Pack fruit tightly in storage containers.

- Dry pack: pack fruit in containers without sugar or syrup. No headspace is necessary.

- Individual quick frozen (IQF): this pack is good for small whole fruit. The fruit is frozen individually without sugar on a shallow metal tray or cookie sheet, then packed in a container for storage.

Ascorbic acid should be used with fruits that tend to darken quickly (peaches, apricots, figs, sweet cherries, pears, and apples). Follow manufacturer's directions as to method and amount.

Freezing fruit allows jelly and jam making anytime of the year.

Refer to Table 13.4 for information on percent recovery.

Table 13.4
WEIGHT CONVERSIONS: FARM TO PROCESSED FROZEN FRUITS[1]

FROZEN FRUITS	% RECOVERY	FROZEN WEIGHT FROM FARM WEIGHT[2]
Apples	60	0.60
Apricots	78	0.91
Berries		
Blackberries	95	0.95
Blueberries	97	0.97
Boysenberries	88	0.88
Gooseberries	97	0.97
Loganberries	88	0.88
Raspberries	95	0.95
Strawberries	93	1.12
Cherries		
sour	75	0.90
sweet	85	0.85
Grapes	85	0.85
Peaches	67	0.80
Pineapples	50	0.625
Prunes	85	0.85

[1] Economic, Statistics, and Cooperative Services, U.S. Department of Agriculture. From *The Almanac of Canning, Freezing, Preserving and Allied Industries*. Edward E. Judge & Sons, Inc., Westminster, MD.

[2] Frozen weight is weight of frozen fruits plus sugar content. Fruit to sugar ratio is used in this computation: apricots 6 to 1; strawberries, sour cherries, peaches 5 to 1; pineapples 4 to 1; other fruits 0.

VEGETABLES

Speed from garden to freezer is the important factor in vegetable freezing. Blanching destroys enzymes that will cause deterioration of quality and vitamin C loss during storage. Blanching also cleanses the surface of microorganisms and softens the product which makes it easier to package. Vegetables are lowered into boiling water or in steam for a specific amount of time and then quickly cooled before packing to freeze. (See Table 13.5 for blanching times and Table 13.6 for yields of frozen vegetables from fresh produce).

Vegetables for freezing can be packed in two ways.

Dry Pack — After vegetables have been blanched, cooled, and drained, place them in meal-size, airtight, moisture-proof containers. After packaging, remove all air possible from the container before it is sealed. Allow headspace for expansion of the vegetables during freezing.

Individual quick frozen (IQF) — After vegetable pieces have been blanched, cooled, and drained, spread them in a single layer on shallow trays or pans. Place trays in the freezer for four to six hours, then quickly package frozen pieces in a suitable resealable container. Unblanched diced onions and peppers may be IQF packed.

Table 13.5
TIMETABLE FOR BLANCHING VEGETABLES PRIOR TO FREEZING

VEGETABLE	MINUTES HEATED IN BOILING WATER [1,2]	VEGETABLE	MINUTES HEATED IN BOILING WATER [1,2]
Asparagus		medium ears — 1 1/4 to 1 1/2	
small stalks	1 1/2	inches (3-3.8 cm) in diameter	6
medium stalks	2	large ears — 1 1/2 to 2 inches	
large stalks	3	(3-5 cm) in diameter	8
Beans, lima		extra large ears (over 2 inches	
small beans or pods	1	(5 cm) in diameter	10
medium beans or pods	2	whole kernel	5 to 6
large beans or pods	3	**Greens, all types**	2
Beans, wax or green	3	**Kohlrabi**	
Beets		1/2 inch (1.2 cm) cubes	2
small	25 to 30	whole, small to medium	3
medium	45 to 50	**Okra**	
Broccoli		small pods	3
florets 1 1/2 inches (3.8 cm)		large pods	5
in diameter	3	**Parsnips**, 1/2 inch (1.2 cm) cubes	
large	4	or slices	5
Brussels sprouts		**Peas**	
small heads	3	black-eyed	
medium	4	small	1
large	5	large	2
Cabbage		green	2
coarse shreds or thin wedges	1 1/2	**Pumpkin**	until soft
wedges	3	**Rutabagas**, 1/2 inch (1.2 cm) cubes	3
Carrots		**Squash**	
whole small	5	summer, 1/2 inch (1.2 cm) slices	3
diced, sliced, strips	3	winter	until soft
Cauliflower		**Sweet potatoes**	until soft
medium	3	**Tomatoes**	
large	4	whole	until soft
Corn, sweet		juice, simmer tomatoes	5
small ears — 1 1/4 inches (3 cm)		**Turnips**, 1/2 inch (1.2 cm) cubes	3
or less in diameter	5		

[1] For each pound of prepared vegetable, use at least 1 gallon of boiling water. After heating the specified time, cool promptly in cold water and drain.

[2] Adjust time for altitude so under-blanching does not occur.

Table 13.6
WEIGHT CONVERSIONS: FARM TO PROCESSED FROZEN VEGETABLES[1]

FROZEN VEGETABLE	% RECOVERY	FROZEN WEIGHT FROM FARM WEIGHT[2]
Asparagus	52	0.52
Lima beans		
shelled	95	0.95
Snap beans	85	0.85
Broccoli	75	0.75
Brussels sprouts	75	0.75
Cauliflower	70	0.70
Corn, cut	27	0.27
Carrots	55	0.55
Okra	85	0.85
Peas, green		
shelled	92	0.92
Peas	50	0.50
Potatoes, white	40	0.40
Peppers, sweet	70	0.70
Spinach	70	0.70
Other greens	75	0.75
Squash	55	0.55
Sweet potatoes	50	0.50

[1] Economic, Statistics, and Cooperative Services, U.S. Department of Agriculture. From *The Almanac of Canning, Freezing, Preserving and Allied Industries*. Edward E. Judge & Sons, Inc., Westminster, MD.

[2] Sugar ratio does not apply

NOTE; Relationships between farm and processed weights for most commodities vary widely from season to season and between localities. Factors shown in the table above represent average relationships for all producing areas.

MEAT

Freezing is the best method of meat storage. Starting with a wholesome, high-quality product will ensure the best results. All meat should be wrapped in moisture-vapor-proof material that is impermeable to oxygen.

THAWING

With the exception of spinach and corn-on-the-cob, vegetables may be taken directly from the freezer, unpacked, and steamed or boiled. Spinach and corn-on-the-cob are better if first thawed in a microwave oven or four hours in the refrigerator.

Meats, fish, shellfish, and vegetables must not be thawed at room temperature. Many bacteria on fresh food will still be present when food is thawed. The nutrients in the drip that forms upon thawing support rapid bacterial growth. Bacteria capable of causing illness are common on vegetables, meats, poultry, and seafood. Improper thawing of these products may lead to illness. Thawing sealed packages of foods rapidly in cold water is an acceptable practice, but the cold water should be changed every 5 to 10 minutes. Proper thawing will help ensure safe food. Leftover frozen foods should be held below 40°F or above 140°F (4°C - 60°C) to avoid possible foodborne illnesses.

FOODS NOT SUITABLE FOR FREEZING

Some foods not suitable for freezing include raw cabbage, cake batters, raw celery, cream pie fillings, custards, cooked egg whites, lettuce, mayonnaise, potato salad, salad dressing, fresh tomatoes, and watermelon.

IF FREEZER STOPS

If power fails or the freezer stops operating normally, try to determine how long it will be before the freezer will be back in operation.

A fully-loaded freezer usually will stay cold enough to keep foods frozen for two days if the cabinet is not opened. In a cabinet with less than half a load, food may not stay frozen more than one day. Some partially thawed foods can be refrozen. Generally, refreezing should not pose a health hazard if the food has not reached 40°F (4°C). If thawed food still contains a few ice crystals, it is safe to refreeze. Quality loss occurs with thawing and refreezing. However, it is least evident in red meats and most evident in fish and seafood.

Meat, Poultry and Vegetables — Refreeze if the temperature is 40°F (4°C) or below and if the color and odor are good. Discard packages that show signs of spoilage, such as off-colors or bad odors.

Fruits — Refreeze if they smell and taste good. Thawed fruits may also be used in cooking or making jellies, jams, and preserves.

Cooked foods — Refreeze if ice crystals are still present or the freezer is 40°F (4°C) or below. If the condition is poor or questionable, throw it out.

If normal operation cannot be resumed before the food will start to thaw, use dry ice. If dry ice is placed in the freezer soon after the power is off, 25 pounds (11 kg) should keep the temperature below freezing for two to three days in a 10-cubic-foot (0.3 m^3) cabinet with half a load, and three to four days in a loaded cabinet. Place the dry ice on cardboard or small boards on top of packages and do not open cabinet again except to put in more dry ice or to remove it when normal operation is resumed.

Another suggestion is to move the food to a locker plant, using insulated boxes or thick layers of paper to prevent thawing while in transit. The locker plant can refreeze the packaged food more quickly, resulting in better quality.

Sources of Information

Additional information on food and food preparation may be obtained from the following:

U.S. GOVERNMENT RESOURCES

Consumer Information Center
Pueblo, CO 81009
719-948-4000
USDA consumer publications such as Home & Garden Bulletins and Buying Guides: topics include food, nutrition and home safety. Complete listing of publications available.

Federal Trade Commission (FTC)
Div. of Advertising Practices
601 Pennsylvania Ave., NW, Room 4221
Washington, DC 20580
202-326-3131
Hotline for questions regarding advertising of food, drugs, cosmetics and tobacco.

Food and Drug Administration (FDA)
Office of Consumer Affairs and Information Staff
5600 Fisher Lane, Room 16-63
Rockville, MD 20857
301-443-3170
Answers consumer inquiries and acts as clearing house for FDA consumer publications.

FDA Seafood Hotline

FDA Center for Food Safety and Applied Nutrition
1-800-FDA-4010
Takes questions and complaints about identity, safety, inspection, labeling and nutrient values of commercial seafood.

Food and Nutrition Information Center
National Agricultural Library, Room 304
Department of Agriculture
Beltsville, MD 20705
301-504-5719 • 301-504-5472 fax
The FNIC offers pathfinders on food and nutrition topics geared to specific user levels: consumer, educator and professional. Resources include bibliographies, databases, computer software, print and audio/visual materials, and contacts for assistance.

National Academy of Sciences
2010 Constitution Avenue
Washington, D.C. 20418
Office of News and Public Information
202-334-2138
Food and Nutrition Board
202-334-2238
National Marine Fisheries Services

Office of Trade and Industry Service
U.S. Department of Commerce
1335 East-West Highway
Silver Spring, MD 20910
301-713-2355 (inspection and safety)
301-713-2358 (nutrition information)
Provides grading and inspection service for fish processors.

Safe Drinking Water Hotline, EPA
202-382-5533 in D.C.
800-426-4791 outside D.C.
Explains federal drinking water regulations; provides information on health issues related to drinking water contaminants.

Superintendent of Documents
U.S. Government Printing Office
Washington, D.C. 20402-9325
202-783-3238
202-275-0019 fax
To order government publications and current lists of publications published by various U.S. agencies.

US Consumer Product Safety Commission
Washington, D.C. 20207
800-638-2772 (CPSC)
To report a hazardous product or product-related injury, or inquire about product recalls.

U.S. Department of Agriculture (USDA)
Office of the Consumer Advisor
12th & Jefferson Drive, SW
Room 207-W, Administration Building
Washington, DC 20250
202-720-3975 or 202-720-9681
Will refer calls to appropriate agency within USDA.

"How to Get Information from the USDA"
This publication lists all USDA agencies with contact names and phone numbers.
For a copy call 202-720-7454.

Human Nutrition Information Service

United States Department of Agriculture
Federal Building, Rooms 360 & 344
6505 Belcrest Road
Hyattsville, MD 20782
301-436-8617, 7725
USDA publications for consumers and professionals.

USDA Information Center
14th and Independence
Washington, D.C. 20250
202-720-2791

USDA Meat and Poultry Hotline
Food Safety and Inspection Service (FSIS)
Department of Agriculture
Washington, D.C. 20250
1-800-535-4555 10-4 EST
Inquiries on food safety, food storage, cooking, labeling and nutrition.

PROFESSIONAL ORGANIZATIONS

American Dietetic Association (ADA)
216 W. Jackson Blvd., Suite 800
Chicago, IL 60606-6995
312-899-0040 Hotline for professionals
800-232-3472 Consumer Hotline
Members are registered dietitians or associates in the health care and related fields.

American Home Economics Association (AHEA)
1555 King Street
Alexandria, VA 22314
703-706-4600
Members are home economics professionals working in such areas as business, education, extension, health care and government.

American Institute of Wine and Food (AIWF)
1550 Bryant, Suite 700
San Francisco, CA 94103
415-255-3000
Members include food and wine professionals.

American School Food Service Association

5600 South Quebec, Suite 300B
Englewood, CO 80111
303-220-8484
Members work in school, food-service operations.

Home Economists in Business (HEIB)
Blendonview Office Park
5008-16 Pine Creek Drive
Westerville, OH 43081-4899
614-890-4342 (HEIB)
A professional section of AHEA, many HEIB members work for various types of food companies. Call the HEIB office for contacts in the food industry.

Institute of Food Technologists (IFT)
221 N. LaSalle Street
Chicago, IL 60601
312-782-8424
Members include food technologists, dietitians and home economists.

International Association of Cooking Professionals (IACP)
304 West Liberty Street, Suite 301
Louisville, KY 40202
502-583-3783
Members are primarily food professionals and cooking school owners/teachers.

INDUSTRY-SPONSORED ORGANIZATIONS TRADE ASSOCIATIONS

Food Marketing Institute (FMI)
1750 K Street N.W.
Washington, D.C. 20006
202-452-8444

Grocery Manufacturers of America (GMA)
1010 Wisconsin Avenue N.W.
Suite 800
Washington, D.C. 20007
202-337-9400

International Microwave Power Institute (IMPI)

13542 Union Village Circle
Clifton, VA 22024
703-830-5588

National Association of Food Equipment Manufacturers
111 East Wacker Drive, Suite 600
Chicago, IL 60601
312-644-6610

National Grocers' Association
1825 Samuel Morse Drive
Reston, VA 22090
703-437-5300

National Restaurant Association (NRA)
311 1st Street NW
Washington, D.C. 20001
202-331-5900

Produce Marketing Association (PMA)
1500 Casho Mill Road (P.O. Box 6036)
Newark, DE 19714-6036
302-738-7100

AGRICULTURAL COMMODITY BOARDS & COMMISSIONS; PRODUCT PROMOTION ASSOCIATIONS

American Dry Bean Board
4502 Avenue I
Scottsbluff, NE 69861
308-632-1258

American Egg Board
1460 Renaissance Drive
Park Ridge, IL 60068
708-296-7044
Egg Nutrition Center
1-800-833-3447

American Lamb Council
200 Clayton Street
Denver, CO 80206
303-771-3500

Apple Institute, International
P.O. Box 1137
McLean, VA 22101
703-442-8850

Canned Food Information Council
National Food Processors Association
1401 New York Avenue NW
Washington, D.C. 20005
312-836-7279

Canned Fruit Promotion Service
P.O. Box 7111
San Francisco, CA 94120
415-541-0100

Cheese Importer's Association
460 Park Avenue
New York, NY 10022
212-753-7500

National Dairy Council/
American Dairy Association
6300 North River Road
Rosemont, IL 60018
708-696-1860

National Fisheries Institute
1525 Wilson Blvd., Suite 500
Arlington, VA 22209
703-524-8881

National Live Stock & Meat Board
444 North Michigan Avenue
Chicago, IL 60611
312-467-5520

National Onion Association
1 Greeley National Plaza, Suite 510
Greeley, CO 80631
303-353-5895

National Pasta Association
2101 Wilson Blvd., Suite 920
Arlington, VA 22201
703-841-0818
National Pork Producers' Council

Div. of Natl. Livestock & Meat Board
P.O. Box 10383
Des Moines, IA 50306
515-223-2600

National Turkey Federation
11319 Sunset Hills Road
Reston, VA 22090
703-435-7206

Papaya Administrative Committee
2211 Hacienda Blvd.
Hacienda Heights, CA 91745
818-961-1856

Peanut Advisory Board
1950 North Park Place, Suite 525
Atlanta, GA 30339
404-933-0357

Pineapple Growers' Association
1150 South King Street, Suite 901D
Honolulu, HI 96814
808-531-5395

The Potato Board
1385 South Colorado Blvd., Suite 512
Denver, CO 80222
303-758-7783

Rice Council of America
P.O.Box 740123
Houston, TX 77274
713-270-6699

United Fresh Fruit & Vegetable Association
272 N. Washington Street
Alexandria, VA 22313
1-800-336-3065

Wheat Foods Council
5500 South Quebec, Suite 111
Englewood, CO 80111
303-694-5828

REFERENCE BOOKS

Cardinal's Handbook of Recipe Development, Evelyn Hullah. Cardinal Biologicals Ltd., Canada, 1984.

Complete Guide to Home Canning, USDA, Agriculture Information Bulletin # 539. Washington, D.C., 1989.

Dictionary of Food Ingredients, Robert S. Igoe. Van Nostrand Reinhold, New York, 1989.

Experimental Food Science, 3rd ed., M.P Penfield and A.M. Campbell. Academic Press, Inc., San Diego, 1990.

Food for Fifty, 8th edition, Grace Shugart and Mary Molt. Macmillan, New York, 1989.

Food Fundamentals, 5th edition, Margaret McWilliams. Plycon Press, Redondo Beach, CA, 1992.

Food:Experimental Perspectives, 2nd edition, Margaret McWilliams. Macmillan, New York, 1993.

Food Theory and Application, 2nd ed., J. Bowers, editor. Macmillan, New York, 1992.
Foundations of Food Preparation, 5th ed., J.H. Freeland-Graves and G.C. Peckham. Macmillan, New York, 1987.

High-altitude cooking write to:
Colorado State University, Cooperative Extension Service, Fort Collins, CO 80523.
Emily Griffith Opportunity School, Public Relations Dept., 1250 Welton St., Denver, CO 80204. Ask for the 1991 publication, The Best of Friends.

Introductory Foods, 9th ed., M. Bennion. Macmillan, New York, 1990.

Larousse Gastronomique, Jennifer Harvey Lang, editor. Crown Publishers, New York, 1988.

The Buying Guide for Fresh Fruits, Vegetables, Herbs and Nuts, Blue Goose Growers Inc. Shepherdstown, West Virginia, 1986.

The Food Professional's Guide, The James Beard Foundation Directory of People, Products and Services, compiled by Irena Chalmers. American Showcase, Inc. and John Wiley & Sons, Inc., New York, 1990.

Uncommon Fruits and Vegetables - A Common Sense Guide, E. Schneider. Harper and Row, New York, 1986.

INDEX

fined, 64
Blini, defined, 64
Blintz, defined, 65
Blueberries,
    buying of, 125
    frozen, 213
Boil, defined, 59
Boiling point, defined,
    56
Boiling temperature of
    water, 14
    *See also Tempera-
    ture; Water*
Bolted white cornmeal,
    146
Bombé, defined, 64
Borscht, defined, 64
Botulism, 54
Bouillabaisse, defined,
    64
Bouillon
    buying of, 196
    defined, 64, 168
Bouquet garni, defined,
    64
Boysenberries,
    buying of, 129
    frozen, 213
Brains, 82
Braising
    defined, 59
    meat, 93
    poultry, 112, 114
Bratwurst, defined, 64
Braunschweiger, de-
    fined, 64
Bread
    buying of, 196
    defined, 59
    flour, 149
    sour dough, 167
Bread crumbs
    defined, 168
Breadfruit, 120
Breaded fish products,
    minimum fish
    weight in, 107
    See also Fish
Breading (coating), 59
Breads
    baking temperatures
    for, 37

basic recipe for, 42-
    43
high-altitude and
    baking of, 18
microwave cooking
    and, 20
*See also individual
products by name*
Brine, defined, 59
Brioche, defined, 64
Broccoli
    buying of, 133, 189
    cooking of, 140
    freezing of, 214, 215
    herbs and, 144
    preservation of, 139
Brochette, defined, 65
Broiling
    charcoal, of fish, 105
    defined, 60
    of fish and shellfish,
    104
    of meat, 88, 89
    of poultry, 112-113
Brown, defined, 60
Brown sugar, 156
    buying of, 195
Browning reactions, 56
Brussels sprouts
    buying of, 133
    cooking of, 140
    freezing of, 214, 215
    herbs and, 144
    preservation, 139,
    140
Buckwheat flour, 151
    See also Flour
Bulgur wheat, 148
    *See also Wheat prod-
    ucts*
Bulgur, defined, 64
Buñuelos, defined, 64
Butter, 71-72
    buying of, 180
    grades and uses of,
    71
Butter and flour sauce
    (roux), 69
Buying guides
    for cereals, 181-183
    for dairy products,
    180

for eggs, 177
for fats and oils, 175
for fish and shellfish,
    178-179
for flours, 181-183
for fruits, 183-187
for herbs, 194
for leavening agents,
    196
for meat, 179
for miscellaneous
    foods, 196-199
for poultry, 176
for spices, 194
for sweetening
    agents, 195
for vegetables, 188-
    193

C

Cabbage
    buying of, 133, 189
    Chinese, buying of,
    134, 189
    freezing of, 214, 215
    herbs and, 144
    preservation, 139,
    140
Café au lait, defined, 64
Café noir, defined, 64
Cakes
    baking temperatures
    for, 37
    basic recipes, 37
    high-altitude and
    baking of, 16-18
    microwave cooking
    and, 22-23
Calcium carbonate, 35
Calcium propionate, 35
Caldo, defined, 64
Calories
    decrease, 7-8
    food labeling and, 29,
    31, 32
    See also Low calorie
Campylobacterosis 53-
    54
Can size, 200
Canapés, defined, 64
Candied, defined, 60

Candy, temperature
    tests for, 161
Canistel, 120
Cane syrup, 156
Canned fish, 98
Canned fruit, 123
Canned vegetables, 131
Canned products
    fish and shellfish, 98
Cannelloni, defined, 64
Canner
    altitude adjustment,
    204
    open kettle, 205-208
    pressure, 203-205
    water bath, 205-208
Canning, 203-208
    at high altitudes, 15
    boiling-water bath
    207-208
    outline of processes
    of, 203-206
    pressure, 203-205
    timetables for, 204,
    207-208
    yield of, 210
Cannoli, defined, 64
Cantaloupes
    buying of, 125
Capers, defined, 64
Cappuccino, defined, 64
Carambola, 120
Caramel, 35, 161
Caramelize, defined, 60
Carbon dioxide, as leav-
    ening agent, 165, 166
Carob, 130
Carrots
    buying of, 133
    canning of, 204
    cooking of, 141
    freezing of, 214, 215
    herbs and, 144
    preservation, 139,
    140
Carotinoids, 56
Casaba,
    buying of, 125
Cassoulet, defined, 65
Catsup
    buying of, 196
    defined, 168

Hydrogenation, 58
Hydrolyzed vegetable protein, 35
Hydrolysis, 58

I

Ice cream, 78-79
Ice milk, 79
Imbottite, defined, 67
Individual quick frozen, 212, 213
Infant foods, 23, 170, 197
Ingredient labeling, 29
Ingredient substitution, 38-40
Inspection and grading fish and shellfish, 106
International culinary terms, 63-70
Irish moss, as gelling agent, 51
Irradiation, 58
Isopropyl citrate, 35

J

Jabotica, 120
Jams, 208-209, 211
defined, 208
equipment, 209-211
freezer, 208
making of, 208
pectin, 209
Jellies, 208-209, 211
defined, 208
freezer test, gelling, 209
gelatin, 211
making of, 208
pectin, 209
spoon test, gelling, 209
testing of, 161, 209
Joule, 6
Julienne, defined, 61
Julienne process, 61

K

Kale
buying of, 135
cooking of, 142

Kabob (kebob, kebab), defined, 67
Kasha, defined, 67
Kidneys, 82
cooking of, 95
Kilocalorie, 58
Kim chee, defined, 67
Kippers, defined, 67
Kiwifruit
buying of, 127, 185
defined, 61
Knead, defined, 61
Kohlrabi
buying of, 190
cooking of, 142
freezing of, 214
Kolachi or Kolachy, defined, 67
Kosher, 58
Kuchen, defined, 67
Kugelhopf, defined, 67

L

Labeling, food, government standards and, 28-33
Lactose, 160
Lamb
cooking of, 88-96
cuts of, 83
microwave cooking and, 21
sources of, 82
types of, 82
See also Meat
Lard
buying of, 175
defined, 61
Lasagna, defined, 67
Leavening agents, 34, 58, 165-167
buying guide for, 196
function, 11
high altitudes and, 16
Lecithin, 35
Leeks, buying of, 136
Lemons, buying of, 127, 185
Lentils, buying of, 190
Lettuce
buying of, 135, 190
Lignin, 153

Lilmonene, 35
Lima beans
buying of, 188
freezing of, 214, 215
herbs and, 144
preservation of, 140
Limes, 121, 127
buying of, 127
Limpa, defined, 67
Linguine, defined, 67
Liquid
function, 11
high altitude and, 17
Listeriosis, 55
Liver, 82
cooking of, 95
Lobster
buying of, 179
cooking of, 105-106
Loganberries
buying of, 129
frozen, 213
Longans, 120
Low calorie
food labeling, 31, 32
sweeteners, 158
Lukewarm, defined, 61
Luau, defined, 67
Lucia buns, defined, 67
Lychee, 120

M

Macaroni and cheese
baking temperatures for, 37
Macerate, defined, 61
Mackerel, 98
Magnesium silicate, 36
Maltose, 160
Mamey, 120
Manicotti, defined 67
Maple sugar, 156
Maple syrup, 157, 195
Margarine, 163
buying of, 175
Marinate,
defined, 61
teriyaki, 70
vinaigrette, 70
Marine oils, 162
Marmalade, defined, 209

Matzos, defined, 67
Mayonnaise
buying of, 198
defined, 170
storage of, 173
Measurements
abbreviations for, 46
butter, 72
dry, 3
equivalents for, 46
of fats and oils, 165
high-altitude cooking and, 16, 17
liquid, 3
utensils for, 3
Meat, 81-96
baking temperatures for, 90-92
buying guide for, 179
canning of, 205
cooking of, 88-95
in high altitudes, 14
curing of, 84
cuts, 83
drying of, 202-203
freezing, 87
frozen, thawing, 87, 215
grades of, 86
inspection of, 85-86
microwave cooking and, 21, 95-96
processed, 82
restructured, 85
sources of, 81-82
storage of, 86-87
variety meats, 82
See also names of specific types of meat
Meat loaf
baking temperature for, 37
Meat pie
baking termperature for, 37
Melons, 120, 122, 185
See also Cantaloupes; Crenshaw; Honeydew; Watermelons
Menu terms, 63-70

herbs and, 145
storage of,
Rye flour, 152, 182
    See also Flour

S
Saccharin, 159, 195
Safe handling
    fish and shellfish,
      102-103
Salad dressings,
    buying of, 198
    defined, 198
    French, 170
    low-calorie, 170
    storage of, 173
Salmon, buying of, 178
Salmonella, 109, 116,
    118
Salmonellosis, 53-54
Salsa, defined, 69
Salt
    buying of, 198
    defined, 171-172
    function, 10
    pickling, 172
    rock, 172
    solubility of, 38
    substitutes, 172
Sapodilla, 120
Sapote, 120
Sardines, 98
Sashimi, defined, 69
SAS-phosphate pow-
    ders, 166, 195
Sassafras, 173
Sauces
    basic recipes, 45
    thickening of, 50-52
Sauerbraten, defined, 69
Sauerkraut
    canned, buying of,
      192
    canning of, 208
Sausage, 82-84
Saute, defined, 62
Scalding process
    defined, 62
Scallions, buying of,
    136
Scallop (baking

method), defined,
    62
Scallops
    buying of, 101, 179
    cooking of, 105
Score, defined, 62
Sear, defined, 62
Seeds, drying of, 203
Semolina, defined, 149
Sesame oil, 162
Shallot
    buying of, 136
    See also Onions
Sheet testing jelly or
    jam, 209
Shellfish, 101
    buying guide for, 178
    cooking of, 105-106
    freshness of, 99-100
    raw, eating of, 102
    safe handling, 102
    See Fish and Shell-
      fish
Sherbet, 79
Shortening, types of,
    162-163
Shrimp
    buying of, 179
    cooking of, 105
Simmer, defined, 62
Simplesse®, 36, 79, 163
Slow-cooker cooking,
    25-27
Smoke point, 58, 164
Smoked poultry, 113
Smorgasbord, defined,
    69
Smorrebrod, defined, 69
Sodium
    decrease in recipes, 9
Sodium bicarbonate,
    165
Sodium erythorbate, 36
Sol, defined, 58
Solution, defined, 58
Sorbic acid, 36
Sorghum, 152, 195
Sorghum syrup, 157,
    195
    See also Syrups
Soufflé
    basic recipe, 44

defined, 69
thickening of, 50
Soup
    basic cream recipes,
      45
    buying of canned/
      frozen, 198-199
    defined, 172
    gazpacho, defined,
      66, 172
    thickening of, 50, 52
    vichyssoise, defined,
      70, 172
Sour Cream, 26, 74-75
Soy Flour, 152, 182
    See also Flour
Soy grits, 152, 181
Spätzle, defined, 69
Specific gravity, 59
Specific heat, 59
Spelt, 152, 182
Spices, defined, 172
    aril, 172
    bark, 172
    berry, 172
    flower stigma, 172
    fruit, 172
    kernel, 172
    leaves, 172
    root, 172
    seed, 172
    stem, 172
    storage of, 173
Spinach
    buying of, 135, 192
    canning of, 204
    cooking of, 143
    herbs and, 145
    See also Greens
Spoon testing jelly or
    jam, 209
Sprouts, 188
Spumoni, defined, 69
Squash all types
    buying of, 137, 193
    canning of, 204
    cooking of, 143
    freezing of, 214, 215
    herbs and, 145
Stabilizers, defined, 34
Standards
    food, defined, 57

for vegetables, 131
Staphylococcal poison-
    ing, 54
Starch cooking
    in high altitudes, 15
Steam, defined, 62
Steaming
    fish and shellfish, 104
Steam pressure
    altitude and, 15-16
Stearyl lactylate, 36
Steep, defined, 62
Sterilize, defined, 59
Stewing process, 62
    meat, 93-94
    poultry and, 114
Stir, defined, 62
Stir-fry, defined, 62, 89
Stollen, defined, 69
Storage
    butter, 71-72
    cheese, 73-74
    cream, 74-75
    eggs, 119
    fish, 101-102
    fruit, 122-123
    grain products, 153
    ice cream, 78
    meats, 86-87
    milk, 78
    poultry, 109-110
    sugar products, 158
    vegetables, 130-131,
      139-140
Strain, defined, 62
Strawberries
    buying of, 129, 187
    frozen, 213
    preservation of, 202,
      209
Stroganoff, defined, 69
Strudel, defined, 69
Stuffing (dressing),
    cooking of, 110
    poultry and, 109, 110
Subgum, defined, 69
Substitute foods, label-
    ing and, 31
Substitution of ingredi-
    ents, 38-40
Sucralose, 159
Sucrose, 36, 160